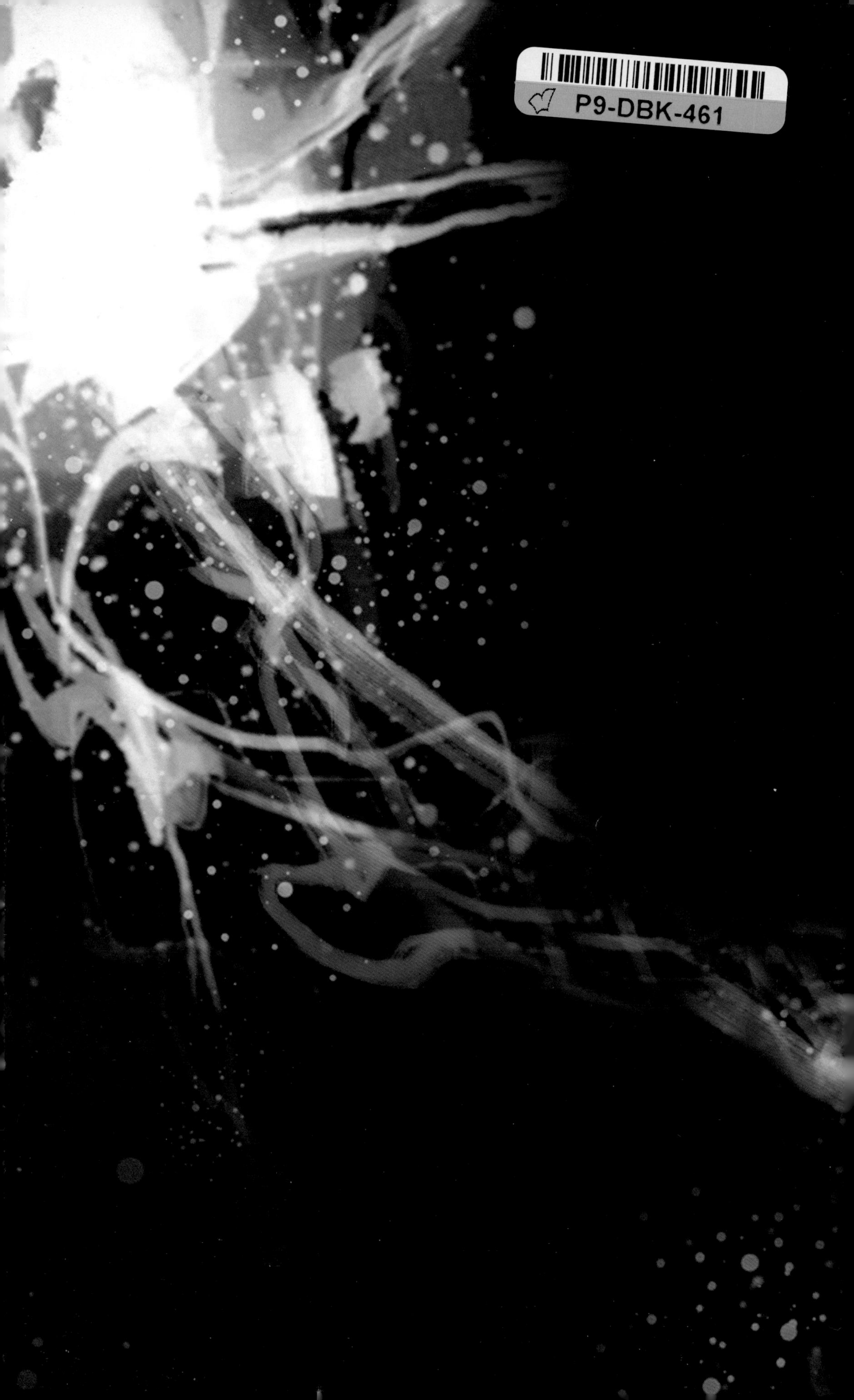

THEY CHANGED THE WORLD

EDISON-TESLA-BELL

Writer	Lewis Helfand
Illustrator	Naresh Kumar
Editorial	Jason Quinn Aadithyan Mohan
Colorist	Vijay Sharma
Letterer	Bhavnath Chaudhary
Design	Era Chawla
Cover Art	Naresh Kumar Pradeep Sherawat

CAMPFIRE®

www.campfire.co.in

Mission Statement

To entertain and educate young minds by creating unique illustrated books
that recount stories of human values, arouse curiosity in the world around us,
and inspire with tales of great deeds of unforgettable people.

Published by Kalyani Navyug Media Pvt Ltd
101 C, Shiv House, Hari Nagar Ashram,
New Delhi 110014, India

ISBN: 978-93-80741-87-1

Printed in India

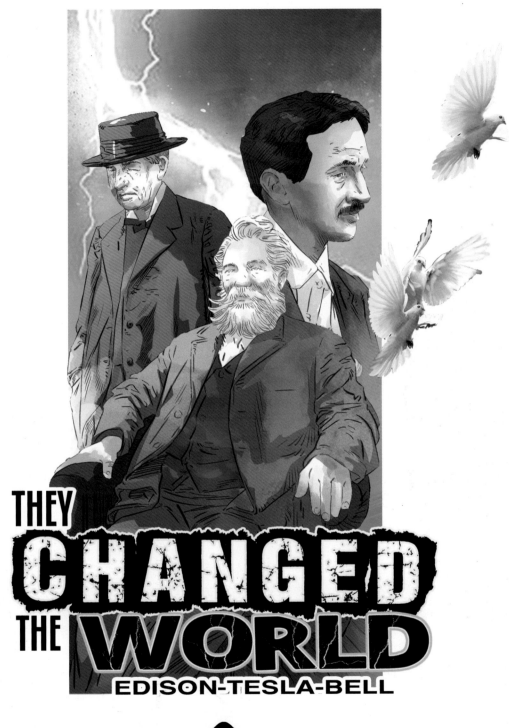

THEY CHANGED THE WORLD

EDISON-TESLA-BELL

CAMPFIRE®

KALYANI NAVYUG MEDIA PVT LTD

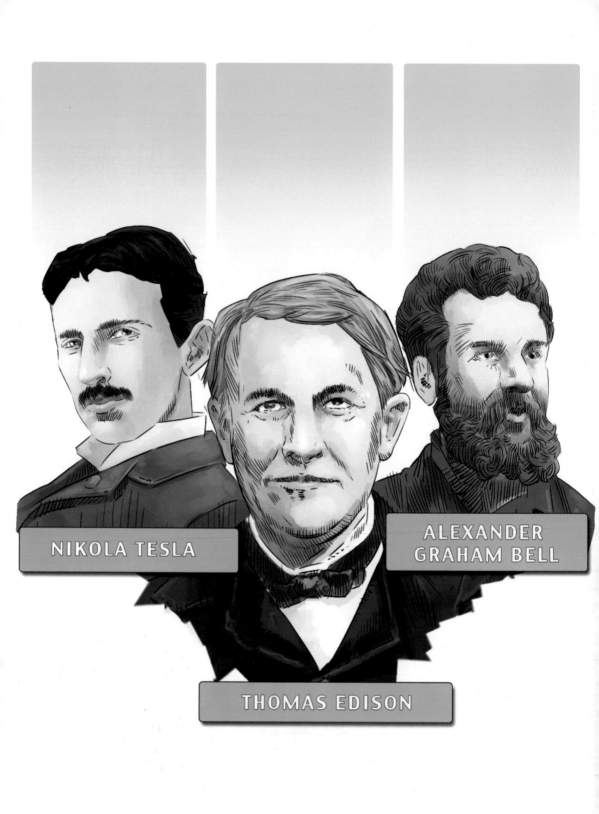

NIKOLA TESLA

ALEXANDER GRAHAM BELL

THOMAS EDISON

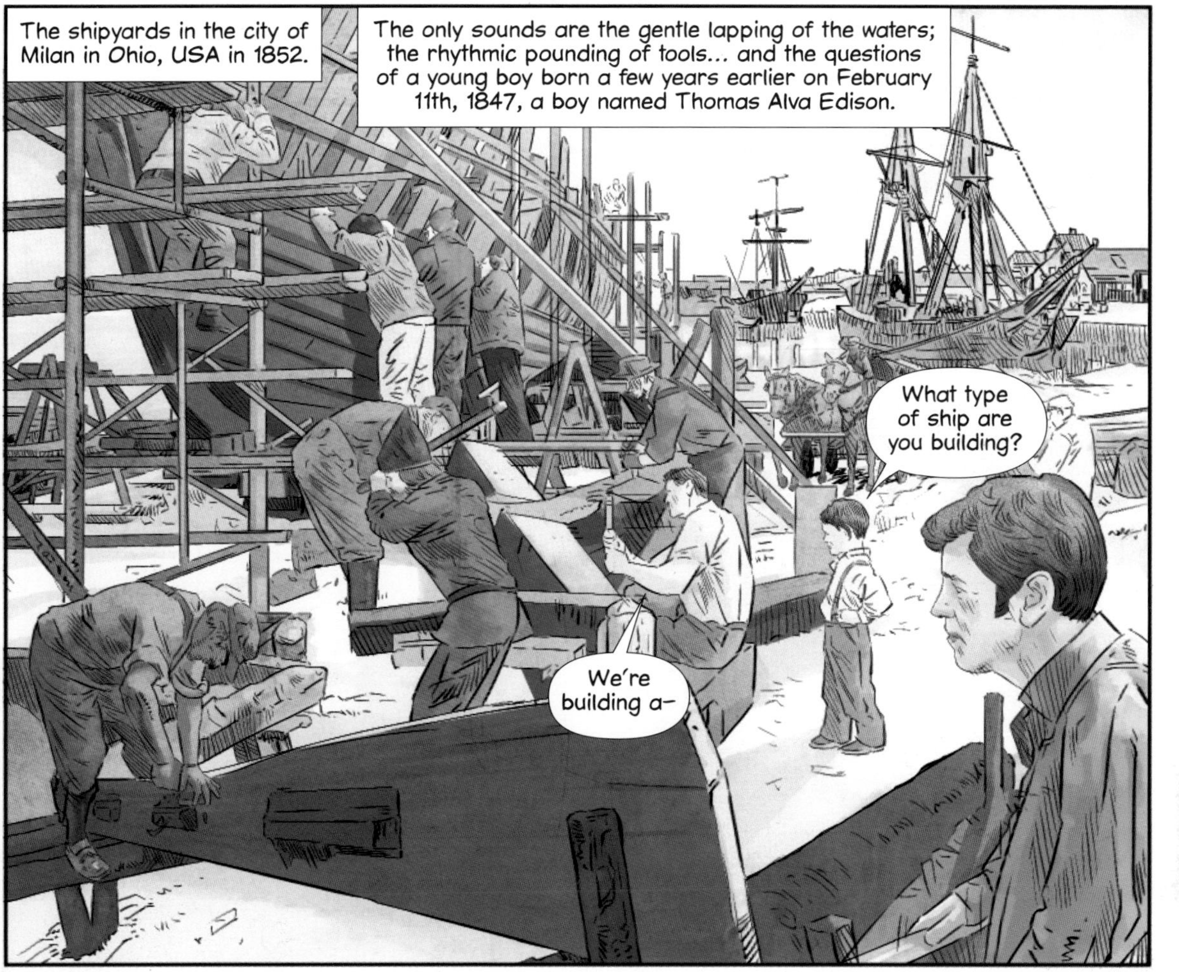
The shipyards in the city of Milan in Ohio, USA in 1852.
The only sounds are the gentle lapping of the waters; the rhythmic pounding of tools... and the questions of a young boy born a few years earlier on February 11th, 1847, a boy named Thomas Alva Edison.
What type of ship are you building?
We're building a–

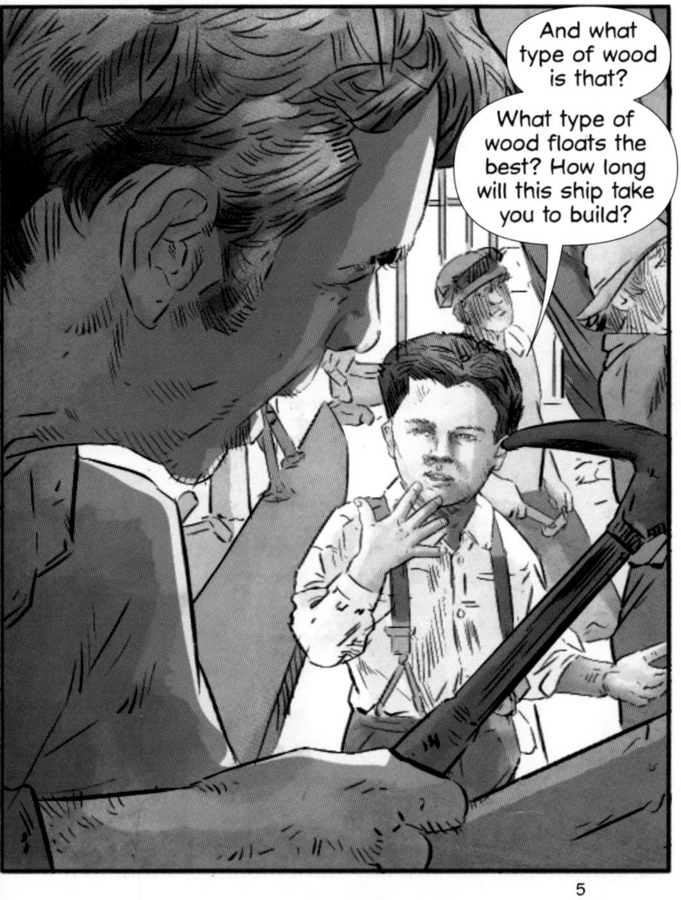
And what type of wood is that?
What type of wood floats the best? How long will this ship take you to build?

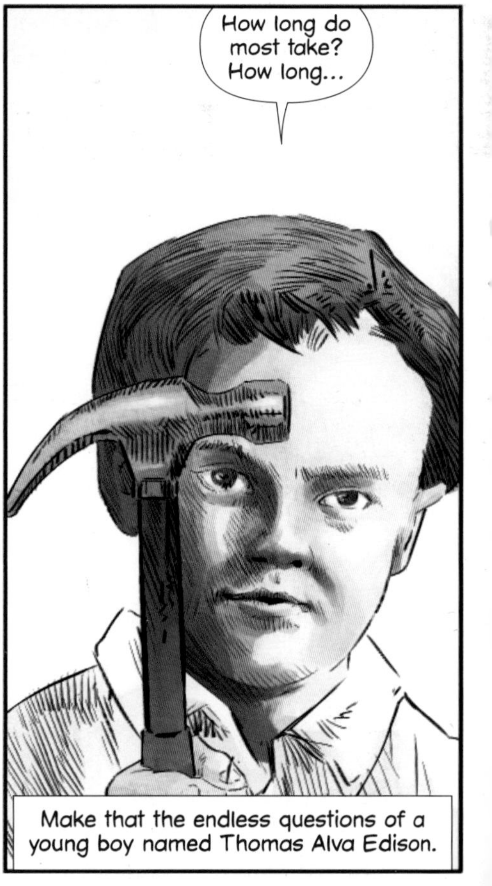
How long do most take? How long...
Make that the endless questions of a young boy named Thomas Alva Edison.

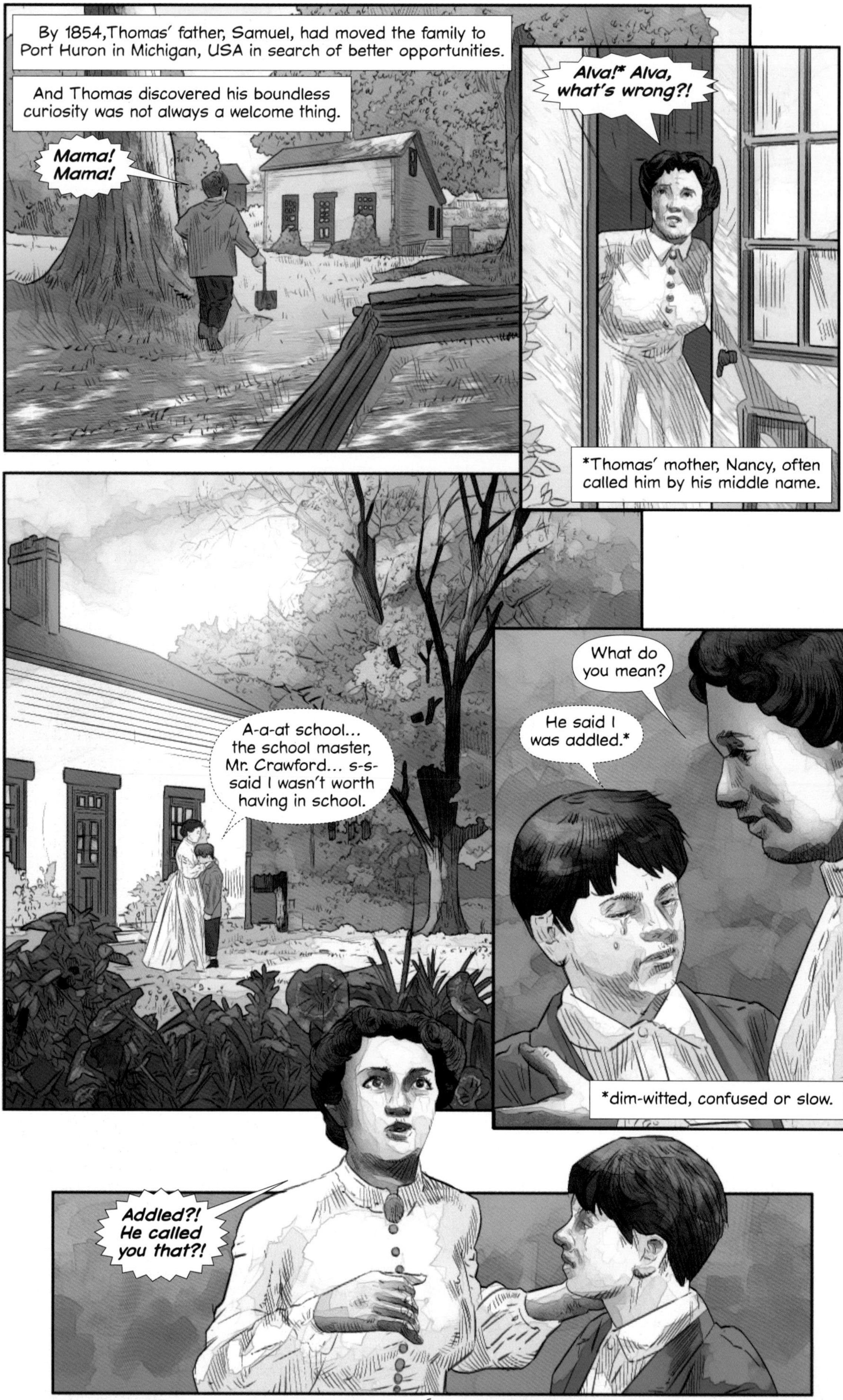
By 1854,Thomas' father, Samuel, had moved the family to Port Huron in Michigan, USA in search of better opportunities.
And Thomas discovered his boundless curiosity was not always a welcome thing.
Mama! Mama!
Alva!* Alva, what's wrong?!
*Thomas' mother, Nancy, often called him by his middle name.
A-a-at school... the school master, Mr. Crawford... s-s-said I wasn't worth having in school.
What do you mean?
He said I was addled.*
*dim-witted, confused or slow.
Addled?! He called you that?!

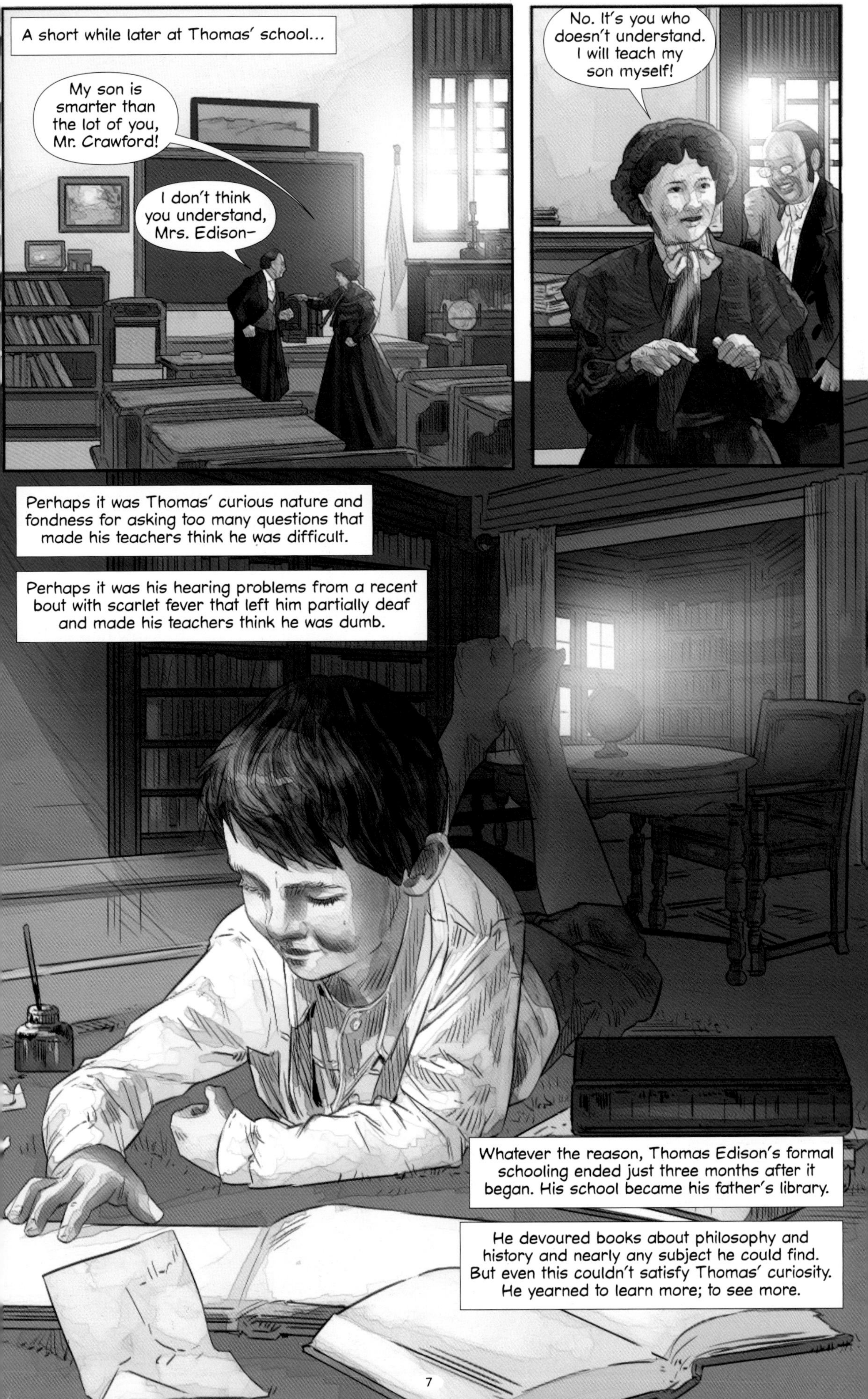

A short while later at Thomas' school...
My son is smarter than the lot of you, Mr. Crawford!
I don't think you understand, Mrs. Edison–
No. It's you who doesn't understand. I will teach my son myself!
Perhaps it was Thomas' curious nature and fondness for asking too many questions that made his teachers think he was difficult.
Perhaps it was his hearing problems from a recent bout with scarlet fever that left him partially deaf and made his teachers think he was dumb.
Whatever the reason, Thomas Edison's formal schooling ended just three months after it began. His school became his father's library.
He devoured books about philosophy and history and nearly any subject he could find. But even this couldn't satisfy Thomas' curiosity. He yearned to learn more; to see more.

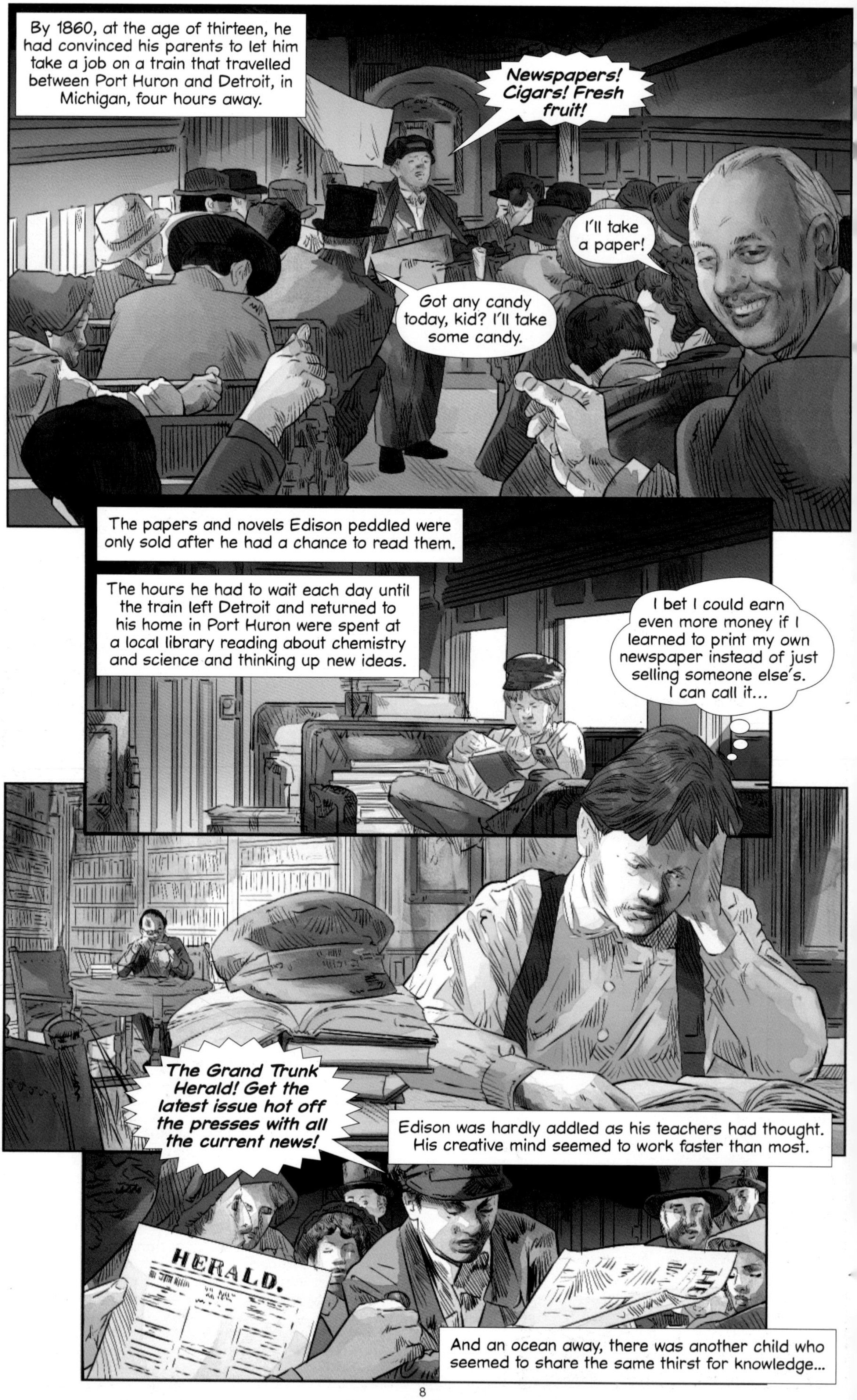
By 1860, at the age of thirteen, he had convinced his parents to let him take a job on a train that travelled between Port Huron and Detroit, in Michigan, four hours away.
Newspapers! Cigars! Fresh fruit!
I'll take a paper!
Got any candy today, kid? I'll take some candy.
The papers and novels Edison peddled were only sold after he had a chance to read them.
The hours he had to wait each day until the train left Detroit and returned to his home in Port Huron were spent at a local library reading about chemistry and science and thinking up new ideas.
I bet I could earn even more money if I learned to print my own newspaper instead of just selling someone else's. I can call it...
The Grand Trunk Herald! Get the latest issue hot off the presses with all the current news!
Edison was hardly addled as his teachers had thought. His creative mind seemed to work faster than most.
HERALD.
And an ocean away, there was another child who seemed to share the same thirst for knowledge...

Boys!!

A twelve-year-old boy by the name of Alexander Graham Bell, born March 3rd, 1847, was doing what young boys do... playing with a friend, a boy named Ben Herdman.

Son, I don't mind if your friend, Aleck*, comes over. But why don't the two of you do something useful instead of causing a commotion?

Like what, Mr. Herdman?

*Alexander's nickname.

Well, you're playing around in my flour mill.

And there's all these piles of wheat that need the husks taken off before it can be ground. You could try doing that.

This is boring, Aleck! It's going to take forever to husk all this wheat one stalk at a time!

Perhaps it would have taken forever had Alexander not noticed a large vat, left over from the days when flour was ground by using water to turn a rotating paddle.

Hey, if we fix these brushes to the paddle we should be able to husk lots of wheat all at once.

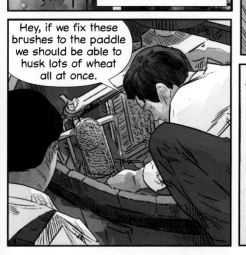

See! The machine is doing our work for us.

Despite Alexander's desire to reduce their workload in the flour mill...

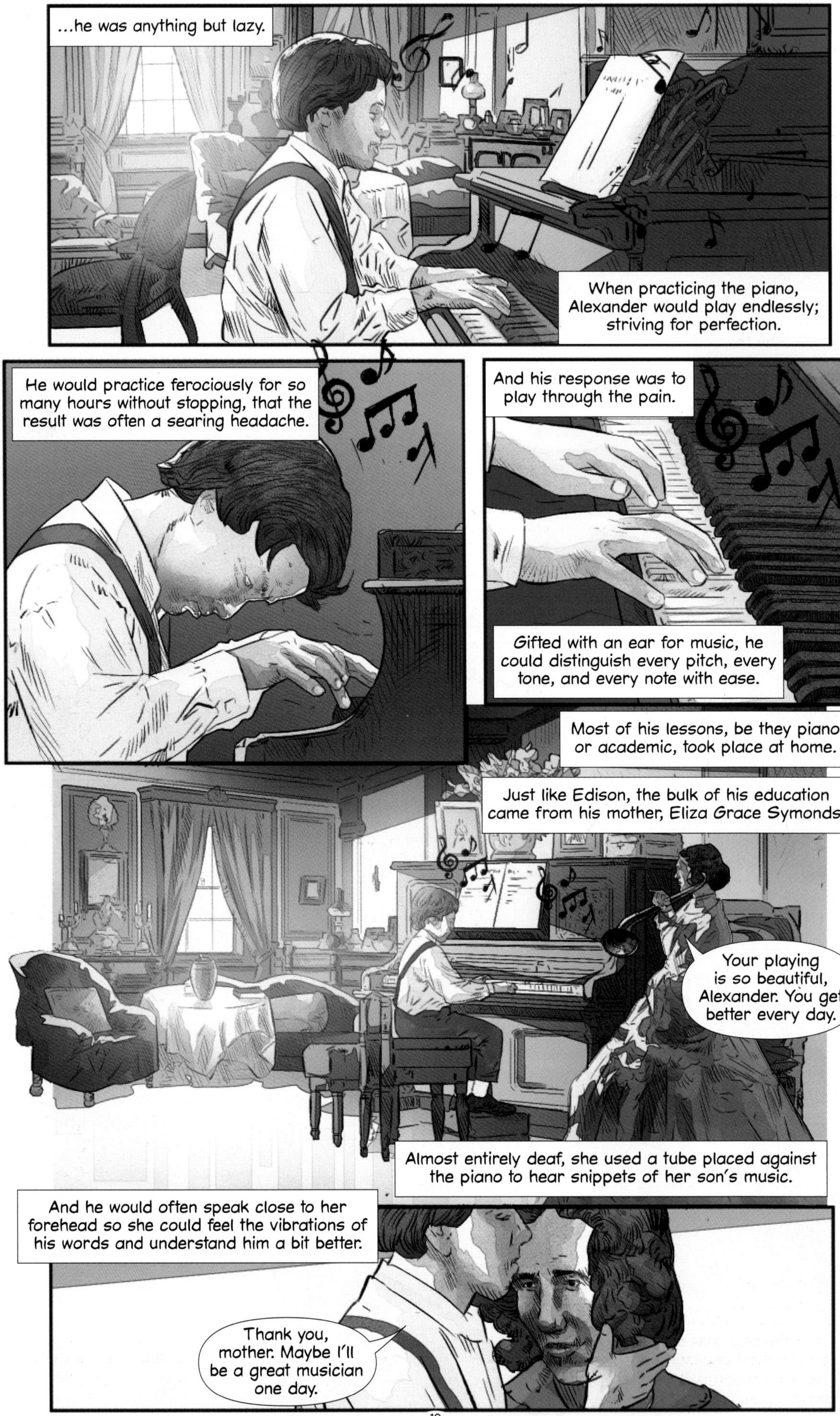
...he was anything but lazy.
When practicing the piano, Alexander would play endlessly; striving for perfection.
He would practice ferociously for so many hours without stopping, that the result was often a searing headache.
And his response was to play through the pain.
Gifted with an ear for music, he could distinguish every pitch, every tone, and every note with ease.
Most of his lessons, be they piano or academic, took place at home.
Just like Edison, the bulk of his education came from his mother, Eliza Grace Symonds.
Your playing is so beautiful, Alexander. You get better every day.
Almost entirely deaf, she used a tube placed against the piano to hear snippets of her son's music.
And he would often speak close to her forehead so she could feel the vibrations of his words and understand him a bit better.
Thank you, mother. Maybe I'll be a great musician one day.

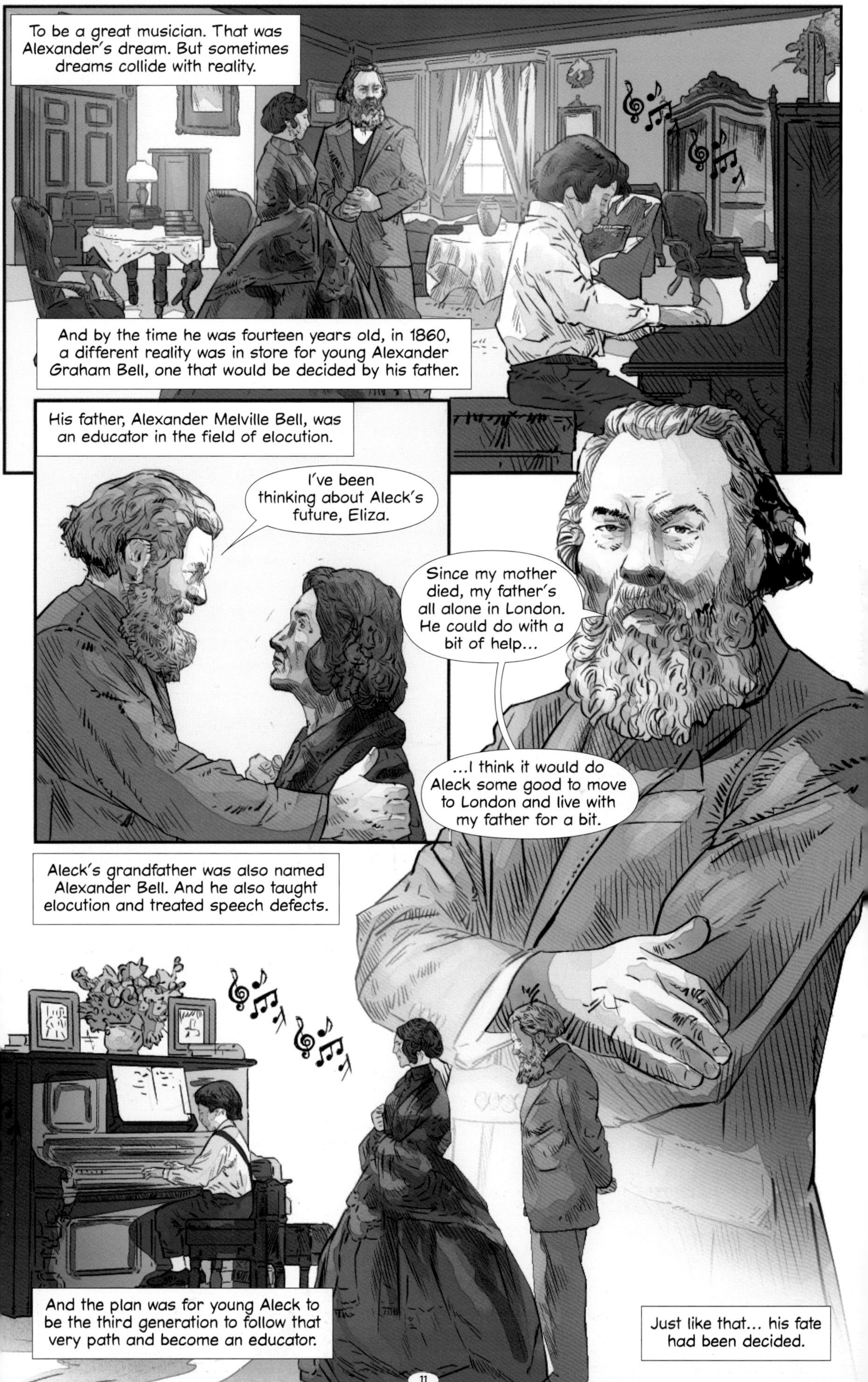

To be a great musician. That was Alexander's dream. But sometimes dreams collide with reality.
And by the time he was fourteen years old, in 1860, a different reality was in store for young Alexander Graham Bell, one that would be decided by his father.
His father, Alexander Melville Bell, was an educator in the field of elocution.
I've been thinking about Aleck's future, Eliza.
Since my mother died, my father's all alone in London. He could do with a bit of help...
...I think it would do Aleck some good to move to London and live with my father for a bit.
Aleck's grandfather was also named Alexander Bell. And he also taught elocution and treated speech defects.
And the plan was for young Aleck to be the third generation to follow that very path and become an educator.
Just like that... his fate had been decided.

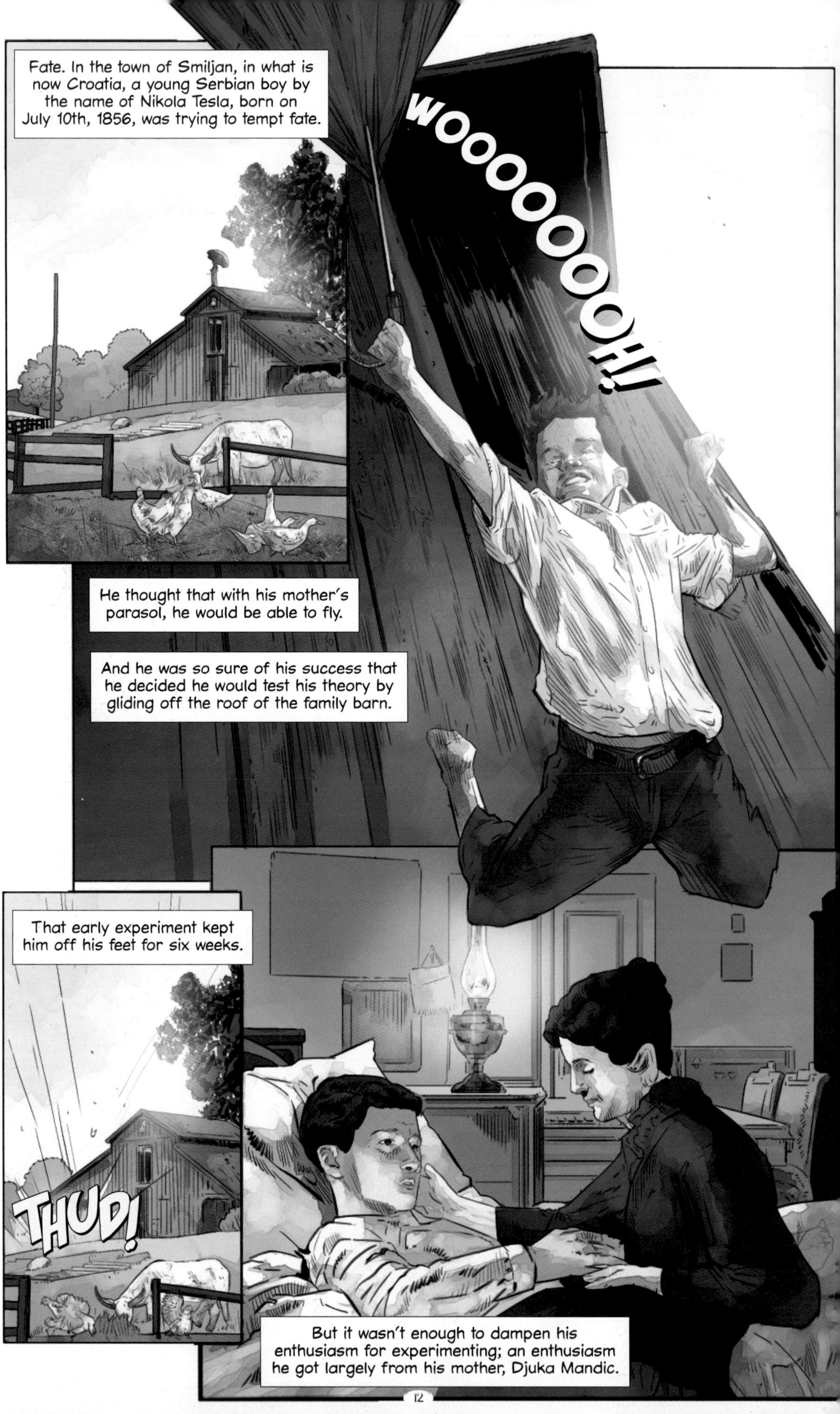

Fate. In the town of Smiljan, in what is now Croatia, a young Serbian boy by the name of Nikola Tesla, born on July 10th, 1856, was trying to tempt fate.
WOOOOOOOH!!
He thought that with his mother's parasol, he would be able to fly.
And he was so sure of his success that he decided he would test his theory by gliding off the roof of the family barn.
That early experiment kept him off his feet for six weeks.
THUD!
But it wasn't enough to dampen his enthusiasm for experimenting; an enthusiasm he got largely from his mother, Djuka Mandic.

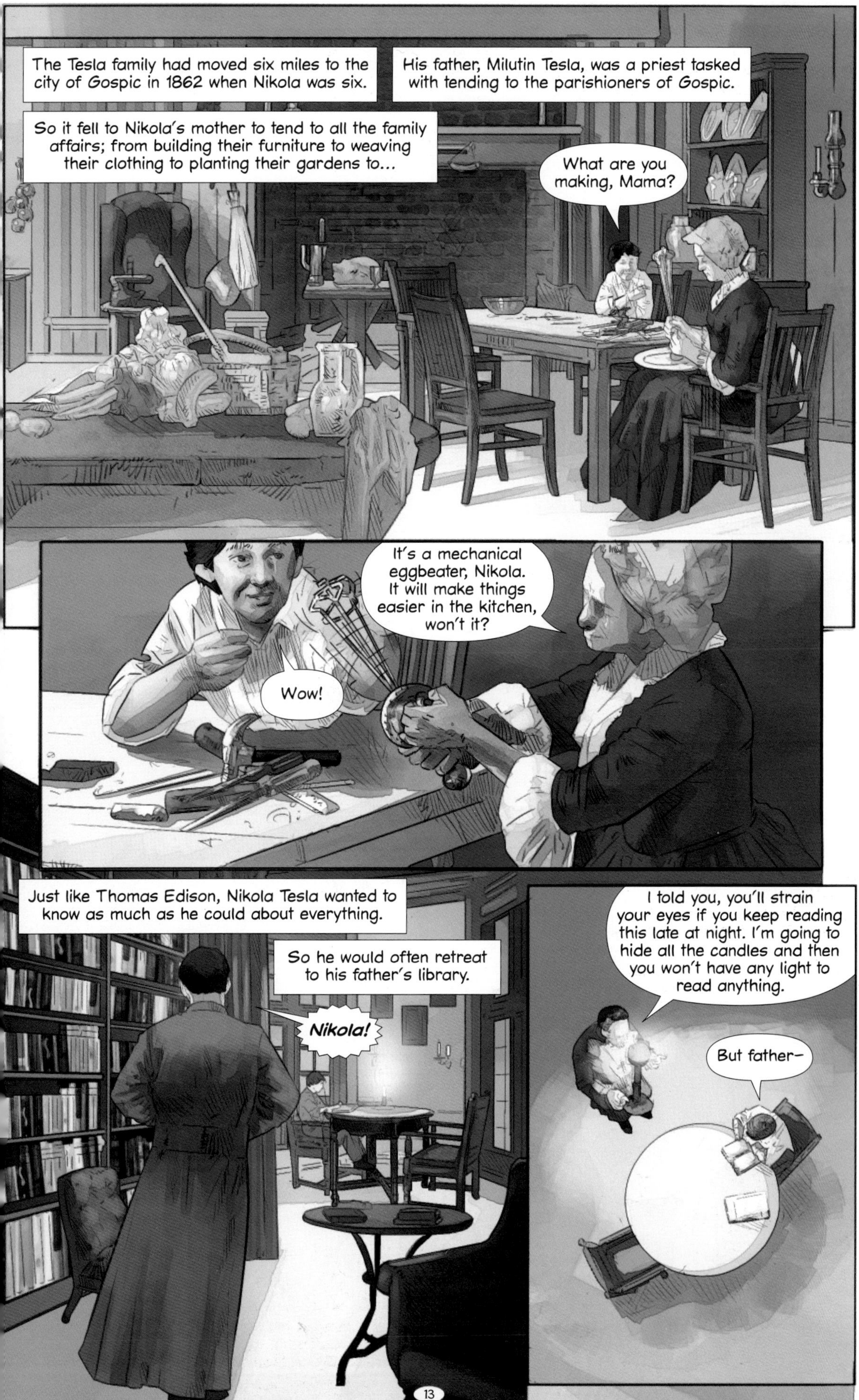
The Tesla family had moved six miles to the city of Gospic in 1862 when Nikola was six.
His father, Milutin Tesla, was a priest tasked with tending to the parishioners of Gospic.
So it fell to Nikola's mother to tend to all the family affairs; from building their furniture to weaving their clothing to planting their gardens to...
What are you making, Mama?
It's a mechanical eggbeater, Nikola. It will make things easier in the kitchen, won't it?
Wow!
Just like Thomas Edison, Nikola Tesla wanted to know as much as he could about everything.
So he would often retreat to his father's library.
Nikola!
I told you, you'll strain your eyes if you keep reading this late at night. I'm going to hide all the candles and then you won't have any light to read anything.
But father–

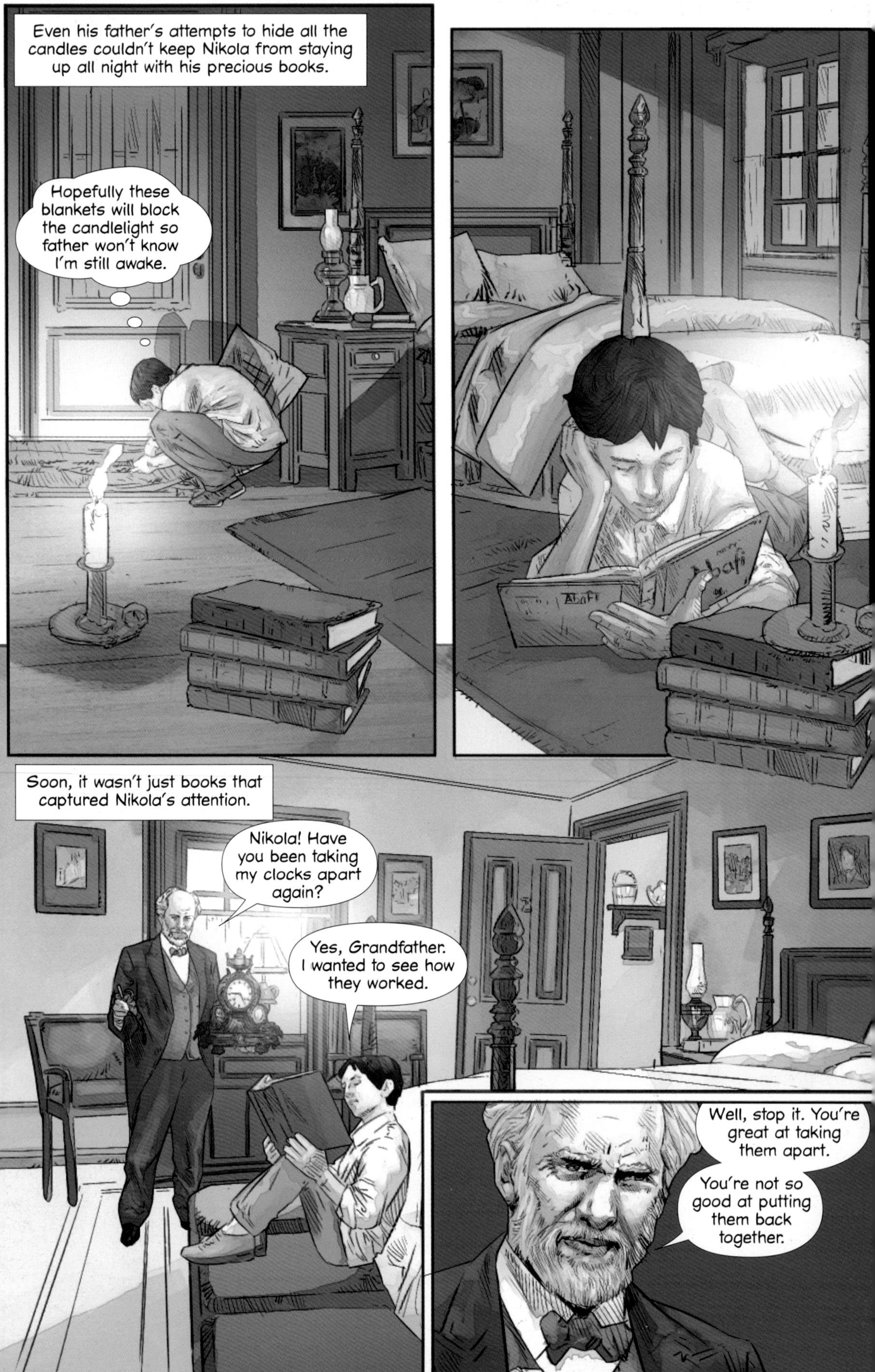
Even his father's attempts to hide all the candles couldn't keep Nikola from staying up all night with his precious books.
Hopefully these blankets will block the candlelight so father won't know I'm still awake.
Soon, it wasn't just books that captured Nikola's attention.
Nikola! Have you been taking my clocks apart again?
Yes, Grandfather. I wanted to see how they worked.
Well, stop it. You're great at taking them apart.
You're not so good at putting them back together.

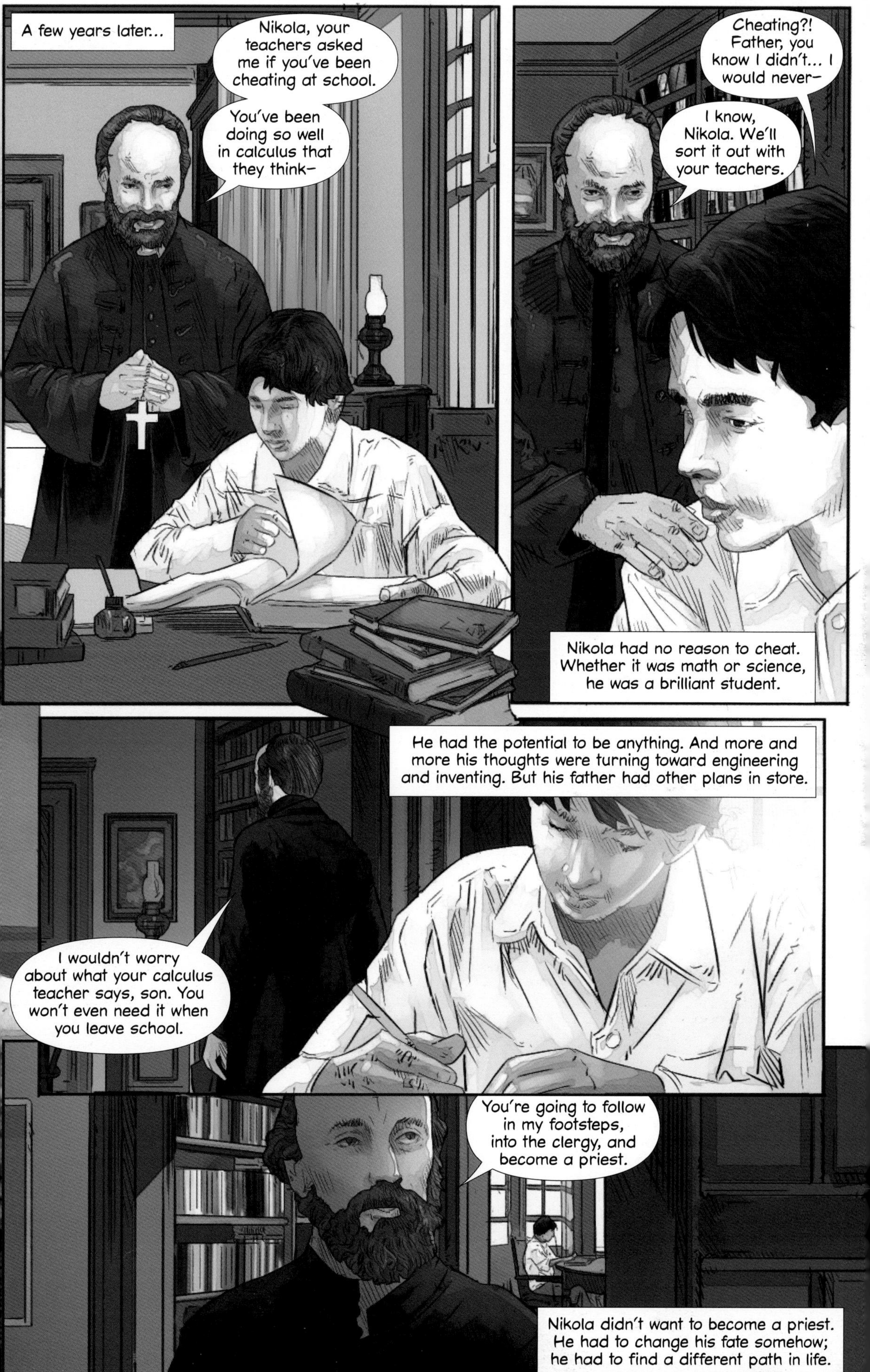

A few years later...
Nikola, your teachers asked me if you've been cheating at school.
You've been doing so well in calculus that they think–
Cheating?! Father, you know I didn't... I would never–
I know, Nikola. We'll sort it out with your teachers.
Nikola had no reason to cheat. Whether it was math or science, he was a brilliant student.
He had the potential to be anything. And more and more his thoughts were turning toward engineering and inventing. But his father had other plans in store.
I wouldn't worry about what your calculus teacher says, son. You won't even need it when you leave school.
You're going to follow in my footsteps, into the clergy, and become a priest.
Nikola didn't want to become a priest. He had to change his fate somehow; he had to find a different path in life.

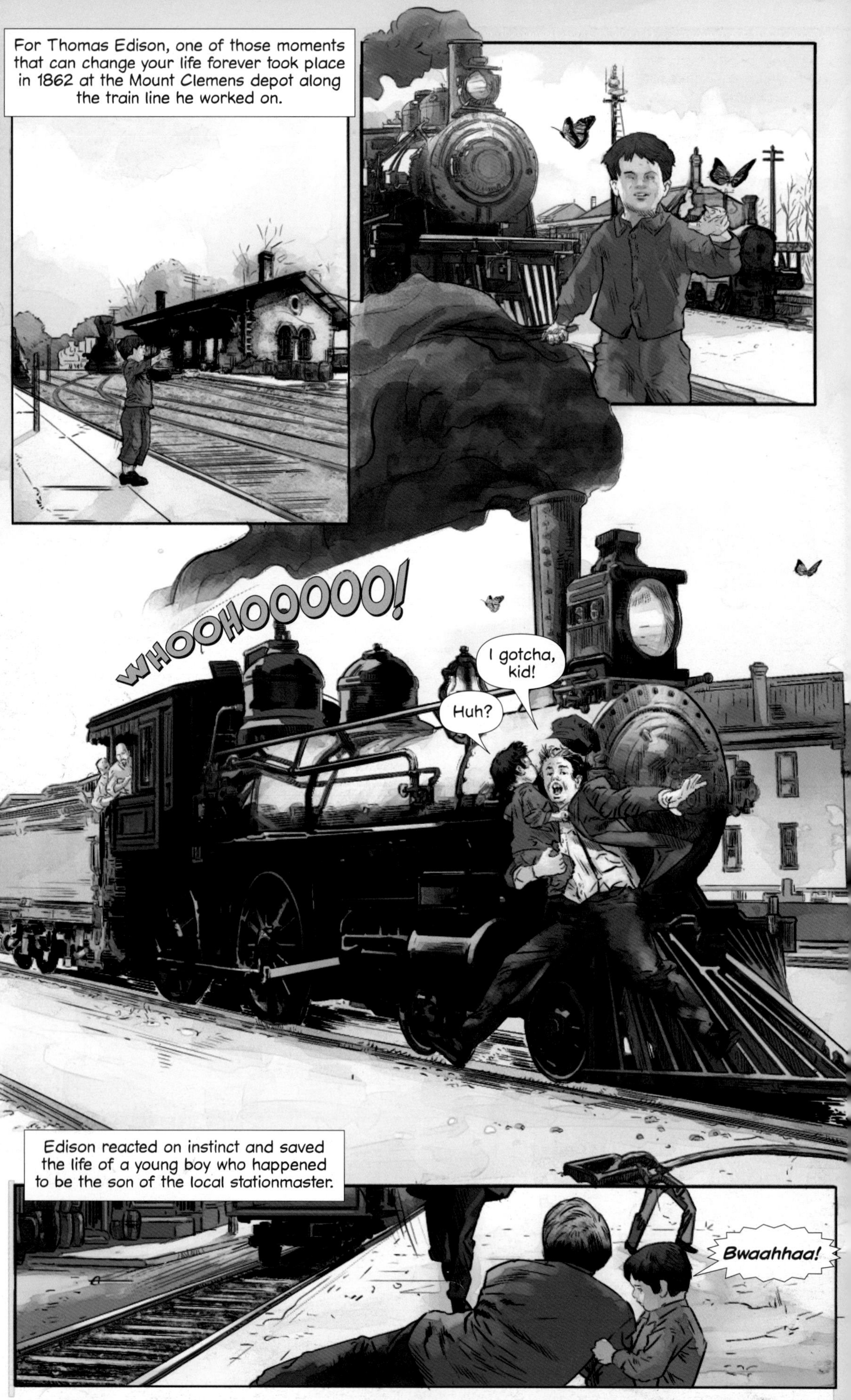
For Thomas Edison, one of those moments that can change your life forever took place in 1862 at the Mount Clemens depot along the train line he worked on.
WHOOHOOOOOO!
Huh?
I gotcha, kid!
Edison reacted on instinct and saved the life of a young boy who happened to be the son of the local stationmaster.
Bwaahhaa!

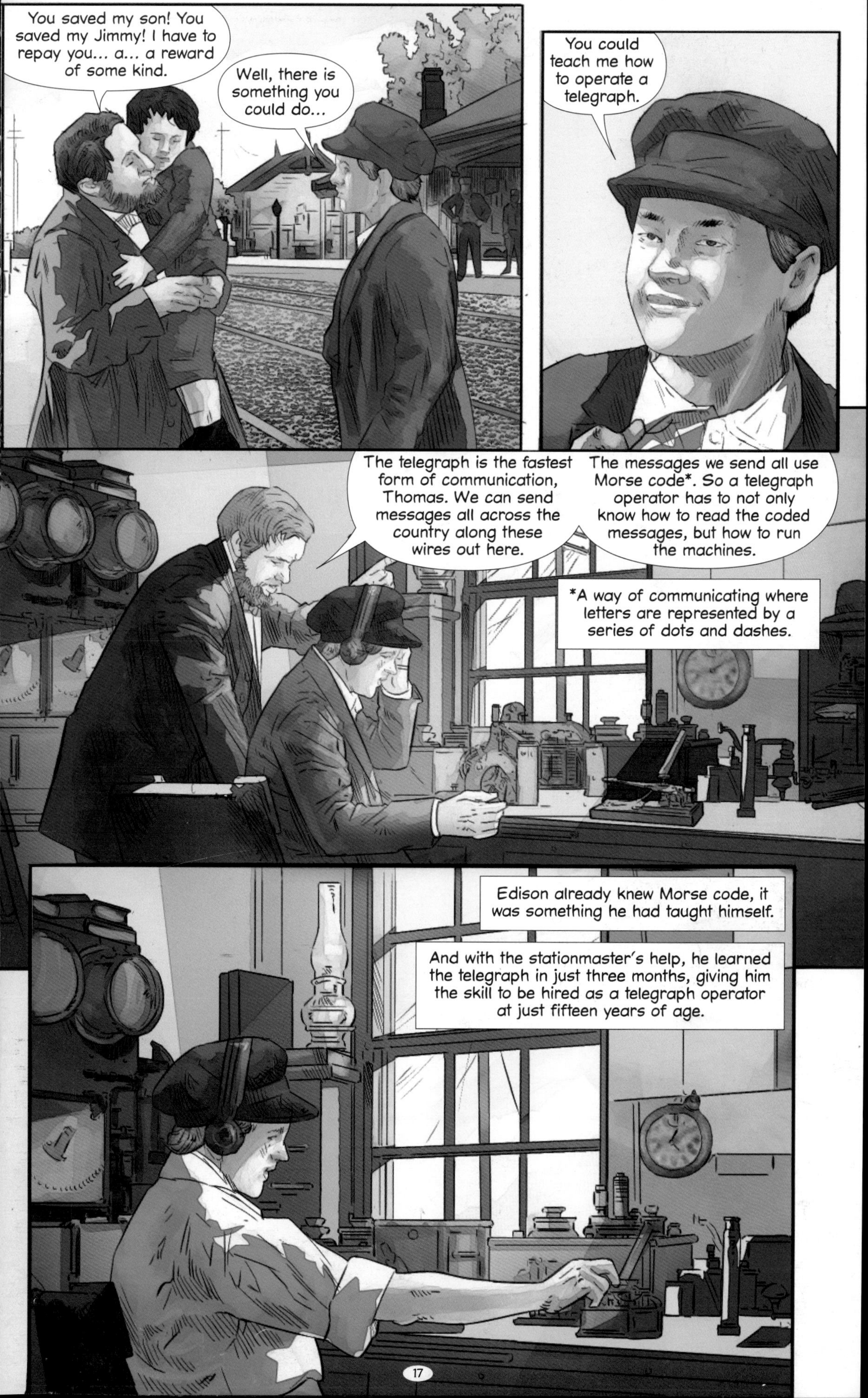
You saved my son! You saved my Jimmy! I have to repay you... a... a reward of some kind.
Well, there is something you could do...
You could teach me how to operate a telegraph.
The telegraph is the fastest form of communication, Thomas. We can send messages all across the country along these wires out here.
The messages we send all use Morse code*. So a telegraph operator has to not only know how to read the coded messages, but how to run the machines.
*A way of communicating where letters are represented by a series of dots and dashes.
Edison already knew Morse code, it was something he had taught himself.
And with the stationmaster's help, he learned the telegraph in just three months, giving him the skill to be hired as a telegraph operator at just fifteen years of age.

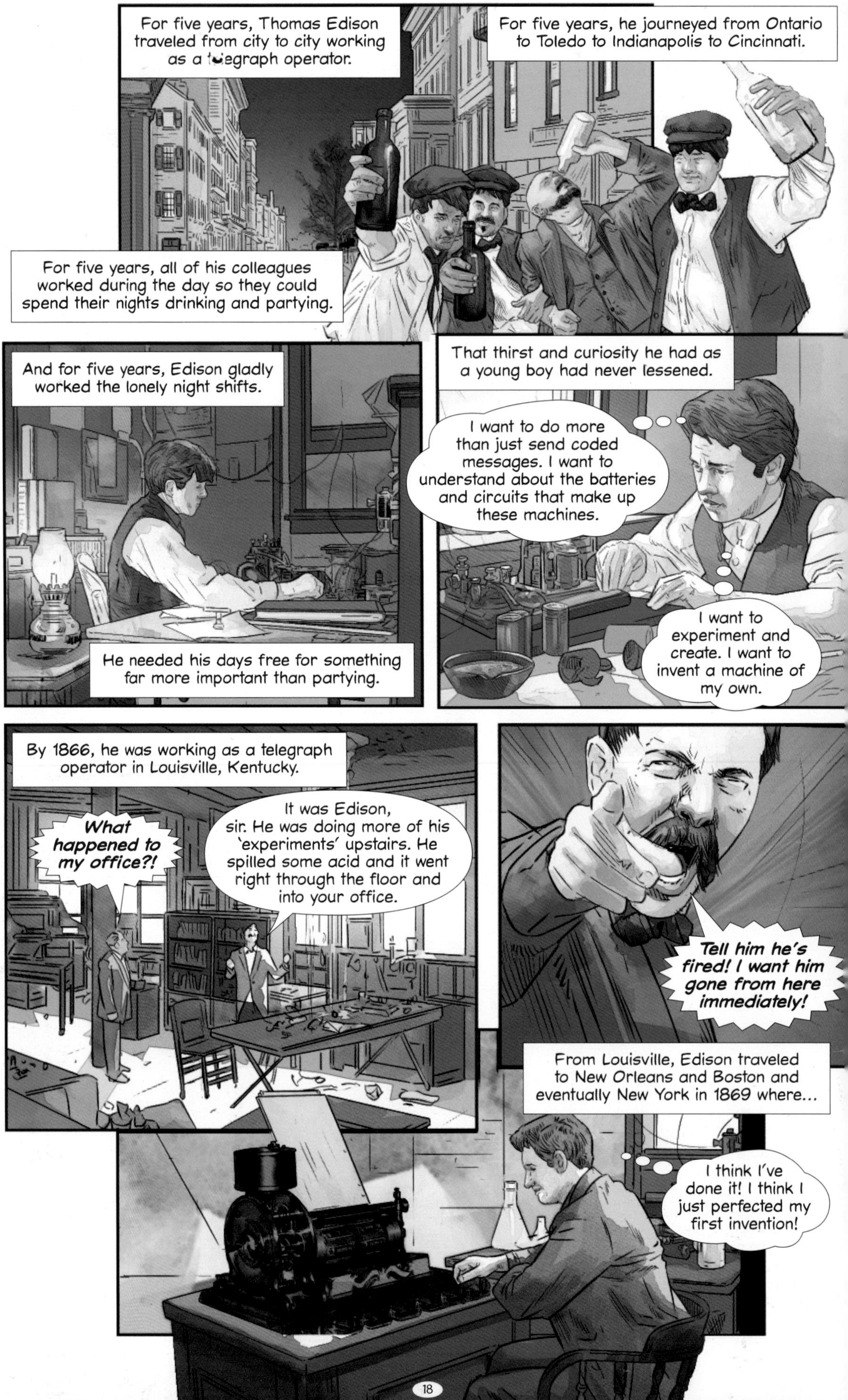

For five years, Thomas Edison traveled from city to city working as a telegraph operator.
For five years, he journeyed from Ontario to Toledo to Indianapolis to Cincinnati.
For five years, all of his colleagues worked during the day so they could spend their nights drinking and partying.
And for five years, Edison gladly worked the lonely night shifts.
He needed his days free for something far more important than partying.
That thirst and curiosity he had as a young boy had never lessened.
I want to do more than just send coded messages. I want to understand about the batteries and circuits that make up these machines.
I want to experiment and create. I want to invent a machine of my own.
By 1866, he was working as a telegraph operator in Louisville, Kentucky.
What happened to my office?!
It was Edison, sir. He was doing more of his 'experiments' upstairs. He spilled some acid and it went right through the floor and into your office.
Tell him he's fired! I want him gone from here immediately!
From Louisville, Edison traveled to New Orleans and Boston and eventually New York in 1869 where...
I think I've done it! I think I just perfected my first invention!

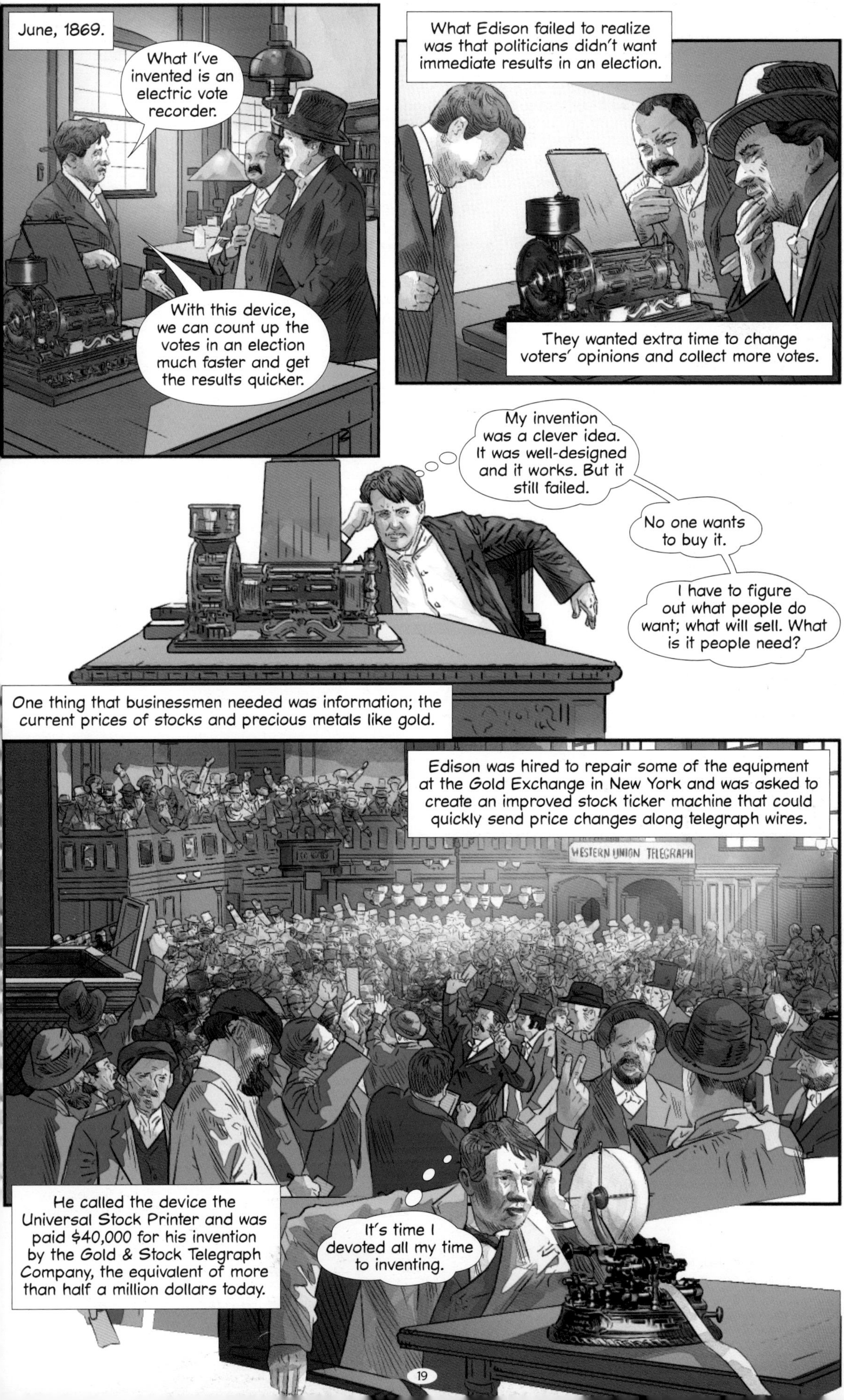
June, 1869.
What I've invented is an electric vote recorder.
With this device, we can count up the votes in an election much faster and get the results quicker.
What Edison failed to realize was that politicians didn't want immediate results in an election.
They wanted extra time to change voters' opinions and collect more votes.
My invention was a clever idea. It was well-designed and it works. But it still failed.
No one wants to buy it.
I have to figure out what people do want; what will sell. What is it people need?
One thing that businessmen needed was information; the current prices of stocks and precious metals like gold.
Edison was hired to repair some of the equipment at the Gold Exchange in New York and was asked to create an improved stock ticker machine that could quickly send price changes along telegraph wires.
WESTERN UNION TELEGRAPH
He called the device the Universal Stock Printer and was paid $40,000 for his invention by the Gold & Stock Telegraph Company, the equivalent of more than half a million dollars today.
It's time I devoted all my time to inventing.

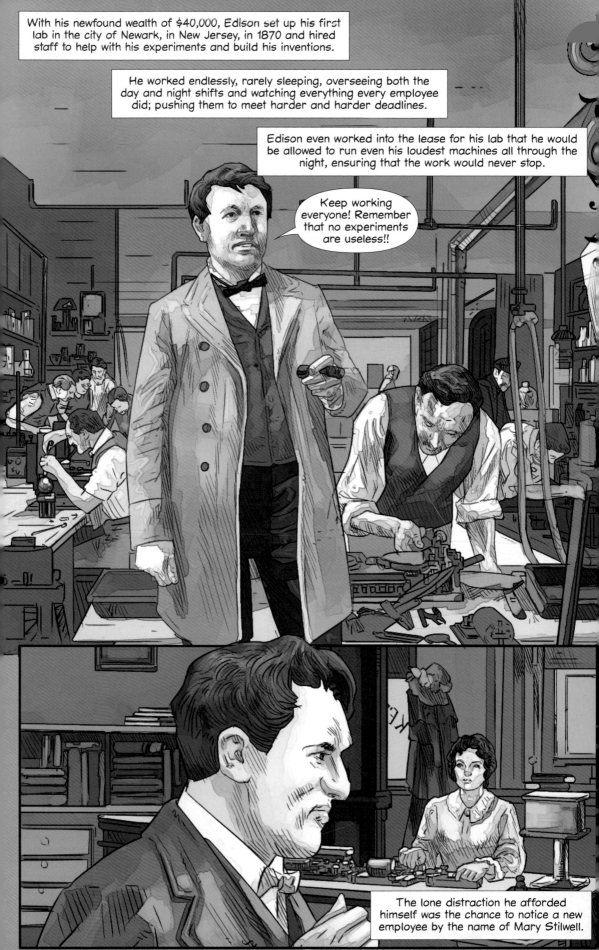

With his newfound wealth of $40,000, Edison set up his first lab in the city of Newark, in New Jersey, in 1870 and hired staff to help with his experiments and build his inventions.

He worked endlessly, rarely sleeping, overseeing both the day and night shifts and watching everything every employee did; pushing them to meet harder and harder deadlines.

Edison even worked into the lease for his lab that he would be allowed to run even his loudest machines all through the night, ensuring that the work would never stop.

Keep working everyone! Remember that no experiments are useless!!

The lone distraction he afforded himself was the chance to notice a new employee by the name of Mary Stilwell.

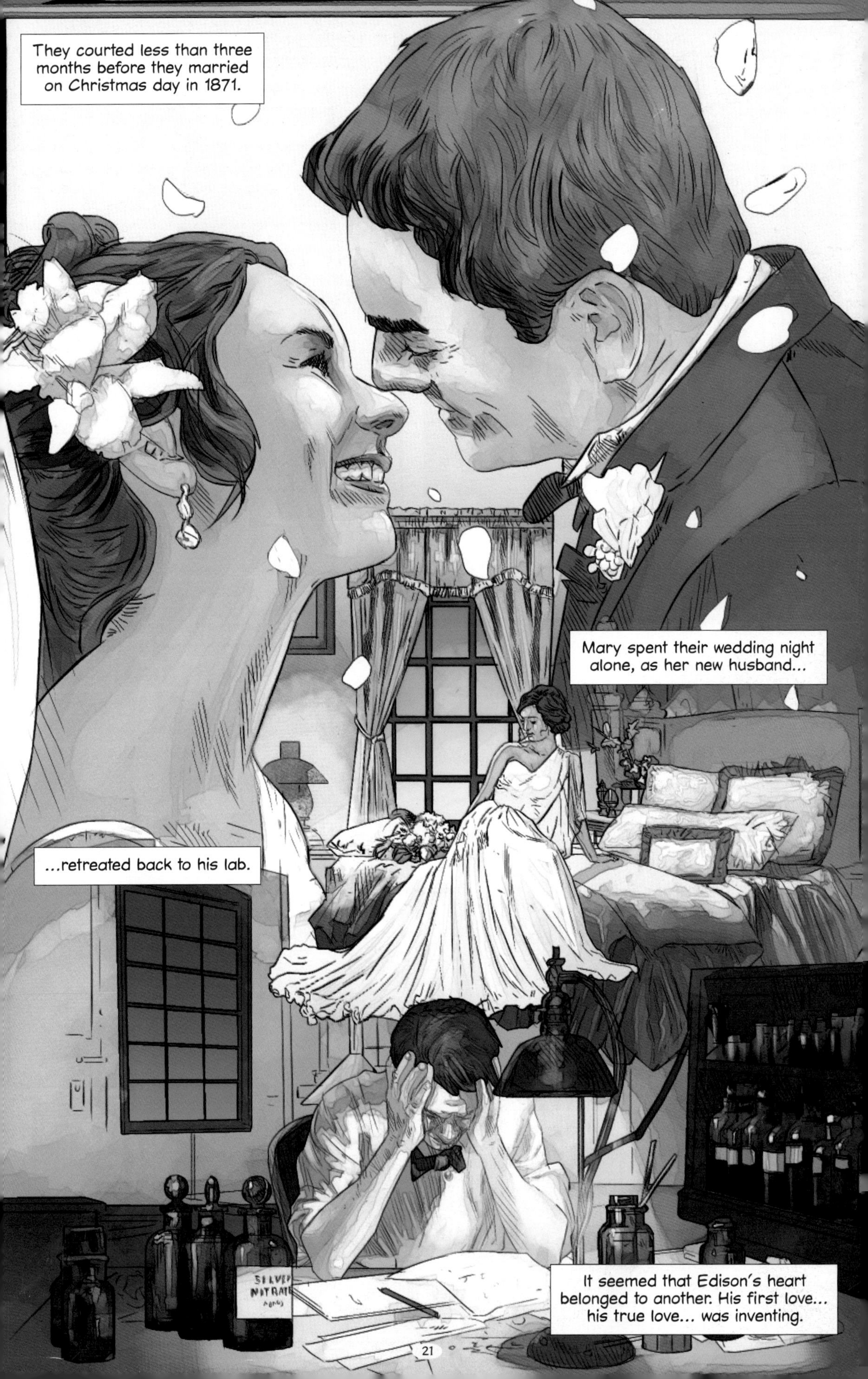
They courted less than three months before they married on Christmas day in 1871.
Mary spent their wedding night alone, as her new husband...
...retreated back to his lab.
It seemed that Edison's heart belonged to another. His first love... his true love... was inventing.

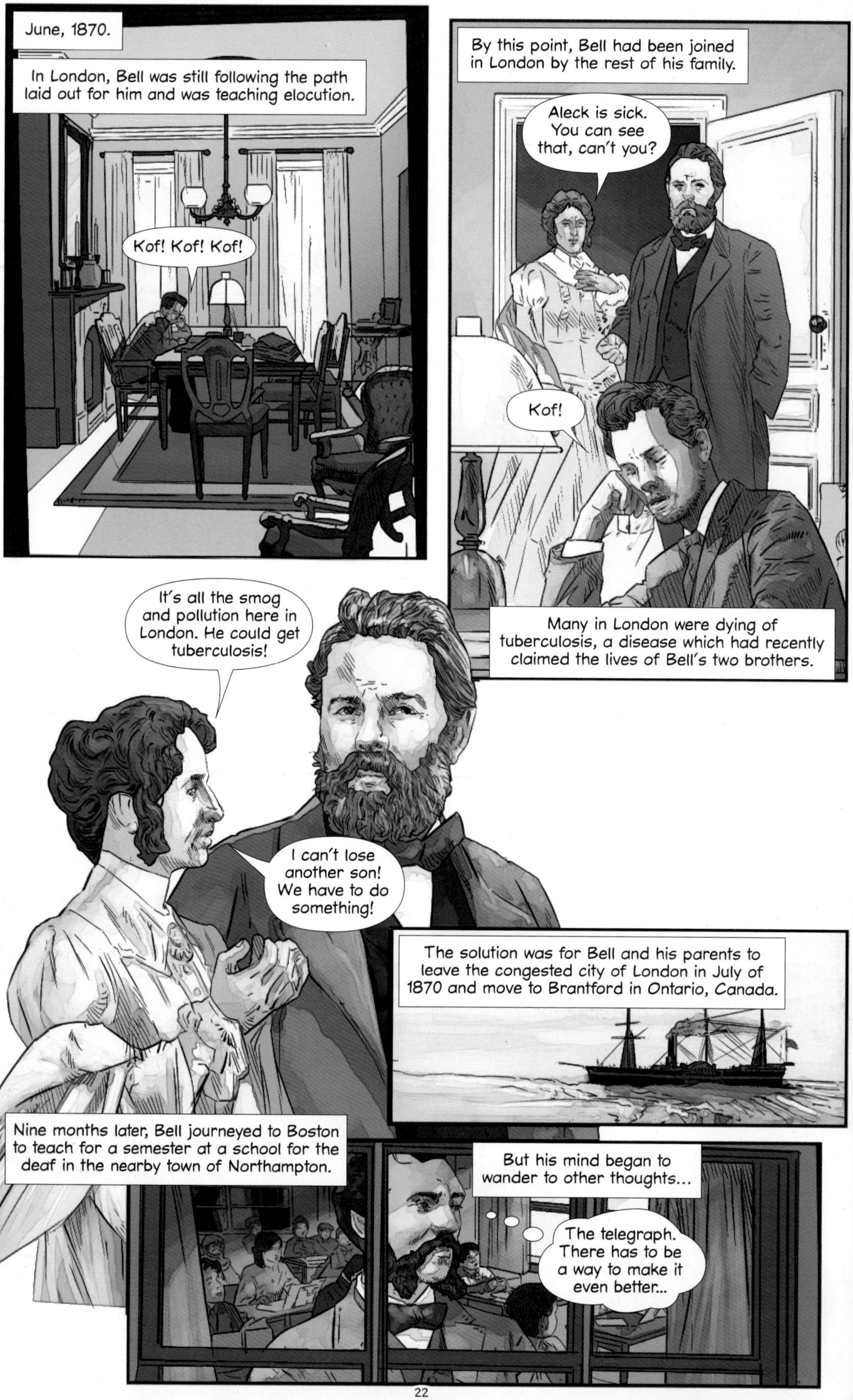

June, 1870.
In London, Bell was still following the path laid out for him and was teaching elocution.
Kof! Kof! Kof!
By this point, Bell had been joined in London by the rest of his family.
Aleck is sick. You can see that, can't you?
Kof!
Many in London were dying of tuberculosis, a disease which had recently claimed the lives of Bell's two brothers.
It's all the smog and pollution here in London. He could get tuberculosis!
I can't lose another son! We have to do something!
The solution was for Bell and his parents to leave the congested city of London in July of 1870 and move to Brantford in Ontario, Canada.
Nine months later, Bell journeyed to Boston to teach for a semester at a school for the deaf in the nearby town of Northampton.
But his mind began to wander to other thoughts...
The telegraph. There has to be a way to make it even better...

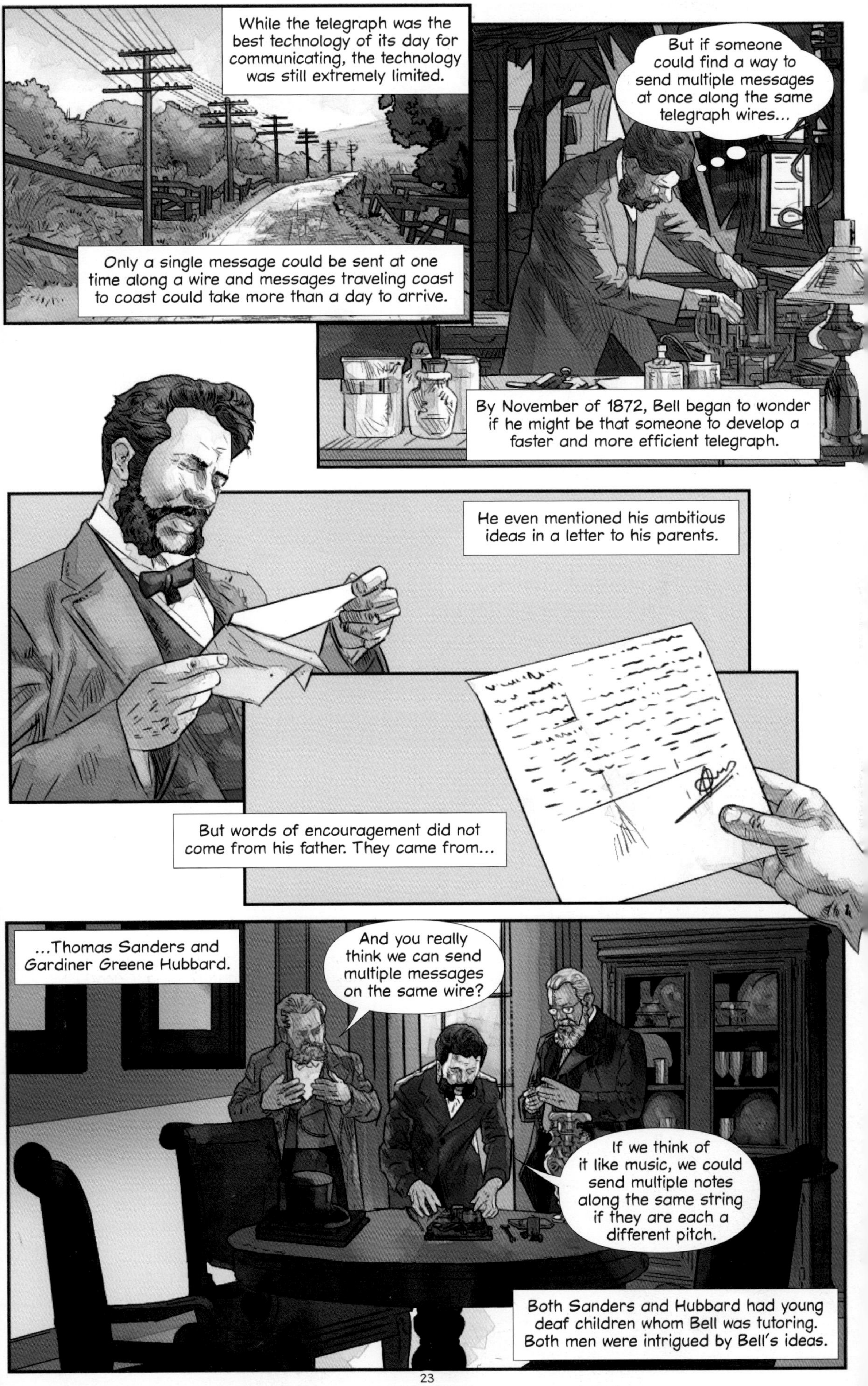
While the telegraph was the best technology of its day for communicating, the technology was still extremely limited.
Only a single message could be sent at one time along a wire and messages traveling coast to coast could take more than a day to arrive.
But if someone could find a way to send multiple messages at once along the same telegraph wires...
By November of 1872, Bell began to wonder if he might be that someone to develop a faster and more efficient telegraph.
He even mentioned his ambitious ideas in a letter to his parents.
But words of encouragement did not come from his father. They came from...
...Thomas Sanders and Gardiner Greene Hubbard.
And you really think we can send multiple messages on the same wire?
If we think of it like music, we could send multiple notes along the same string if they are each a different pitch.
Both Sanders and Hubbard had young deaf children whom Bell was tutoring. Both men were intrigued by Bell's ideas.

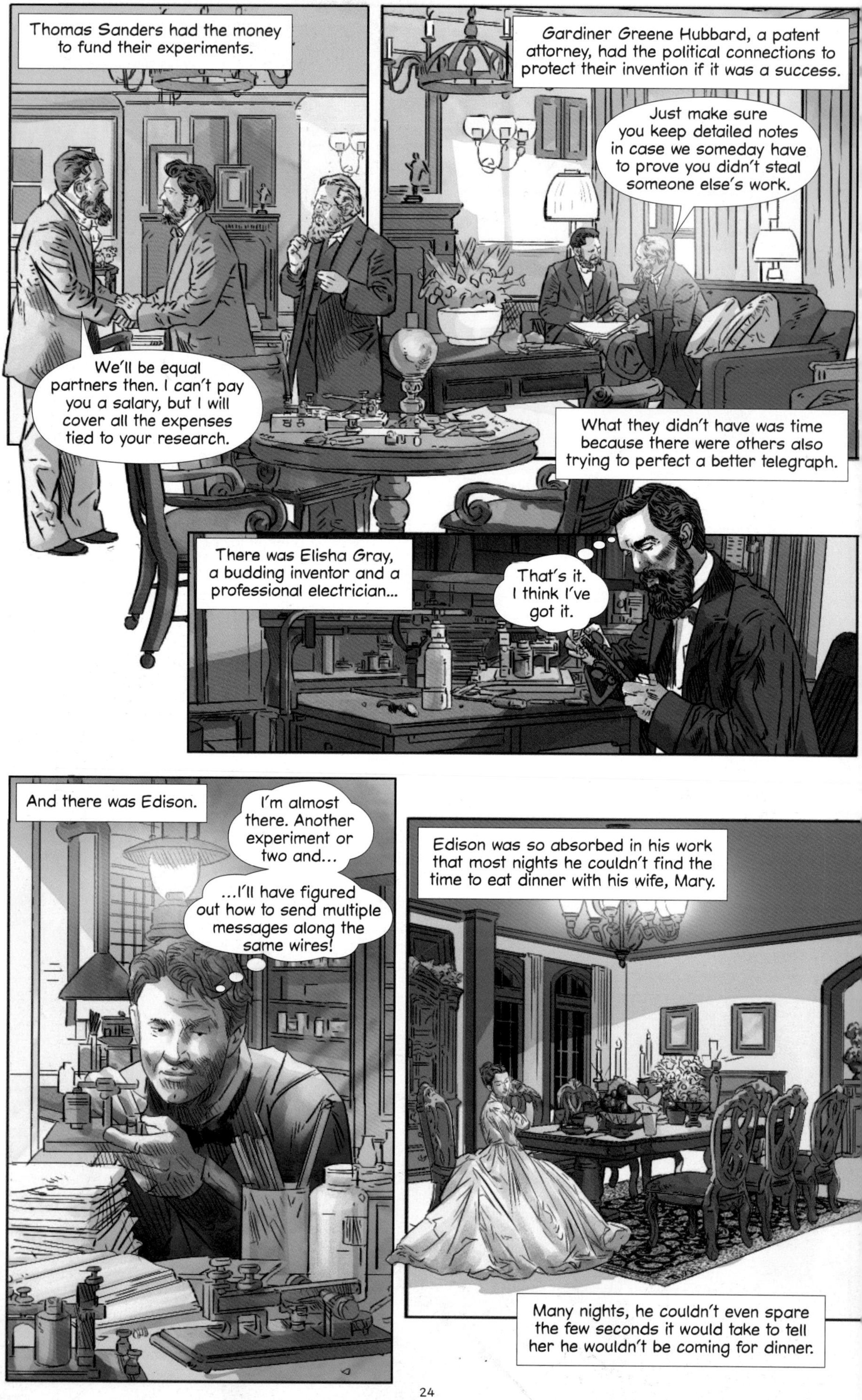
Thomas Sanders had the money to fund their experiments.
We'll be equal partners then. I can't pay you a salary, but I will cover all the expenses tied to your research.
Gardiner Greene Hubbard, a patent attorney, had the political connections to protect their invention if it was a success.
Just make sure you keep detailed notes in case we someday have to prove you didn't steal someone else's work.
What they didn't have was time because there were others also trying to perfect a better telegraph.
There was Elisha Gray, a budding inventor and a professional electrician...
That's it. I think I've got it.
And there was Edison.
I'm almost there. Another experiment or two and...
...I'll have figured out how to send multiple messages along the same wires!
Edison was so absorbed in his work that most nights he couldn't find the time to eat dinner with his wife, Mary.
Many nights, he couldn't even spare the few seconds it would take to tell her he wouldn't be coming for dinner.

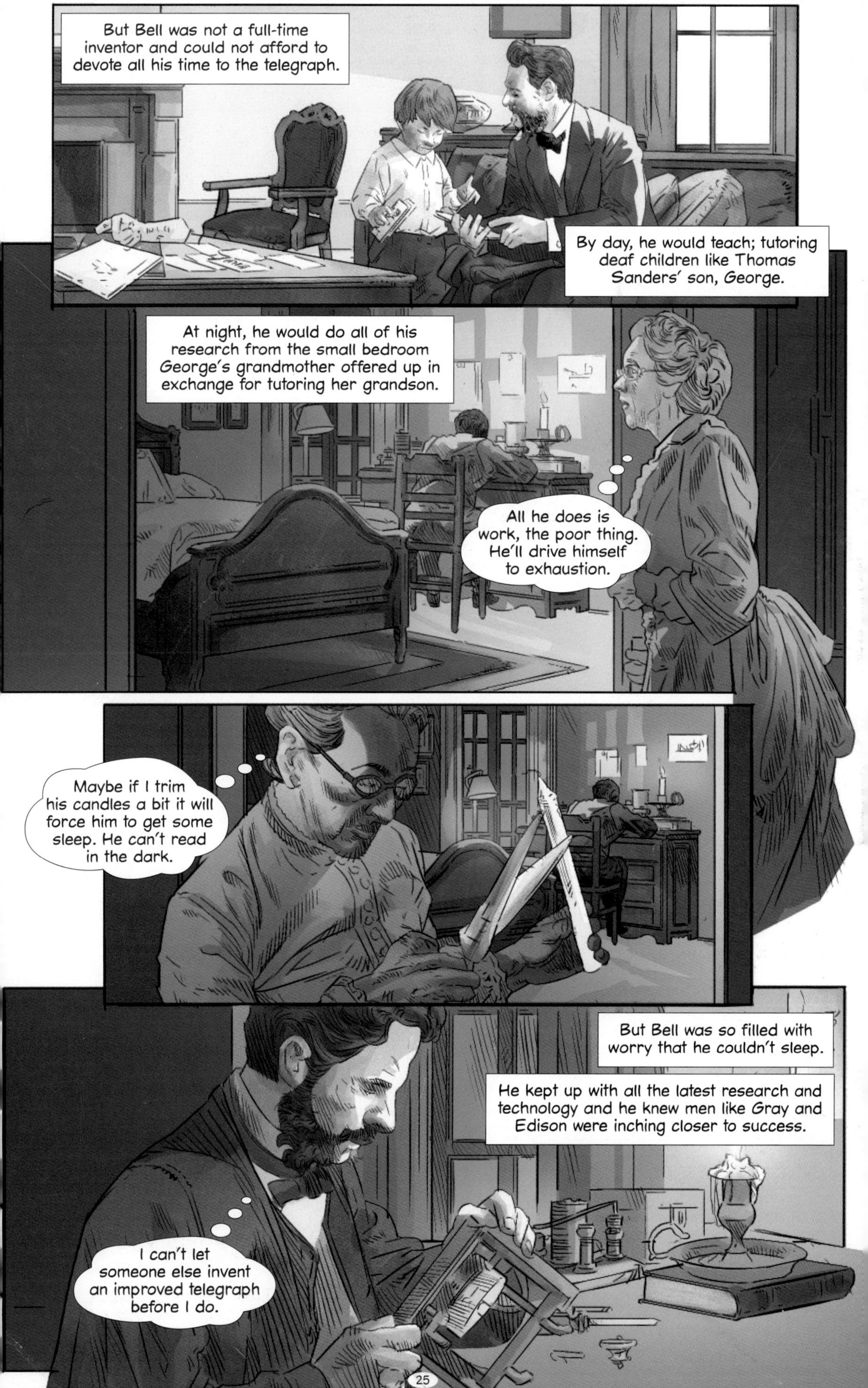
But Bell was not a full-time inventor and could not afford to devote all his time to the telegraph.
By day, he would teach; tutoring deaf children like Thomas Sanders' son, George.
At night, he would do all of his research from the small bedroom George's grandmother offered up in exchange for tutoring her grandson.
All he does is work, the poor thing. He'll drive himself to exhaustion.
Maybe if I trim his candles a bit it will force him to get some sleep. He can't read in the dark.
But Bell was so filled with worry that he couldn't sleep.
He kept up with all the latest research and technology and he knew men like Gray and Edison were inching closer to success.
I can't let someone else invent an improved telegraph before I do.

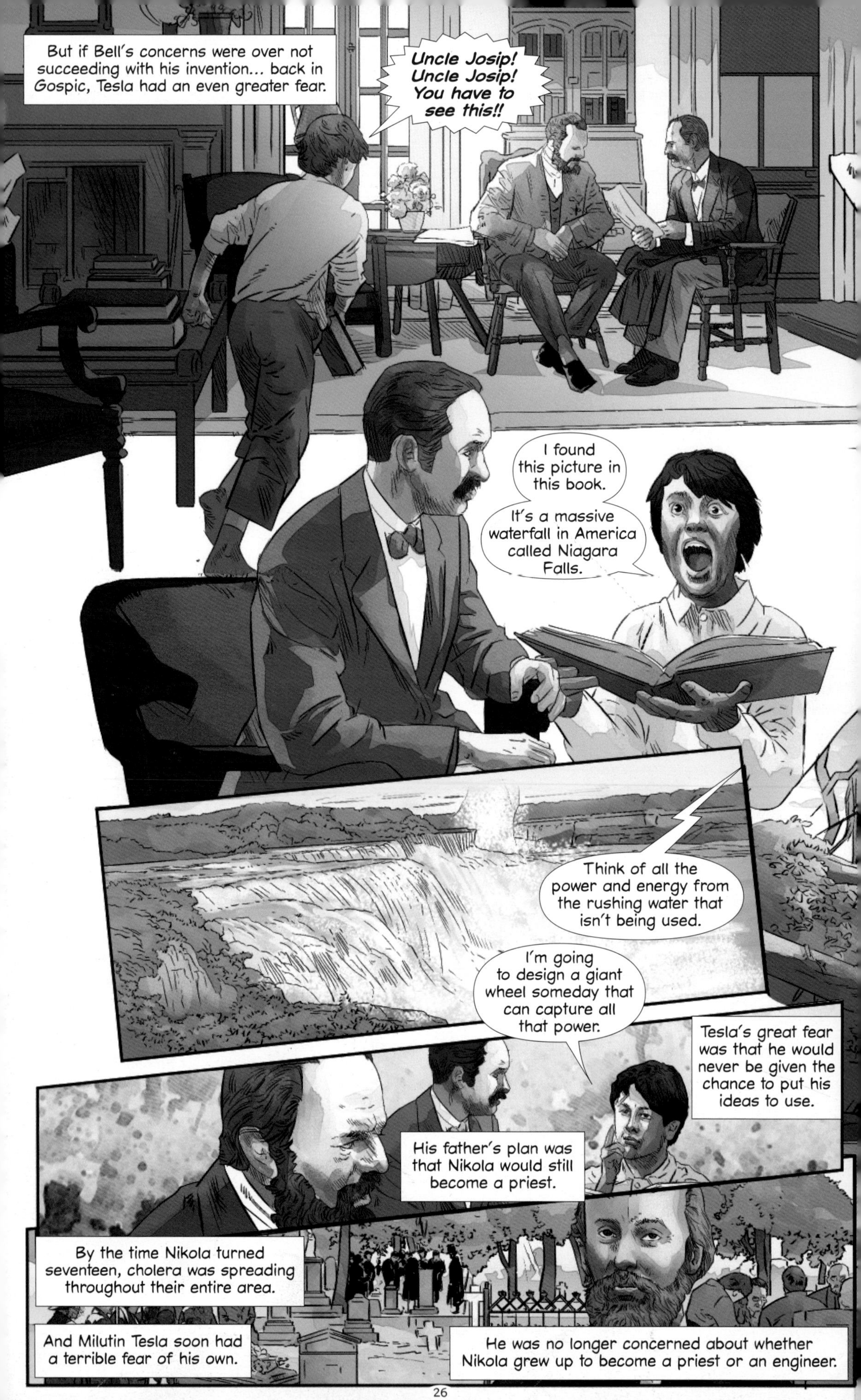
But if Bell's concerns were over not succeeding with his invention... back in Gospic, Tesla had an even greater fear.
Uncle Josip! Uncle Josip! You have to see this!!
I found this picture in this book.
It's a massive waterfall in America called Niagara Falls.
Think of all the power and energy from the rushing water that isn't being used.
I'm going to design a giant wheel someday that can capture all that power.
Tesla's great fear was that he would never be given the chance to put his ideas to use.
His father's plan was that Nikola would still become a priest.
By the time Nikola turned seventeen, cholera was spreading throughout their entire area.
And Milutin Tesla soon had a terrible fear of his own.
He was no longer concerned about whether Nikola grew up to become a priest or an engineer.

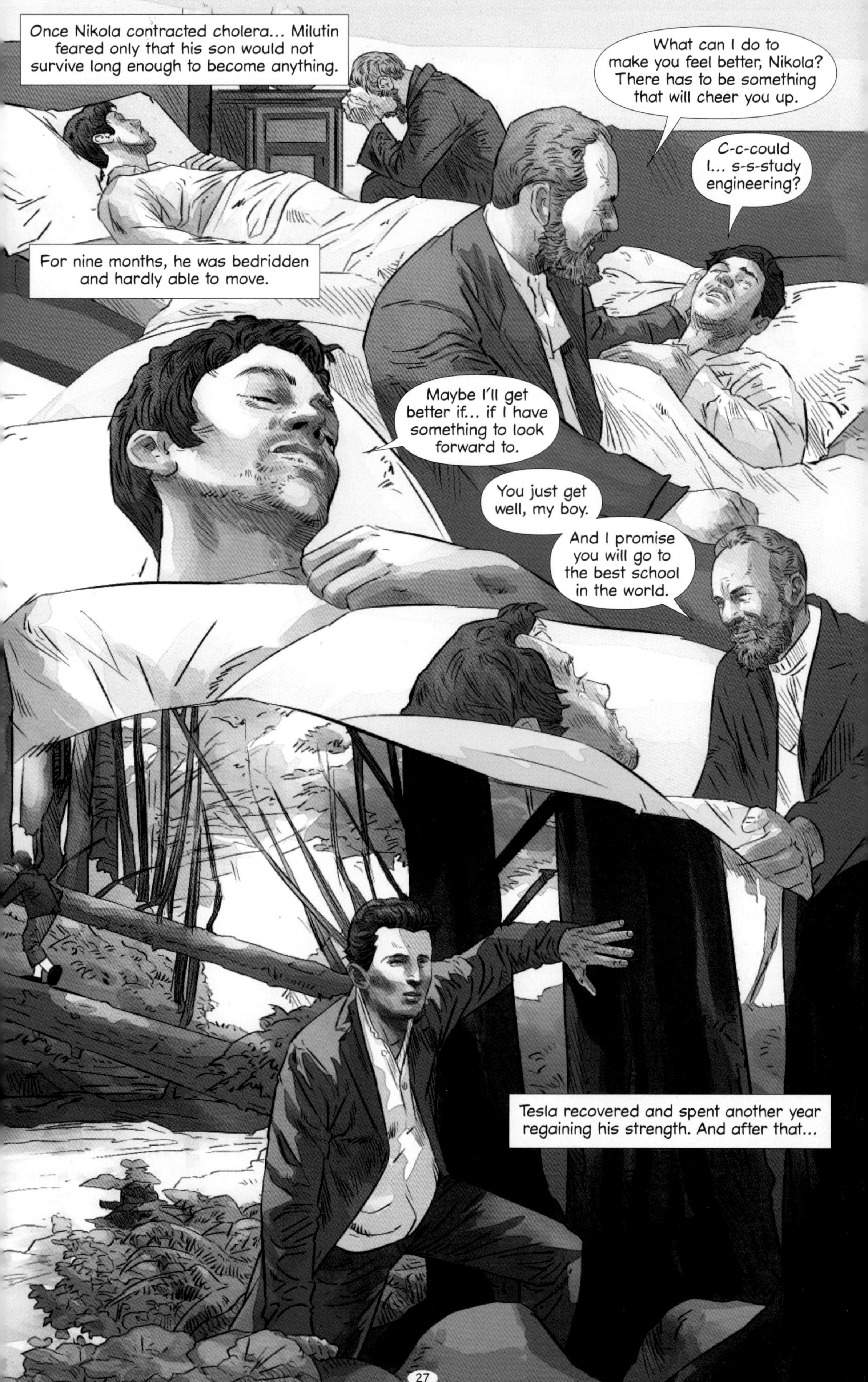
Once Nikola contracted cholera... Milutin feared only that his son would not survive long enough to become anything.
What can I do to make you feel better, Nikola? There has to be something that will cheer you up.
C-c-could I... s-s-study engineering?
For nine months, he was bedridden and hardly able to move.
Maybe I'll get better if... if I have something to look forward to.
You just get well, my boy.
And I promise you will go to the best school in the world.
Tesla recovered and spent another year regaining his strength. And after that...

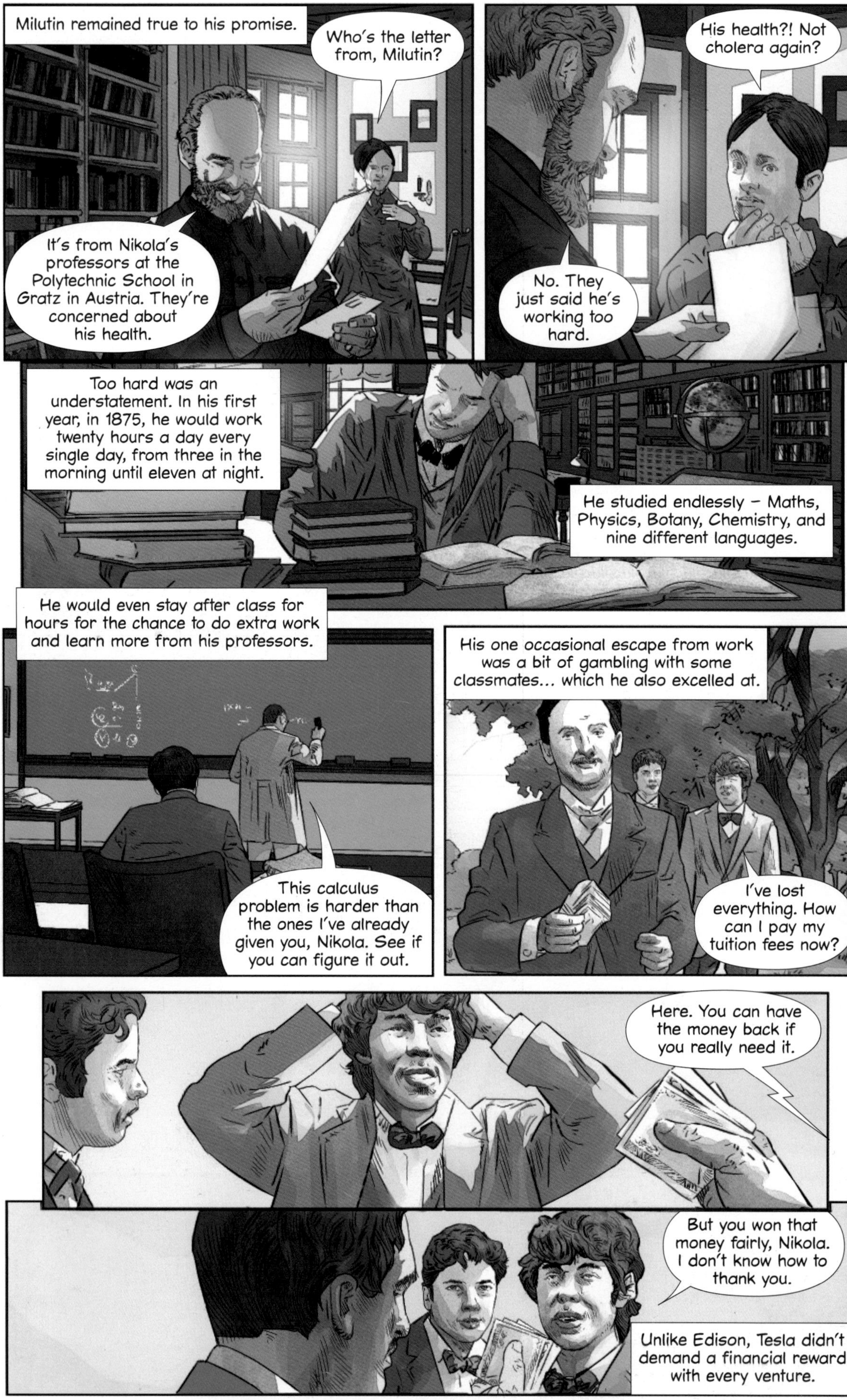

Milutin remained true to his promise.
Who's the letter from, Milutin?
It's from Nikola's professors at the Polytechnic School in Gratz in Austria. They're concerned about his health.
His health?! Not cholera again?
No. They just said he's working too hard.
Too hard was an understatement. In his first year, in 1875, he would work twenty hours a day every single day, from three in the morning until eleven at night.
He studied endlessly – Maths, Physics, Botany, Chemistry, and nine different languages.
He would even stay after class for hours for the chance to do extra work and learn more from his professors.
This calculus problem is harder than the ones I've already given you, Nikola. See if you can figure it out.
His one occasional escape from work was a bit of gambling with some classmates... which he also excelled at.
I've lost everything. How can I pay my tuition fees now?
Here. You can have the money back if you really need it.
But you won that money fairly, Nikola. I don't know how to thank you.
Unlike Edison, Tesla didn't demand a financial reward with every venture.

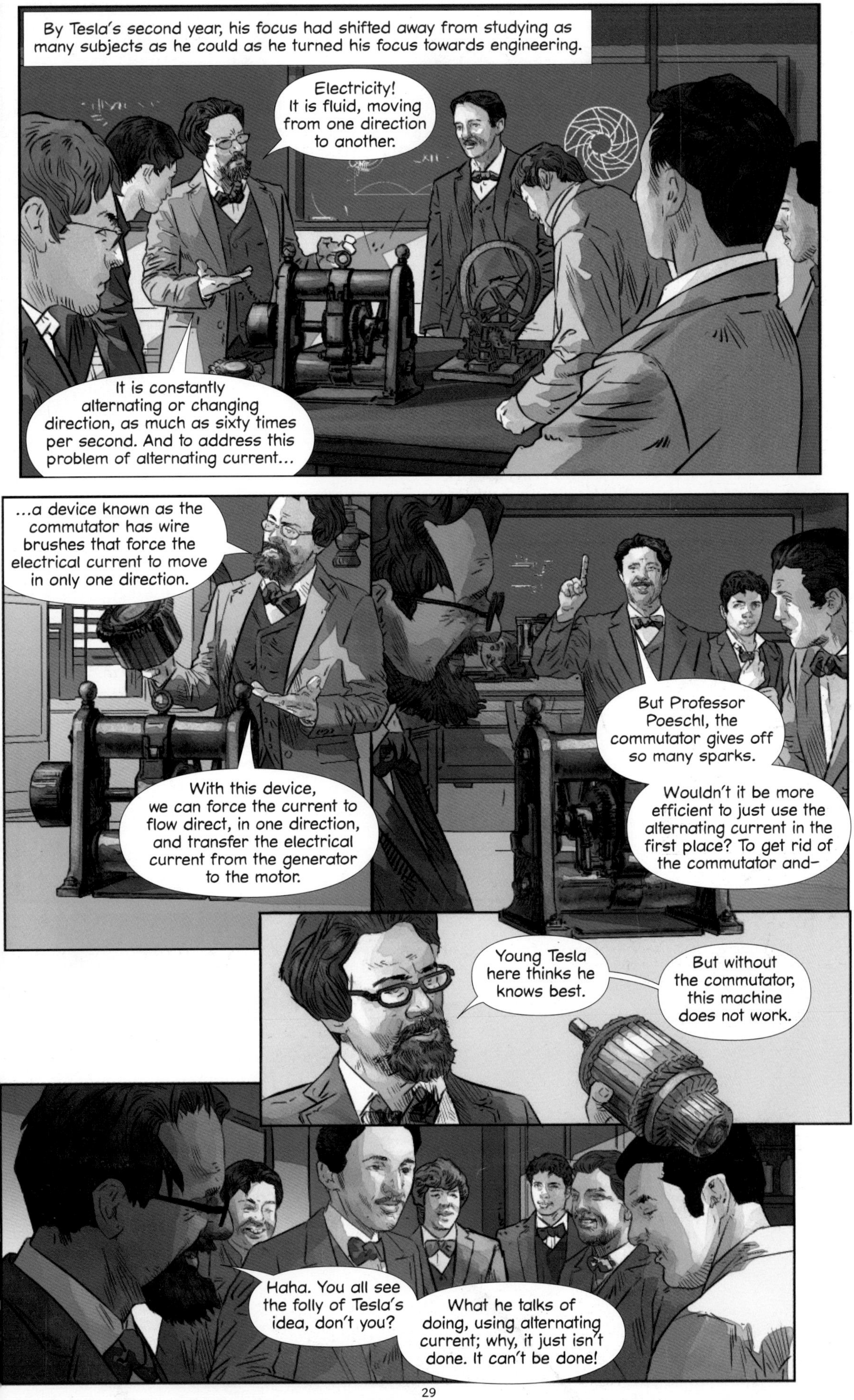
By Tesla's second year, his focus had shifted away from studying as many subjects as he could as he turned his focus towards engineering.
Electricity! It is fluid, moving from one direction to another.
It is constantly alternating or changing direction, as much as sixty times per second. And to address this problem of alternating current...
...a device known as the commutator has wire brushes that force the electrical current to move in only one direction.
With this device, we can force the current to flow direct, in one direction, and transfer the electrical current from the generator to the motor.
But Professor Poeschl, the commutator gives off so many sparks.
Wouldn't it be more efficient to just use the alternating current in the first place? To get rid of the commutator and–
Young Tesla here thinks he knows best.
But without the commutator, this machine does not work.
Haha. You all see the folly of Tesla's idea, don't you?
What he talks of doing, using alternating current; why, it just isn't done. It can't be done!

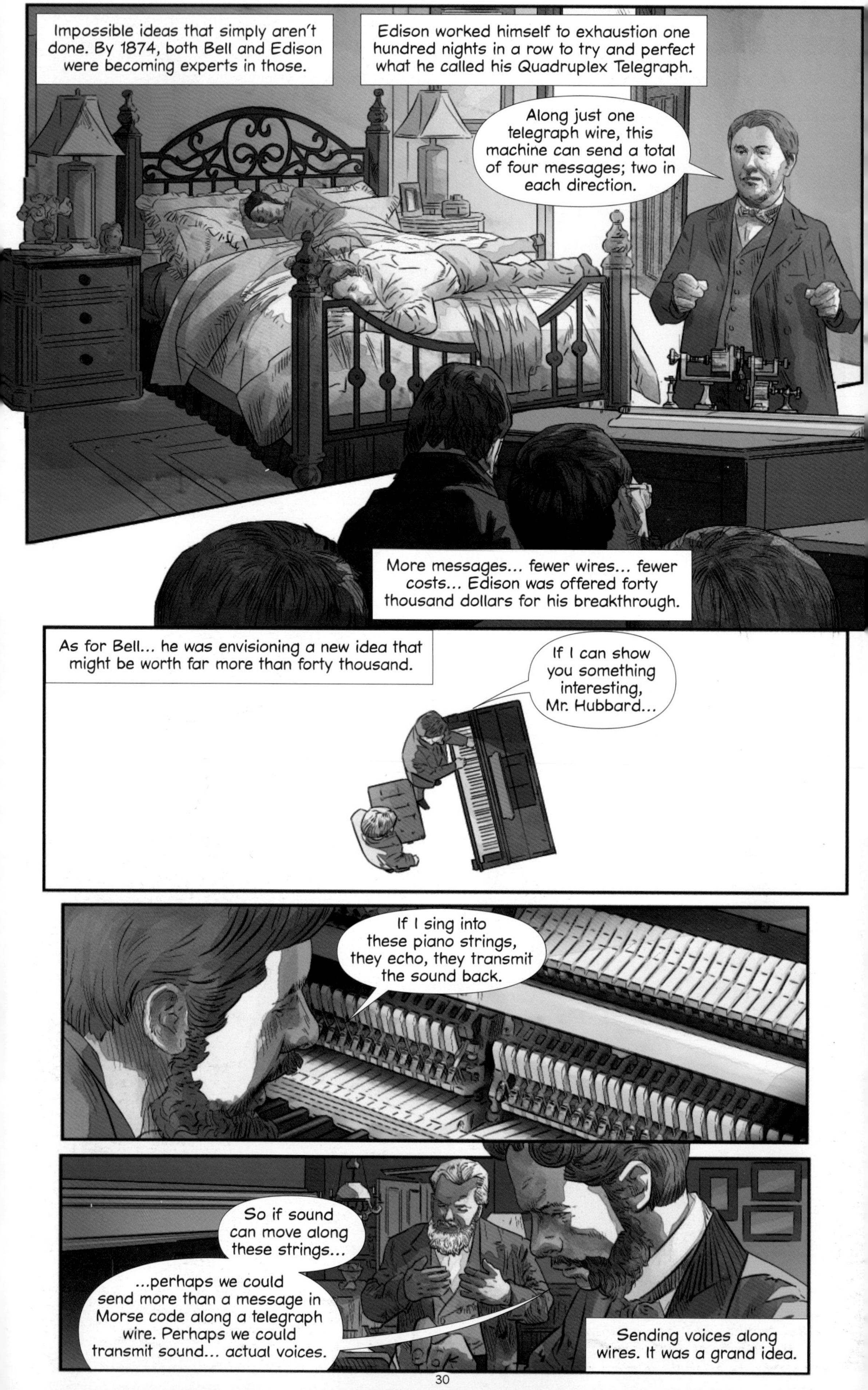
Impossible ideas that simply aren't done. By 1874, both Bell and Edison were becoming experts in those.
Edison worked himself to exhaustion one hundred nights in a row to try and perfect what he called his Quadruplex Telegraph.
Along just one telegraph wire, this machine can send a total of four messages; two in each direction.
More messages... fewer wires... fewer costs... Edison was offered forty thousand dollars for his breakthrough.
As for Bell... he was envisioning a new idea that might be worth far more than forty thousand.
If I can show you something interesting, Mr. Hubbard...
If I sing into these piano strings, they echo, they transmit the sound back.
So if sound can move along these strings...
...perhaps we could send more than a message in Morse code along a telegraph wire. Perhaps we could transmit sound... actual voices.
Sending voices along wires. It was a grand idea.

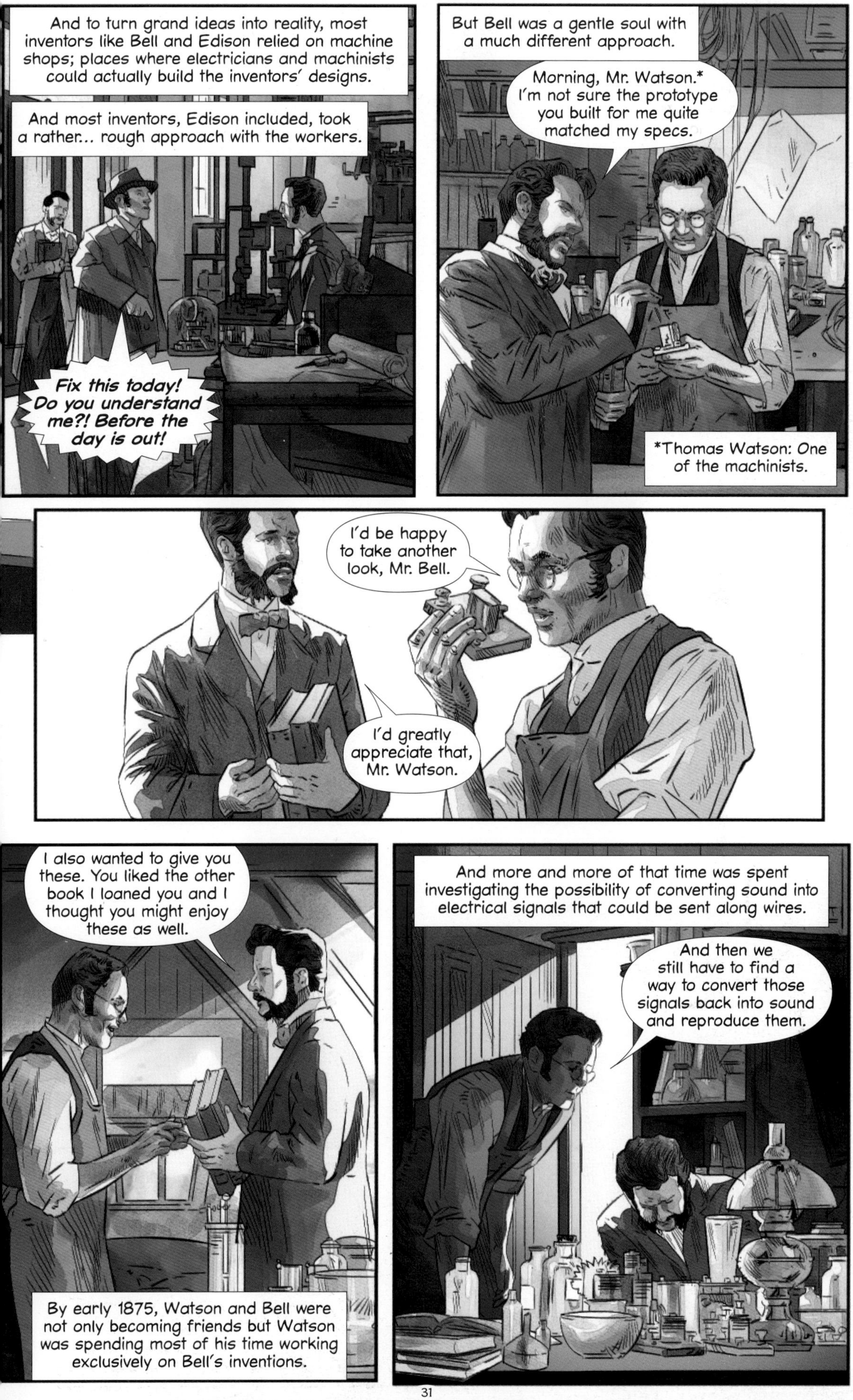
And to turn grand ideas into reality, most inventors like Bell and Edison relied on machine shops; places where electricians and machinists could actually build the inventors' designs.
And most inventors, Edison included, took a rather... rough approach with the workers.
Fix this today! Do you understand me?! Before the day is out!
But Bell was a gentle soul with a much different approach.
Morning, Mr. Watson.* I'm not sure the prototype you built for me quite matched my specs.
*Thomas Watson: One of the machinists.
I'd be happy to take another look, Mr. Bell.
I'd greatly appreciate that, Mr. Watson.
I also wanted to give you these. You liked the other book I loaned you and I thought you might enjoy these as well.
By early 1875, Watson and Bell were not only becoming friends but Watson was spending most of his time working exclusively on Bell's inventions.
And more and more of that time was spent investigating the possibility of converting sound into electrical signals that could be sent along wires.
And then we still have to find a way to convert those signals back into sound and reproduce them.

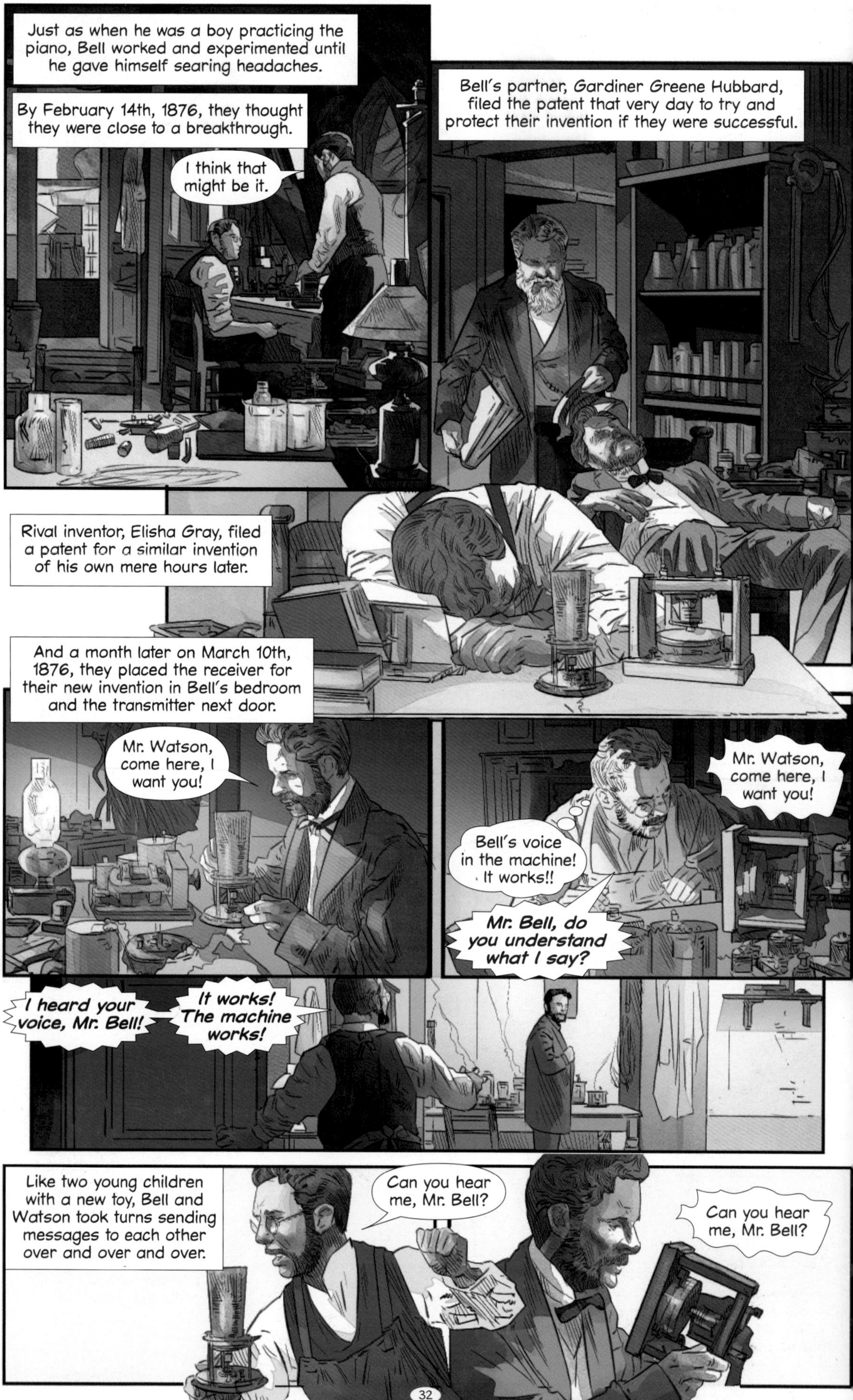
Just as when he was a boy practicing the piano, Bell worked and experimented until he gave himself searing headaches.
By February 14th, 1876, they thought they were close to a breakthrough.
I think that might be it.
Bell's partner, Gardiner Greene Hubbard, filed the patent that very day to try and protect their invention if they were successful.
Rival inventor, Elisha Gray, filed a patent for a similar invention of his own mere hours later.
And a month later on March 10th, 1876, they placed the receiver for their new invention in Bell's bedroom and the transmitter next door.
Mr. Watson, come here, I want you!
Mr. Watson, come here, I want you!
Bell's voice in the machine! It works!!
Mr. Bell, do you understand what I say?
I heard your voice, Mr. Bell!
It works! The machine works!
Like two young children with a new toy, Bell and Watson took turns sending messages to each other over and over and over.
Can you hear me, Mr. Bell?
Can you hear me, Mr. Bell?

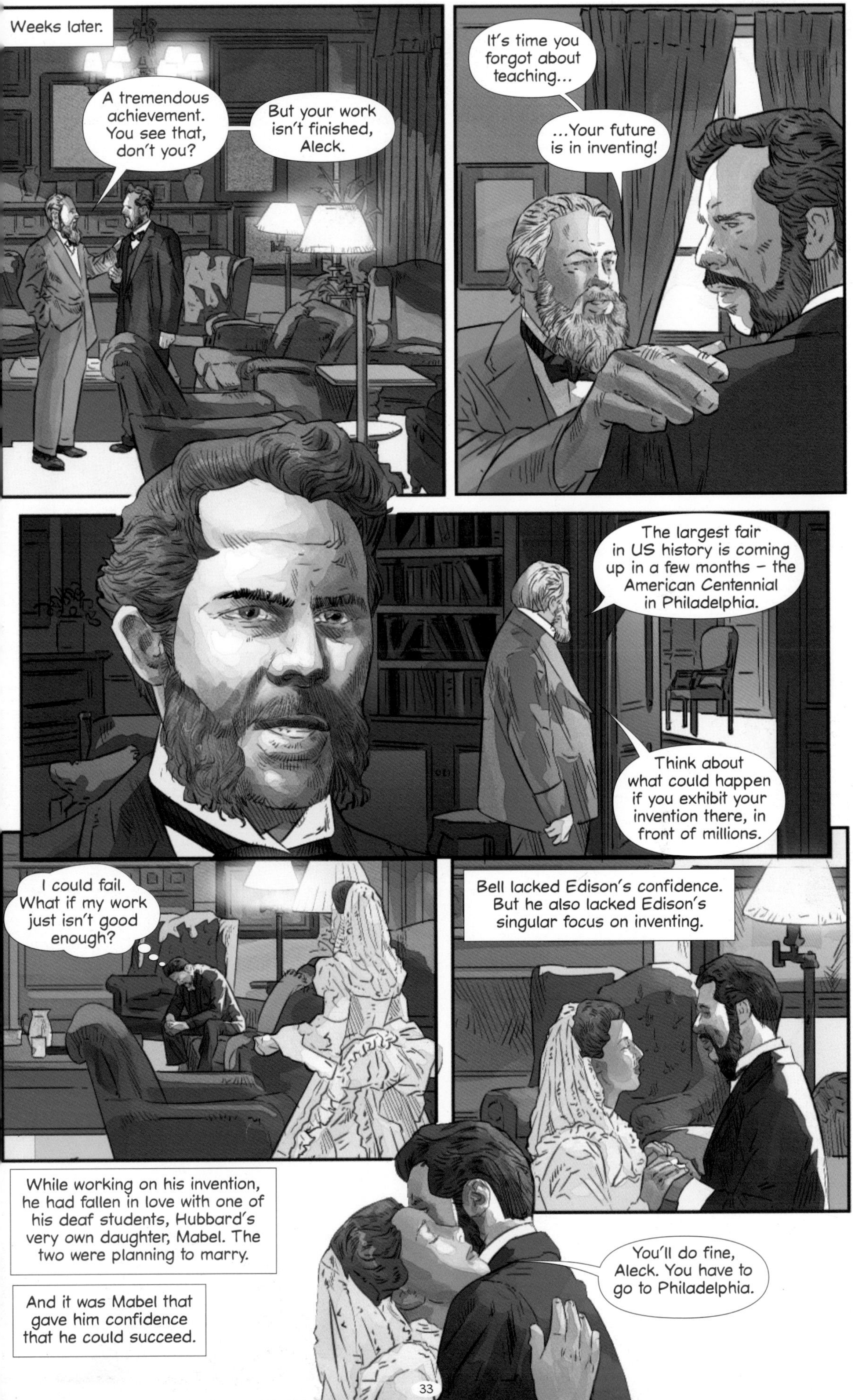
Weeks later.
A tremendous achievement. You see that, don't you?
But your work isn't finished, Aleck.
It's time you forgot about teaching...
...Your future is in inventing!
The largest fair in US history is coming up in a few months – the American Centennial in Philadelphia.
Think about what could happen if you exhibit your invention there, in front of millions.
I could fail. What if my work just isn't good enough?
Bell lacked Edison's confidence. But he also lacked Edison's singular focus on inventing.
While working on his invention, he had fallen in love with one of his deaf students, Hubbard's very own daughter, Mabel. The two were planning to marry.
And it was Mabel that gave him confidence that he could succeed.
You'll do fine, Aleck. You have to go to Philadelphia.

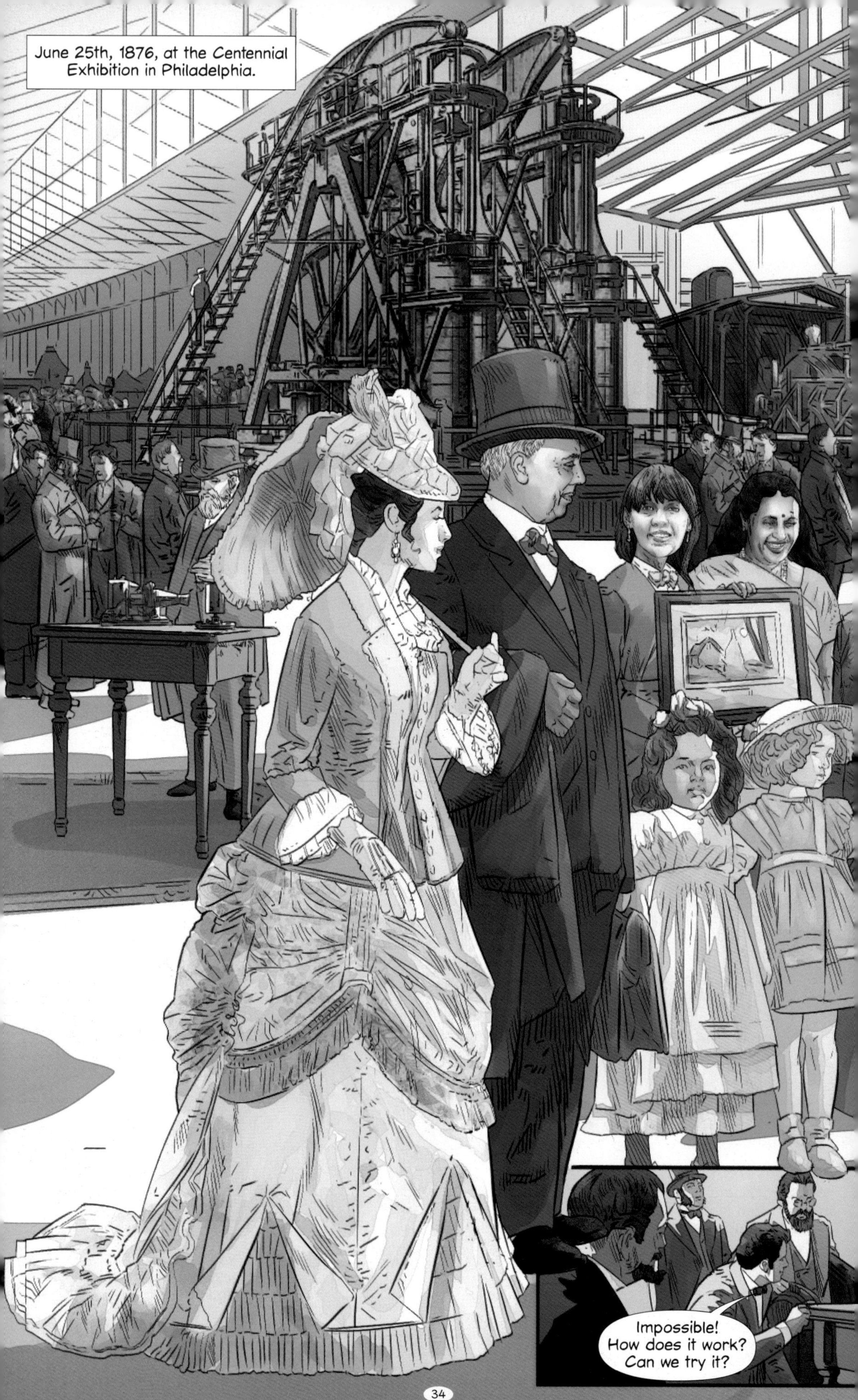
June 25th, 1876, at the Centennial Exhibition in Philadelphia.
Impossible! How does it work? Can we try it?

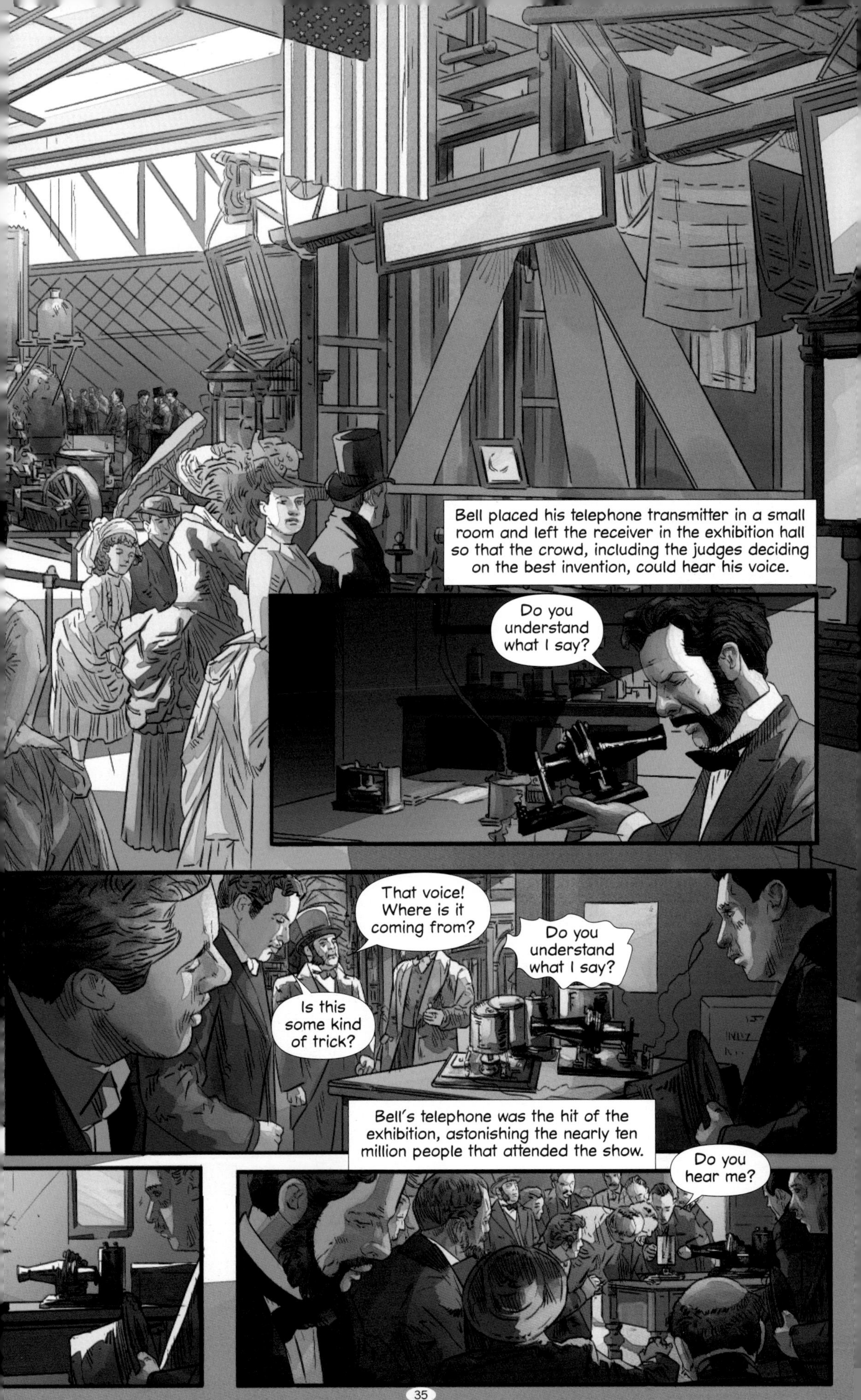
Bell placed his telephone transmitter in a small room and left the receiver in the exhibition hall so that the crowd, including the judges deciding on the best invention, could hear his voice.
Do you understand what I say?
That voice! Where is it coming from?
Do you understand what I say?
Is this some kind of trick?
Bell's telephone was the hit of the exhibition, astonishing the nearly ten million people that attended the show.
Do you hear me?

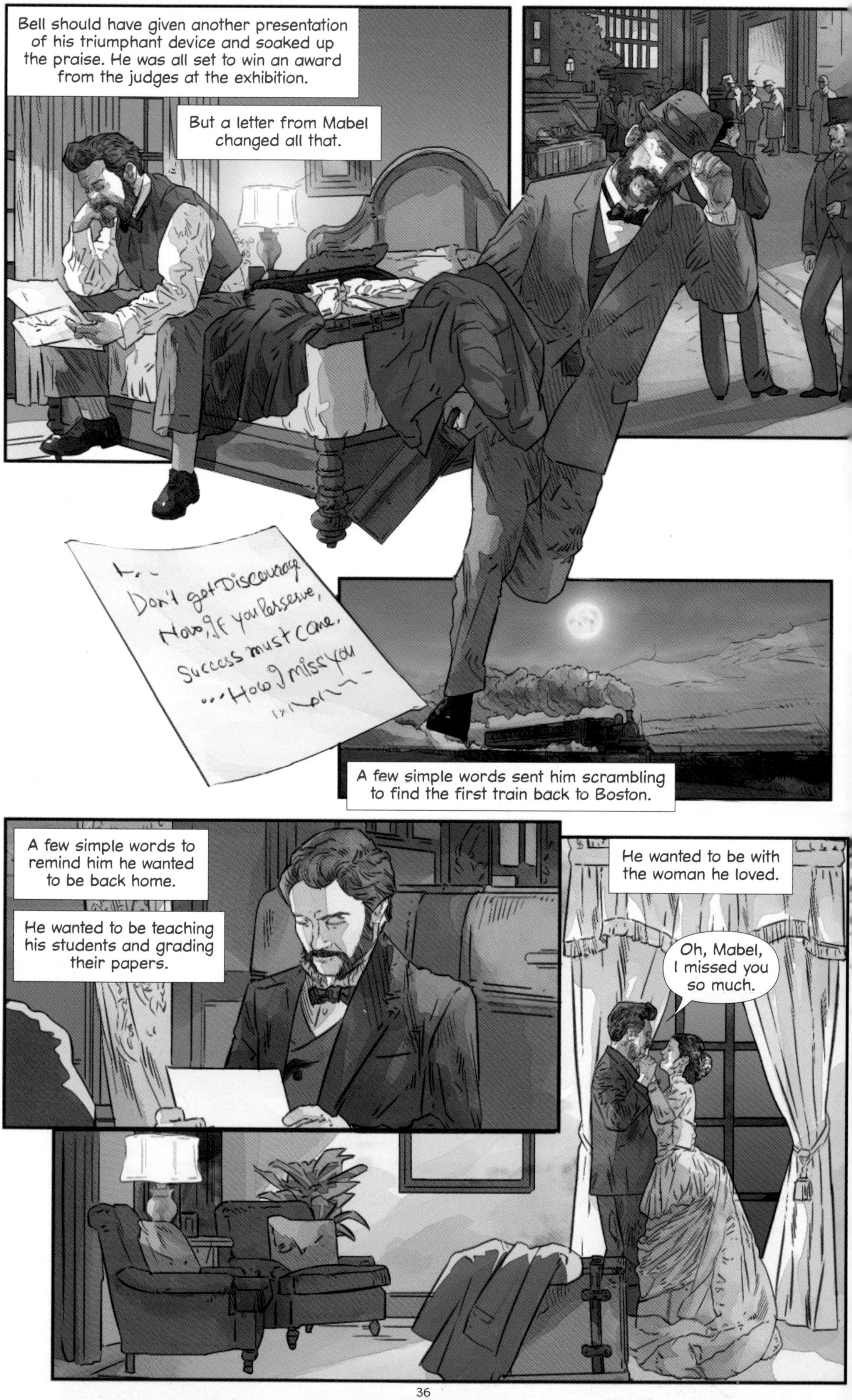

Bell should have given another presentation of his triumphant device and soaked up the praise. He was all set to win an award from the judges at the exhibition.
But a letter from Mabel changed all that.
Don't get Discourag
Now, if you persevere,
Success must come.
...How I miss you
A few simple words sent him scrambling to find the first train back to Boston.
A few simple words to remind him he wanted to be back home.
He wanted to be teaching his students and grading their papers.
He wanted to be with the woman he loved.
Oh, Mabel, I missed you so much.

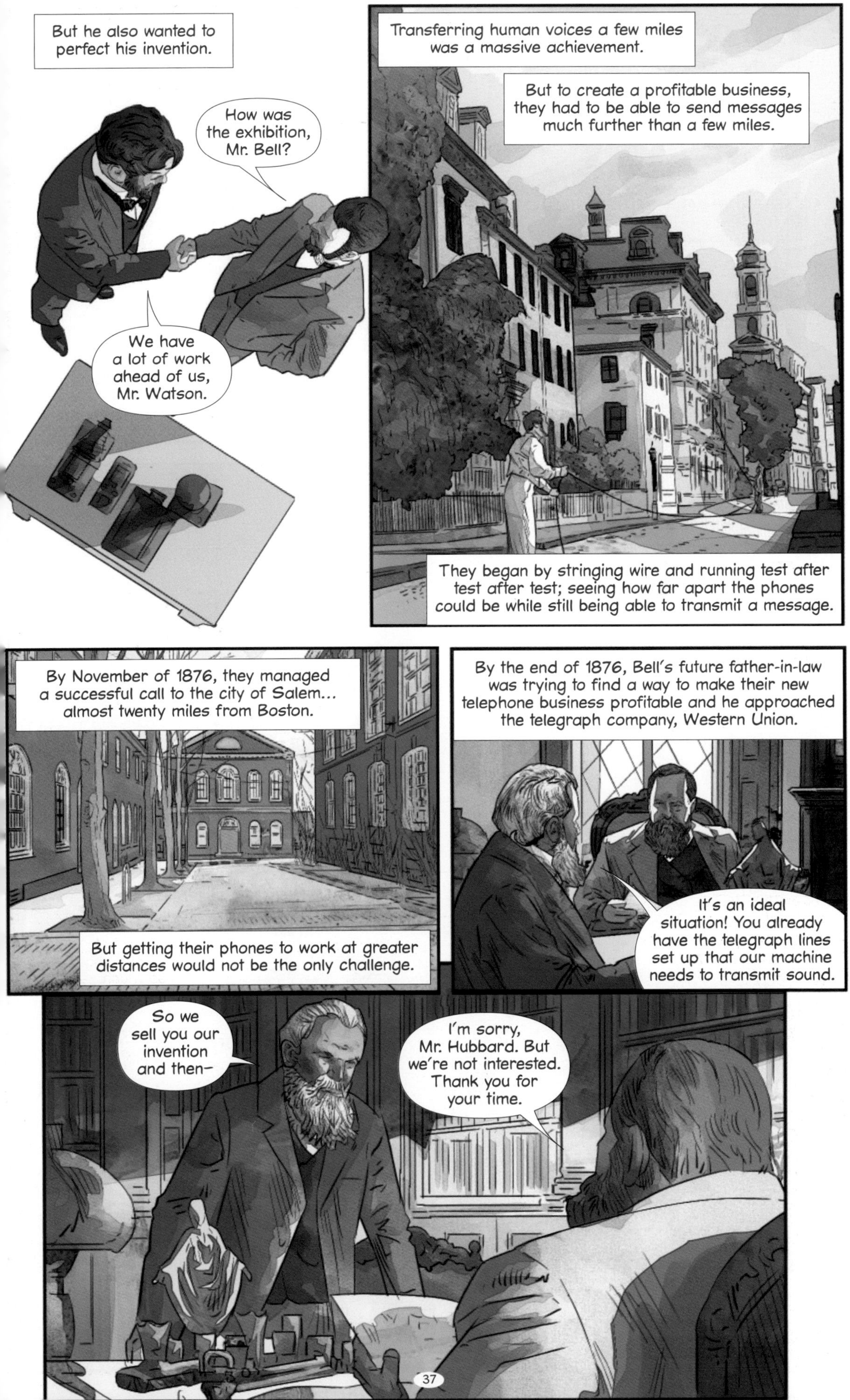
But he also wanted to perfect his invention.
How was the exhibition, Mr. Bell?
We have a lot of work ahead of us, Mr. Watson.
Transferring human voices a few miles was a massive achievement.
But to create a profitable business, they had to be able to send messages much further than a few miles.
They began by stringing wire and running test after test after test; seeing how far apart the phones could be while still being able to transmit a message.
By November of 1876, they managed a successful call to the city of Salem... almost twenty miles from Boston.
But getting their phones to work at greater distances would not be the only challenge.
By the end of 1876, Bell's future father-in-law was trying to find a way to make their new telephone business profitable and he approached the telegraph company, Western Union.
It's an ideal situation! You already have the telegraph lines set up that our machine needs to transmit sound.
So we sell you our invention and then–
I'm sorry, Mr. Hubbard. But we're not interested. Thank you for your time.

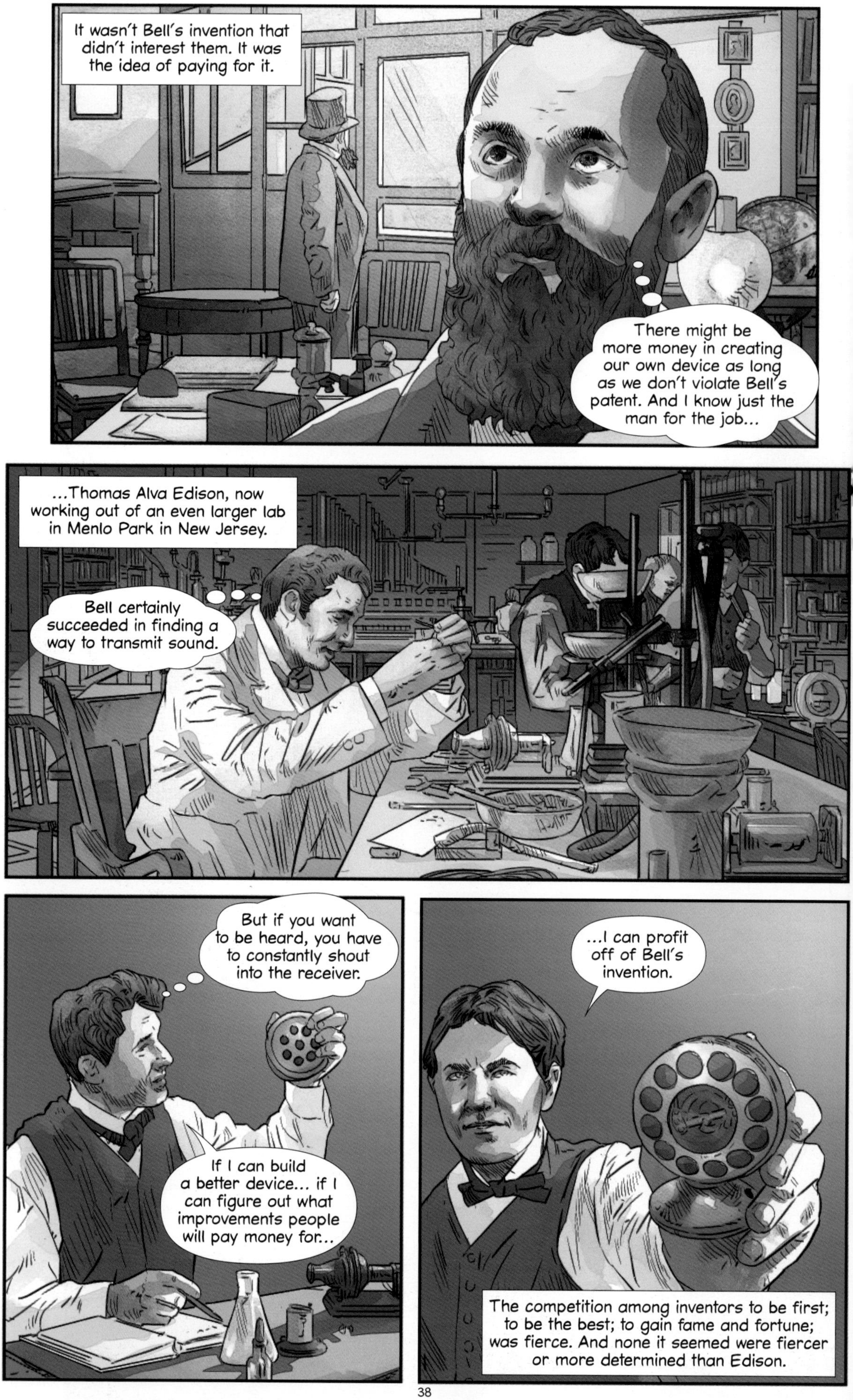
It wasn't Bell's invention that didn't interest them. It was the idea of paying for it.
There might be more money in creating our own device as long as we don't violate Bell's patent. And I know just the man for the job...
...Thomas Alva Edison, now working out of an even larger lab in Menlo Park in New Jersey.
Bell certainly succeeded in finding a way to transmit sound.
But if you want to be heard, you have to constantly shout into the receiver.
If I can build a better device... if I can figure out what improvements people will pay money for...
...I can profit off of Bell's invention.
The competition among inventors to be first; to be the best; to gain fame and fortune; was fierce. And none it seemed were fiercer or more determined than Edison.

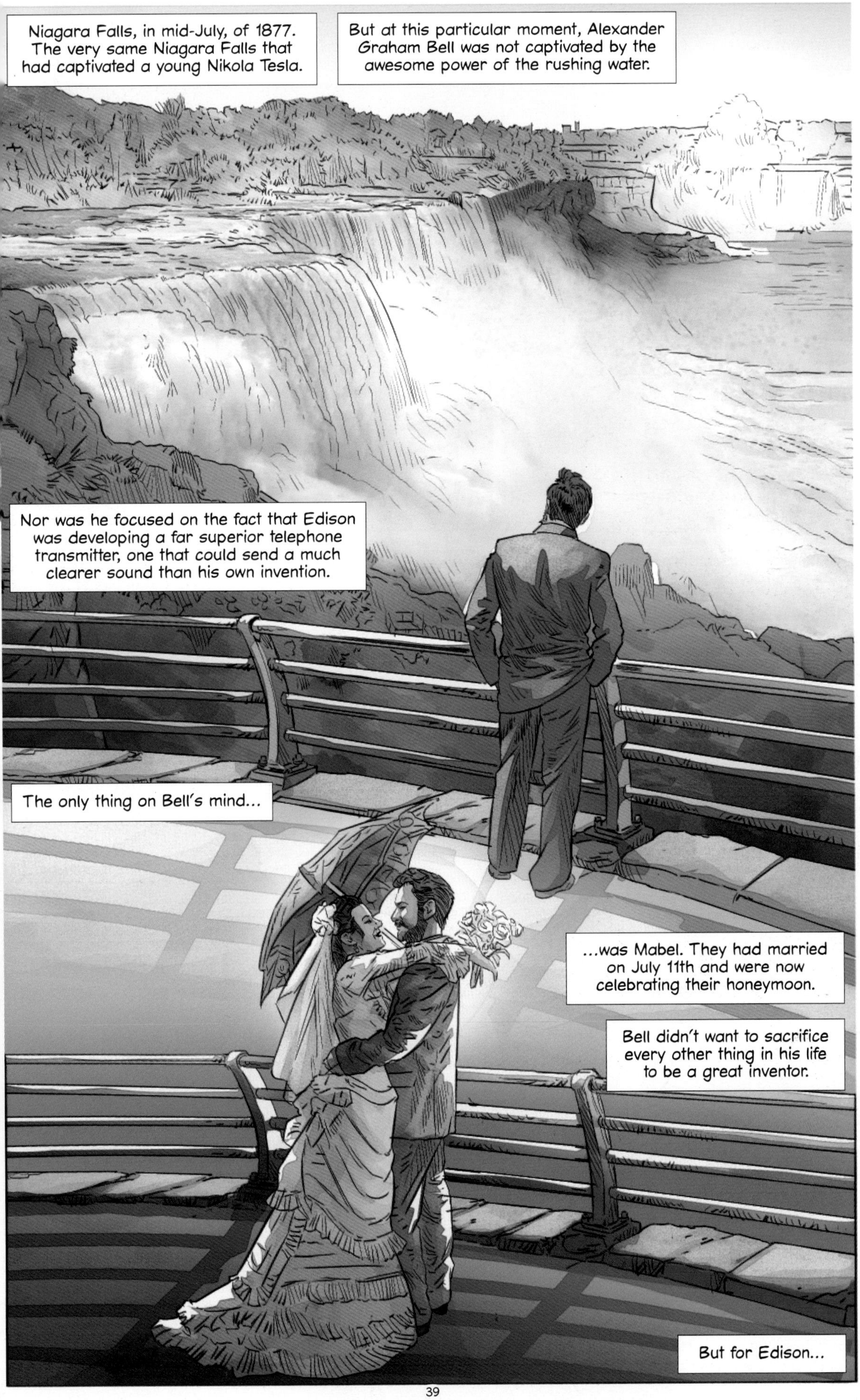
Niagara Falls, in mid-July, of 1877. The very same Niagara Falls that had captivated a young Nikola Tesla.
But at this particular moment, Alexander Graham Bell was not captivated by the awesome power of the rushing water.
Nor was he focused on the fact that Edison was developing a far superior telephone transmitter, one that could send a much clearer sound than his own invention.
The only thing on Bell's mind...
...was Mabel. They had married on July 11th and were now celebrating their honeymoon.
Bell didn't want to sacrifice every other thing in his life to be a great inventor.
But for Edison...

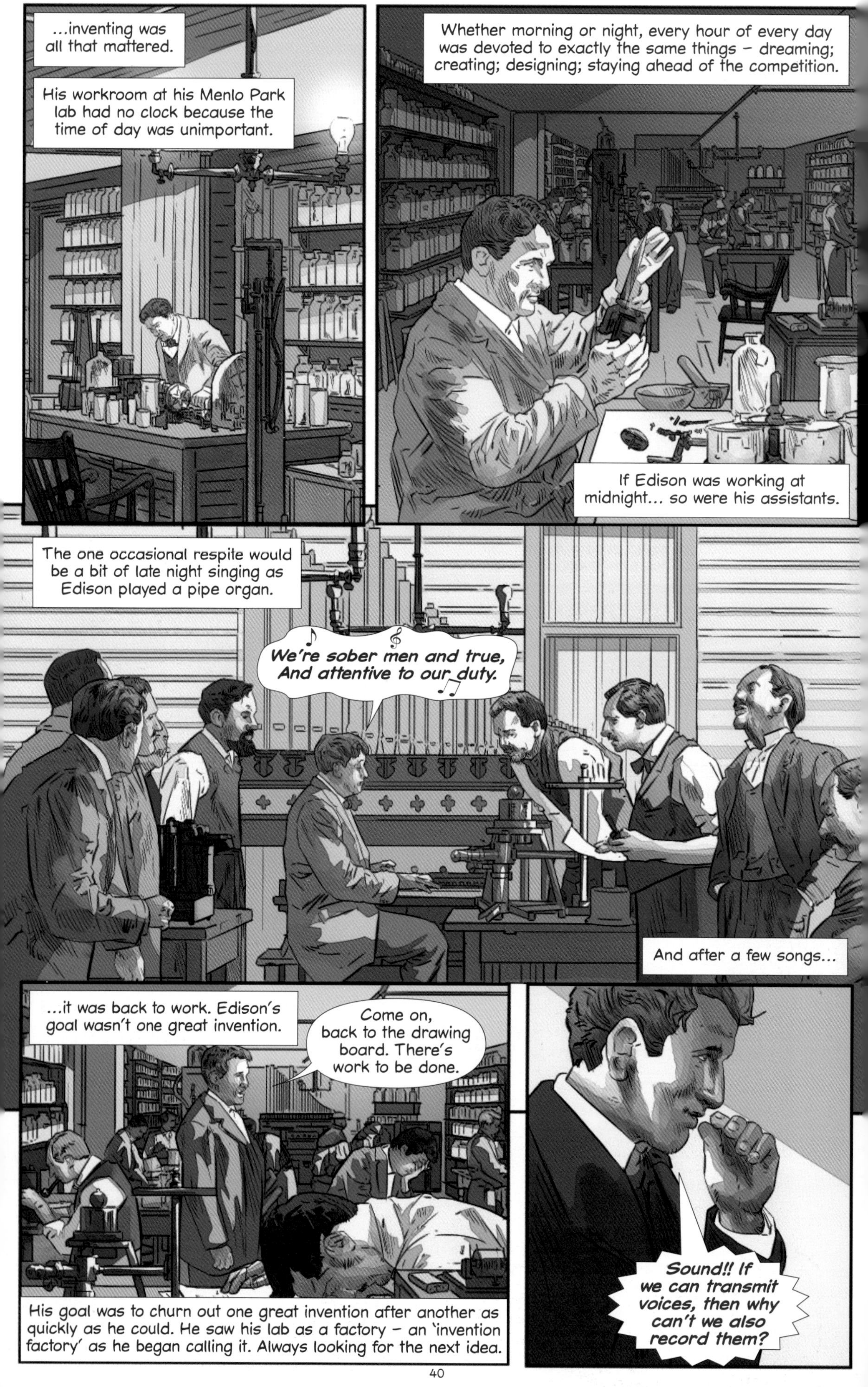
...inventing was all that mattered.
His workroom at his Menlo Park lab had no clock because the time of day was unimportant.
Whether morning or night, every hour of every day was devoted to exactly the same things – dreaming; creating; designing; staying ahead of the competition.
If Edison was working at midnight... so were his assistants.
The one occasional respite would be a bit of late night singing as Edison played a pipe organ.
We're sober men and true, And attentive to our duty.
And after a few songs...
...it was back to work. Edison's goal wasn't one great invention.
Come on, back to the drawing board. There's work to be done.
His goal was to churn out one great invention after another as quickly as he could. He saw his lab as a factory – an 'invention factory' as he began calling it. Always looking for the next idea.
Sound!! If we can transmit voices, then why can't we also record them?

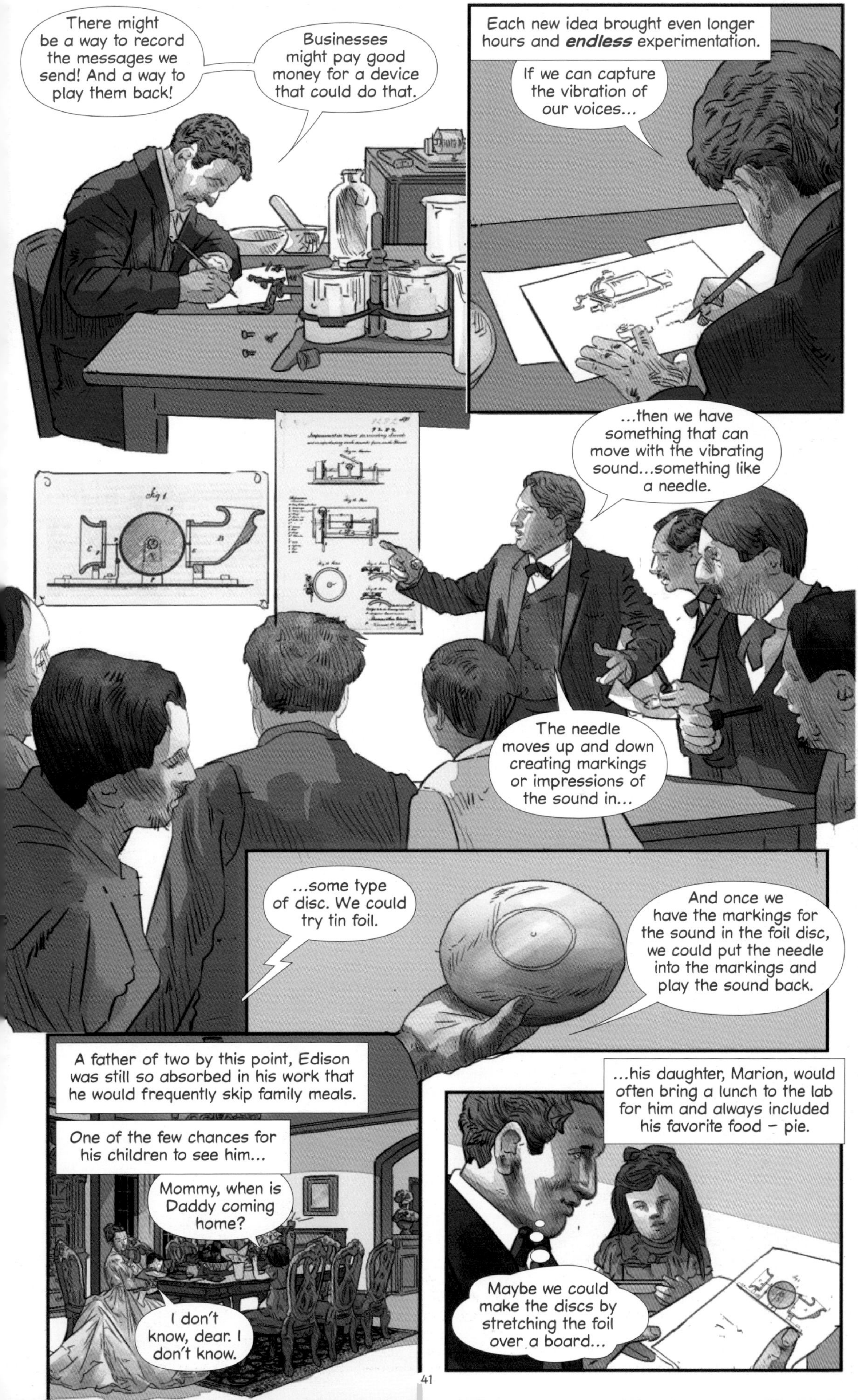
There might be a way to record the messages we send! And a way to play them back!
Businesses might pay good money for a device that could do that.
Each new idea brought even longer hours and ***endless*** experimentation.
If we can capture the vibration of our voices...
...then we have something that can move with the vibrating sound...something like a needle.
The needle moves up and down creating markings or impressions of the sound in...
...some type of disc. We could try tin foil.
And once we have the markings for the sound in the foil disc, we could put the needle into the markings and play the sound back.
A father of two by this point, Edison was still so absorbed in his work that he would frequently skip family meals.
One of the few chances for his children to see him...
Mommy, when is Daddy coming home?
I don't know, dear. I don't know.
...his daughter, Marion, would often bring a lunch to the lab for him and always included his favorite food – pie.
Maybe we could make the discs by stretching the foil over a board...

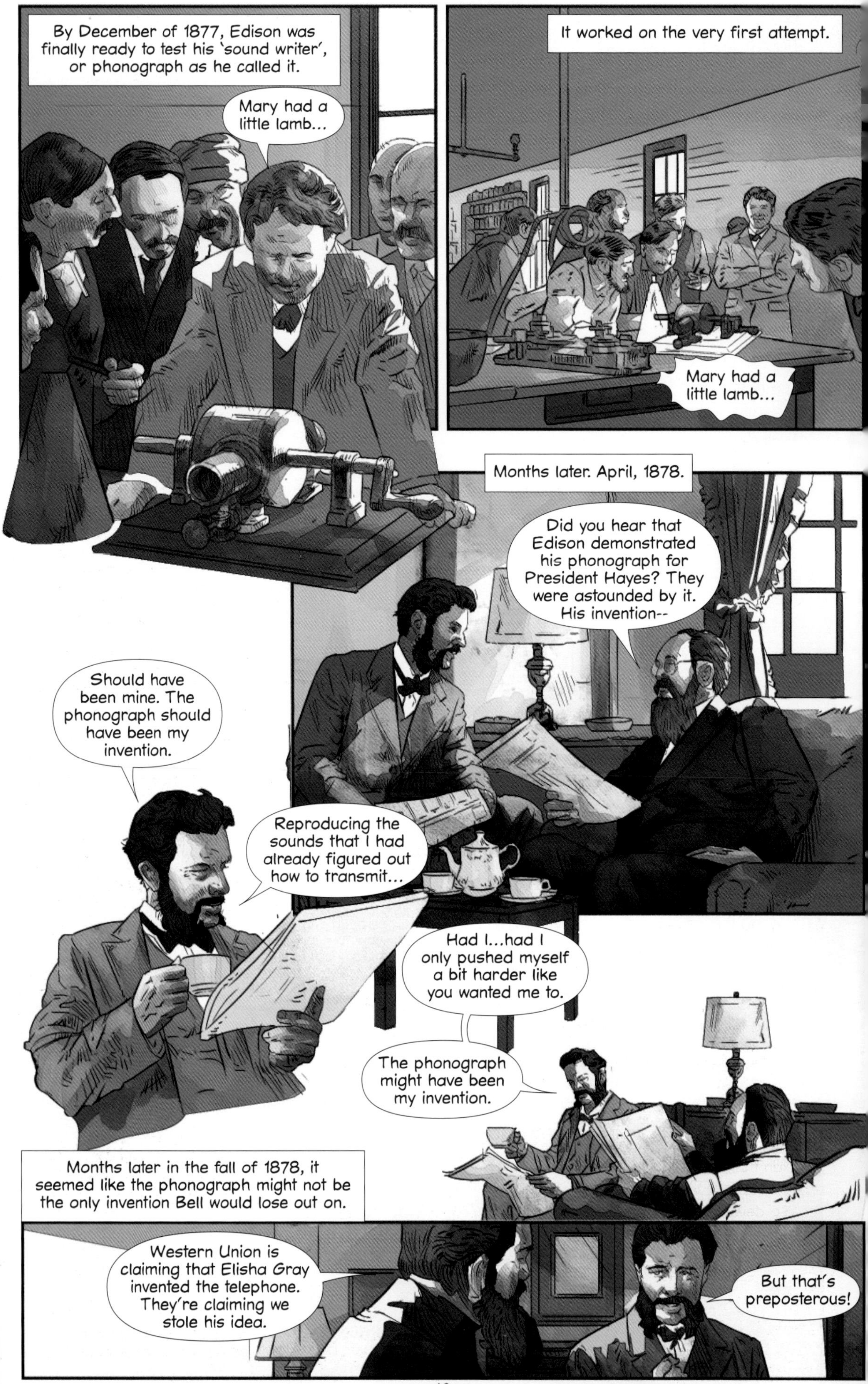

By December of 1877, Edison was finally ready to test his 'sound writer', or phonograph as he called it.
Mary had a little lamb...
It worked on the very first attempt.
Mary had a little lamb...
Months later. April, 1878.
Did you hear that Edison demonstrated his phonograph for President Hayes? They were astounded by it. His invention--
Should have been mine. The phonograph should have been my invention.
Reproducing the sounds that I had already figured out how to transmit...
Had I...had I only pushed myself a bit harder like you wanted me to.
The phonograph might have been my invention.
Months later in the fall of 1878, it seemed like the phonograph might not be the only invention Bell would lose out on.
Western Union is claiming that Elisha Gray invented the telephone. They're claiming we stole his idea.
But that's preposterous!

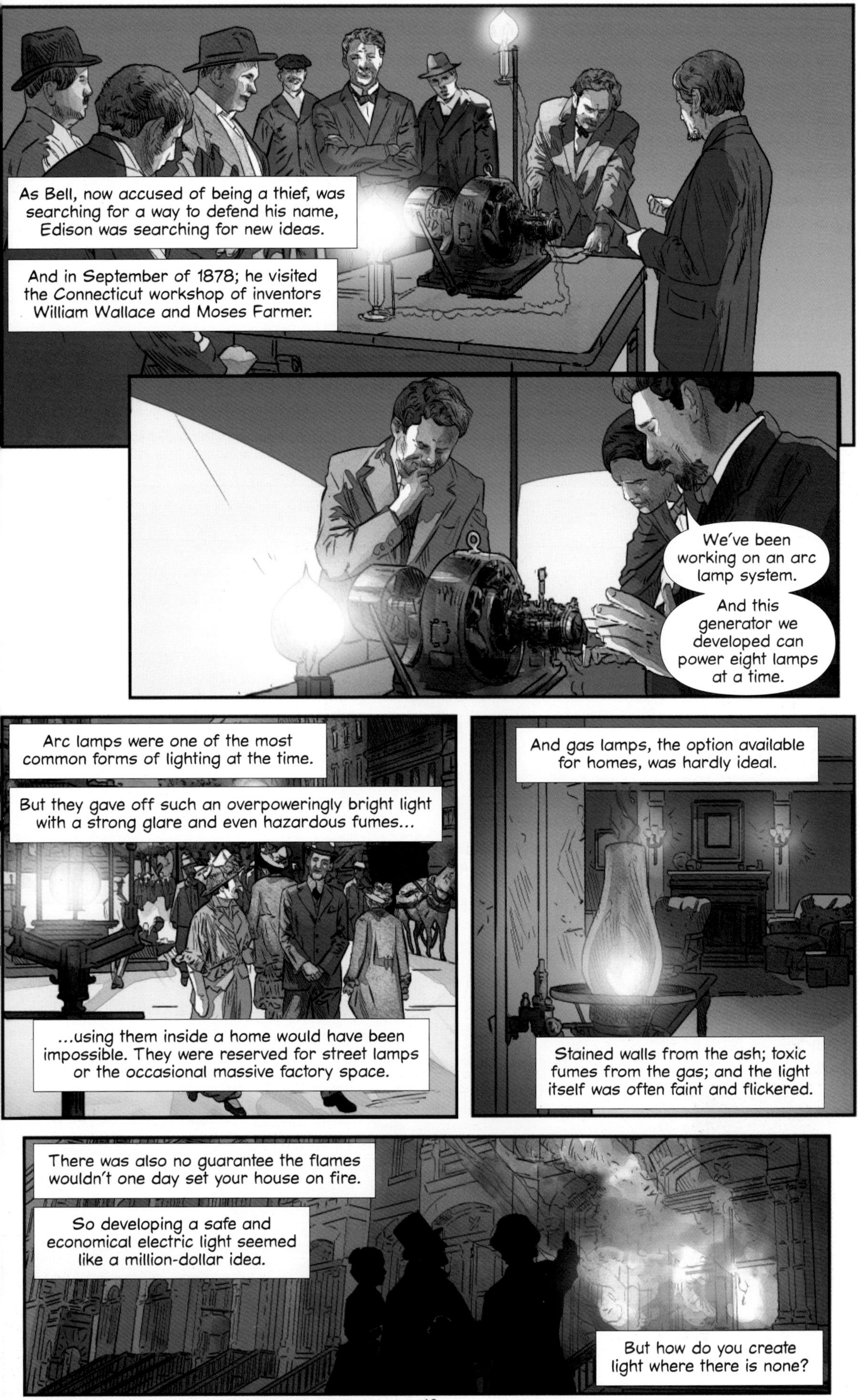
As Bell, now accused of being a thief, was searching for a way to defend his name, Edison was searching for new ideas.
And in September of 1878; he visited the Connecticut workshop of inventors William Wallace and Moses Farmer.
We've been working on an arc lamp system.
And this generator we developed can power eight lamps at a time.
Arc lamps were one of the most common forms of lighting at the time.
But they gave off such an overpoweringly bright light with a strong glare and even hazardous fumes...
...using them inside a home would have been impossible. They were reserved for street lamps or the occasional massive factory space.
And gas lamps, the option available for homes, was hardly ideal.
Stained walls from the ash; toxic fumes from the gas; and the light itself was often faint and flickered.
There was also no guarantee the flames wouldn't one day set your house on fire.
So developing a safe and economical electric light seemed like a million-dollar idea.
But how do you create light where there is none?

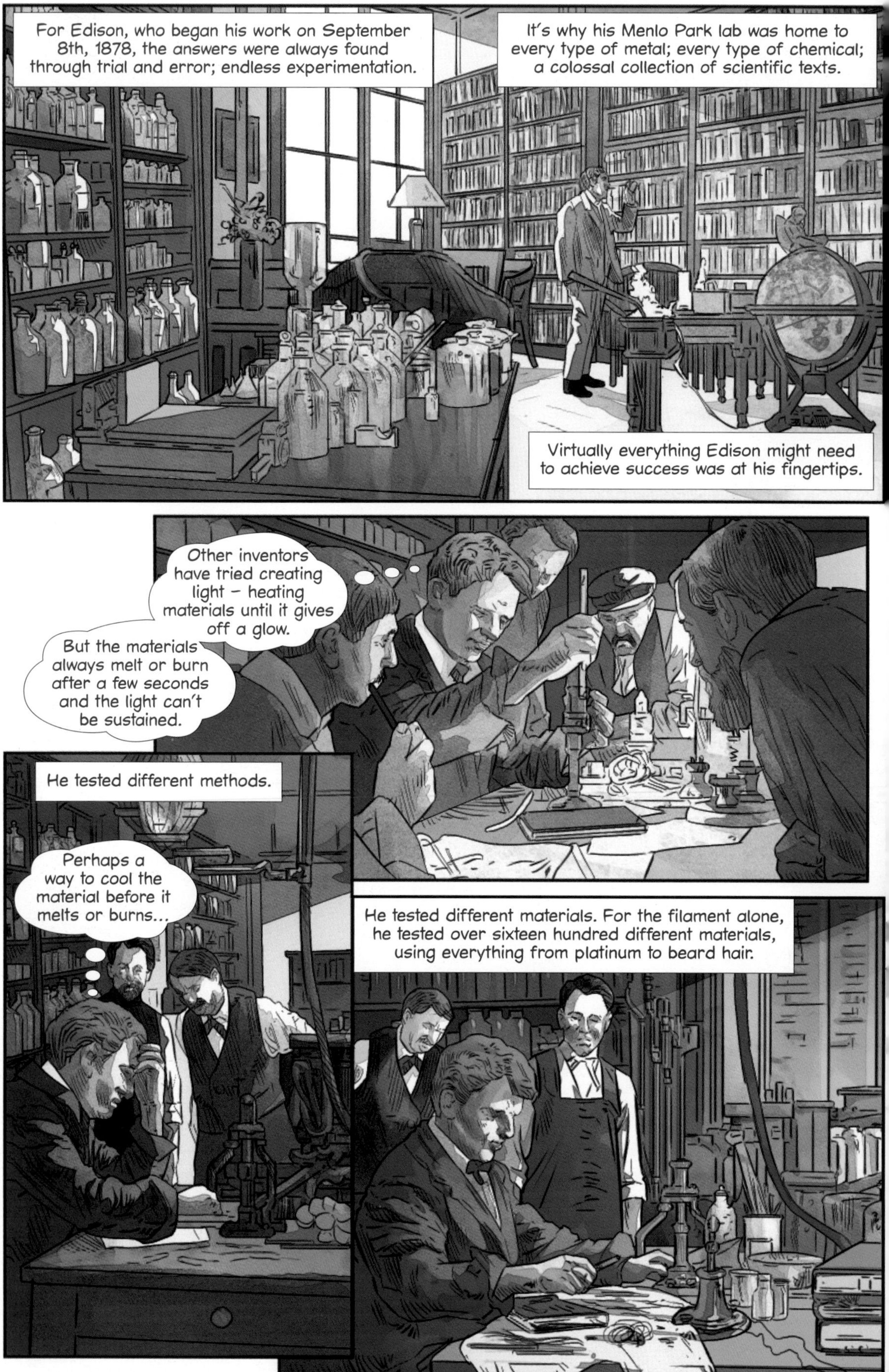

For Edison, who began his work on September 8th, 1878, the answers were always found through trial and error; endless experimentation.
It's why his Menlo Park lab was home to every type of metal; every type of chemical; a colossal collection of scientific texts.
Virtually everything Edison might need to achieve success was at his fingertips.
Other inventors have tried creating light – heating materials until it gives off a glow.
But the materials always melt or burn after a few seconds and the light can't be sustained.
He tested different methods.
Perhaps a way to cool the material before it melts or burns...
He tested different materials. For the filament alone, he tested over sixteen hundred different materials, using everything from platinum to beard hair.
And when he needed more money to keep funding his experiments...

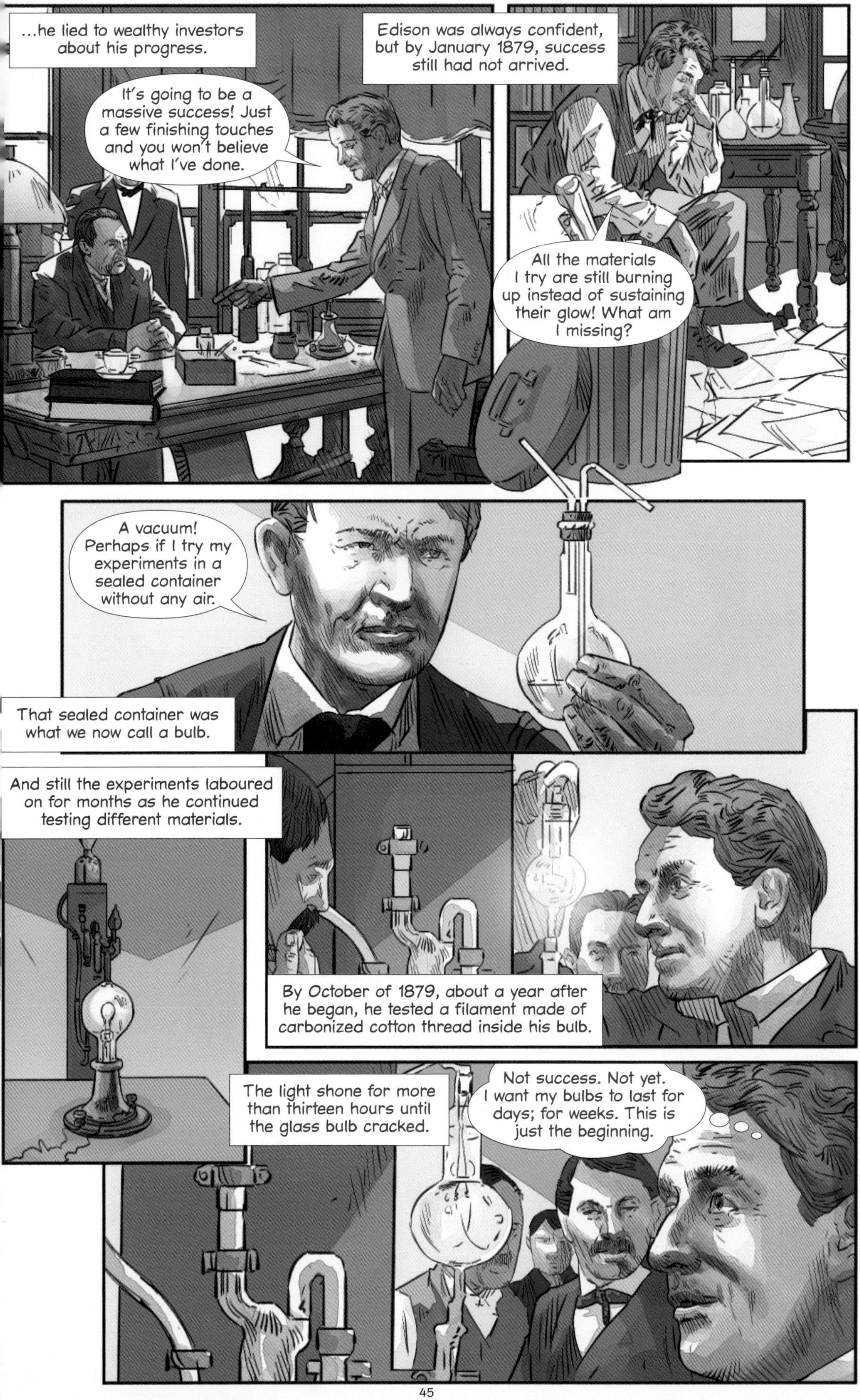
...he lied to wealthy investors about his progress.
It's going to be a massive success! Just a few finishing touches and you won't believe what I've done.
Edison was always confident, but by January 1879, success still had not arrived.
All the materials I try are still burning up instead of sustaining their glow! What am I missing?
A vacuum! Perhaps if I try my experiments in a sealed container without any air.
That sealed container was what we now call a bulb.
And still the experiments laboured on for months as he continued testing different materials.
By October of 1879, about a year after he began, he tested a filament made of carbonized cotton thread inside his bulb.
The light shone for more than thirteen hours until the glass bulb cracked.
Not success. Not yet. I want my bulbs to last for days; for weeks. This is just the beginning.

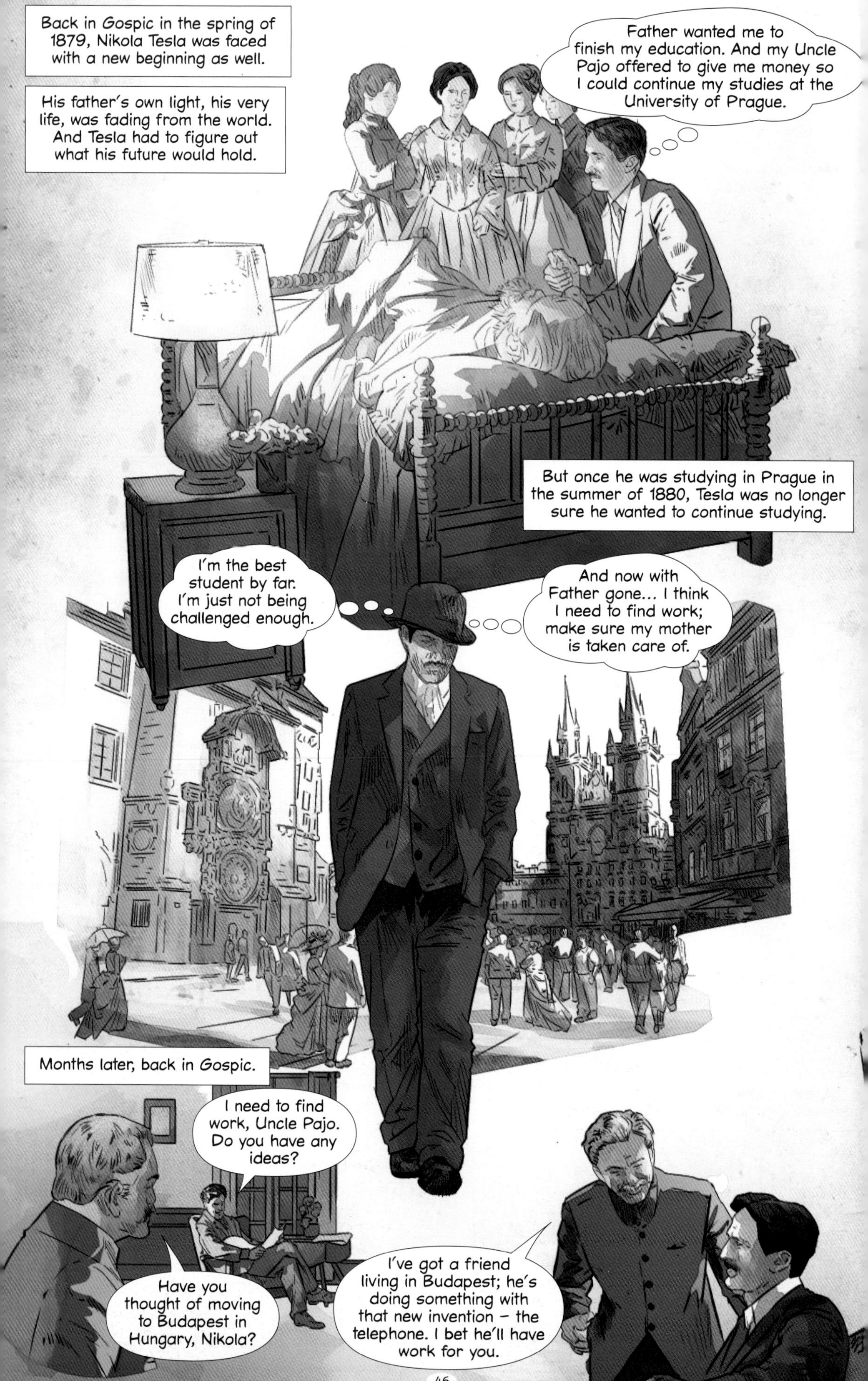
Back in Gospic in the spring of 1879, Nikola Tesla was faced with a new beginning as well.
His father's own light, his very life, was fading from the world. And Tesla had to figure out what his future would hold.
Father wanted me to finish my education. And my Uncle Pajo offered to give me money so I could continue my studies at the University of Prague.
But once he was studying in Prague in the summer of 1880, Tesla was no longer sure he wanted to continue studying.
I'm the best student by far. I'm just not being challenged enough.
And now with Father gone... I think I need to find work; make sure my mother is taken care of.
Months later, back in Gospic.
I need to find work, Uncle Pajo. Do you have any ideas?
Have you thought of moving to Budapest in Hungary, Nikola?
I've got a friend living in Budapest; he's doing something with that new invention – the telephone. I bet he'll have work for you.

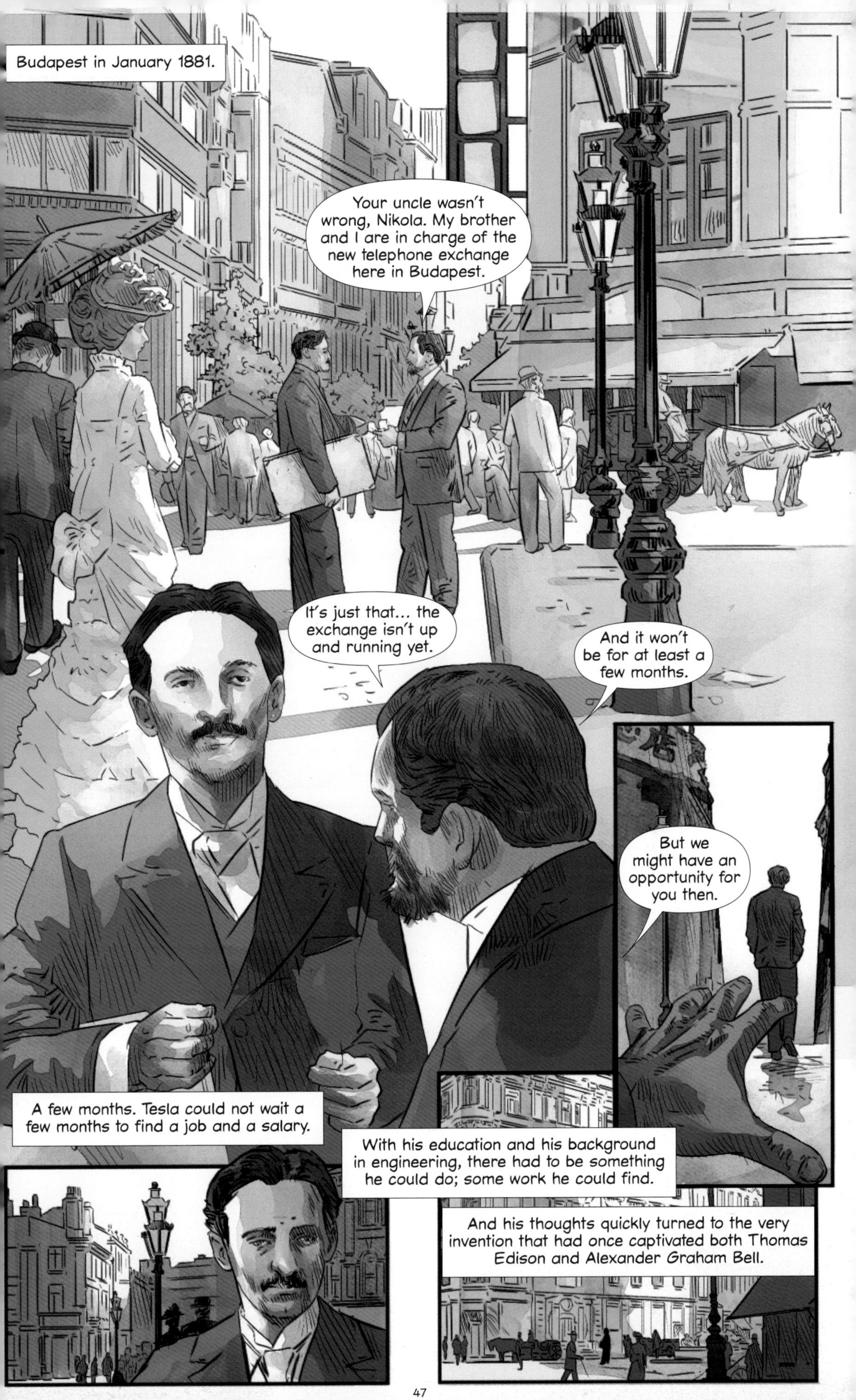
Budapest in January 1881.
Your uncle wasn't wrong, Nikola. My brother and I are in charge of the new telephone exchange here in Budapest.
It's just that... the exchange isn't up and running yet.
And it won't be for at least a few months.
But we might have an opportunity for you then.
A few months. Tesla could not wait a few months to find a job and a salary.
With his education and his background in engineering, there had to be something he could do; some work he could find.
And his thoughts quickly turned to the very invention that had once captivated both Thomas Edison and Alexander Graham Bell.

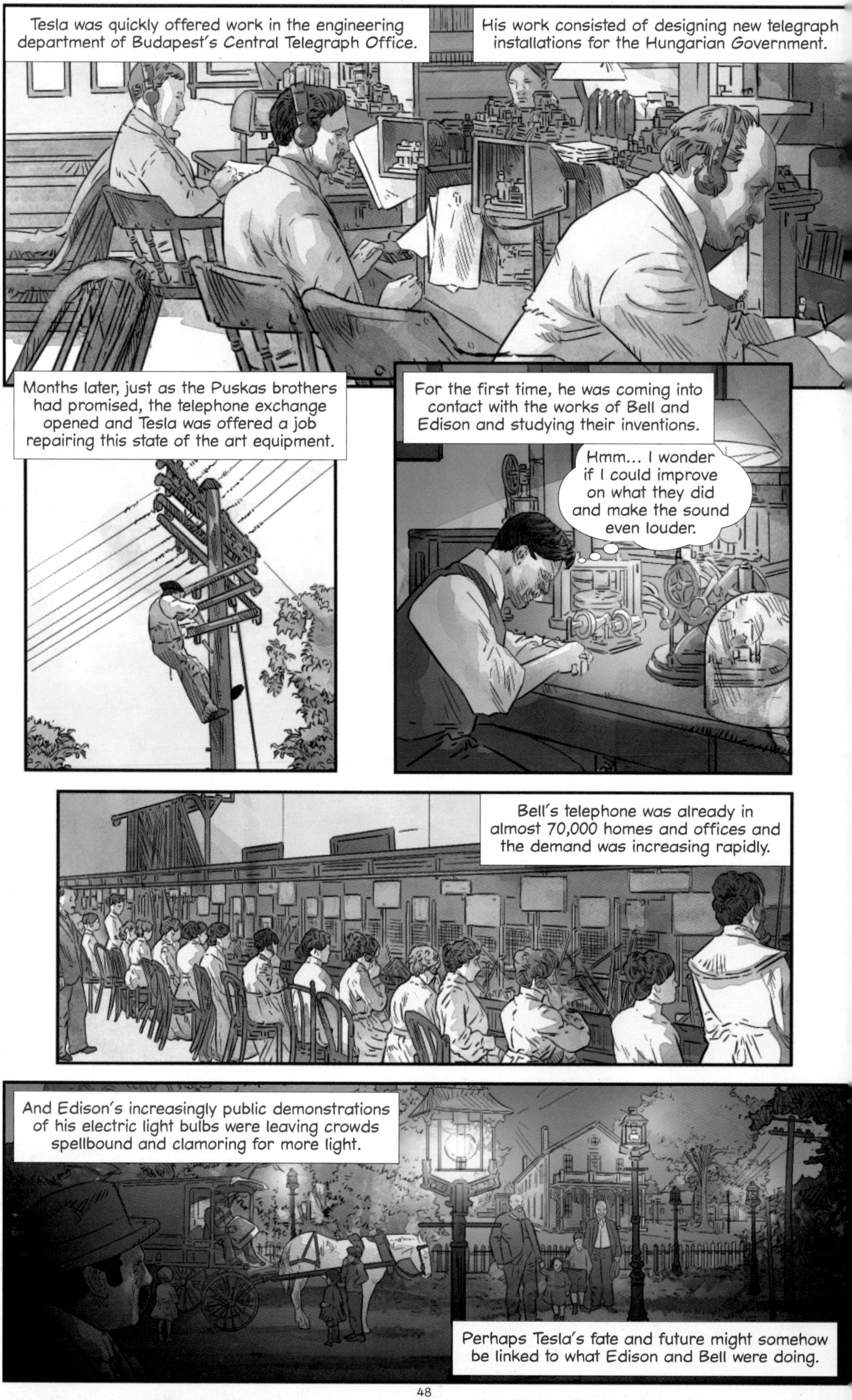
Tesla was quickly offered work in the engineering department of Budapest's Central Telegraph Office.
His work consisted of designing new telegraph installations for the Hungarian Government.
Months later, just as the Puskas brothers had promised, the telephone exchange opened and Tesla was offered a job repairing this state of the art equipment.
For the first time, he was coming into contact with the works of Bell and Edison and studying their inventions.
Hmm... I wonder if I could improve on what they did and make the sound even louder.
Bell's telephone was already in almost 70,000 homes and offices and the demand was increasing rapidly.
And Edison's increasingly public demonstrations of his electric light bulbs were leaving crowds spellbound and clamoring for more light.
Perhaps Tesla's fate and future might somehow be linked to what Edison and Bell were doing.

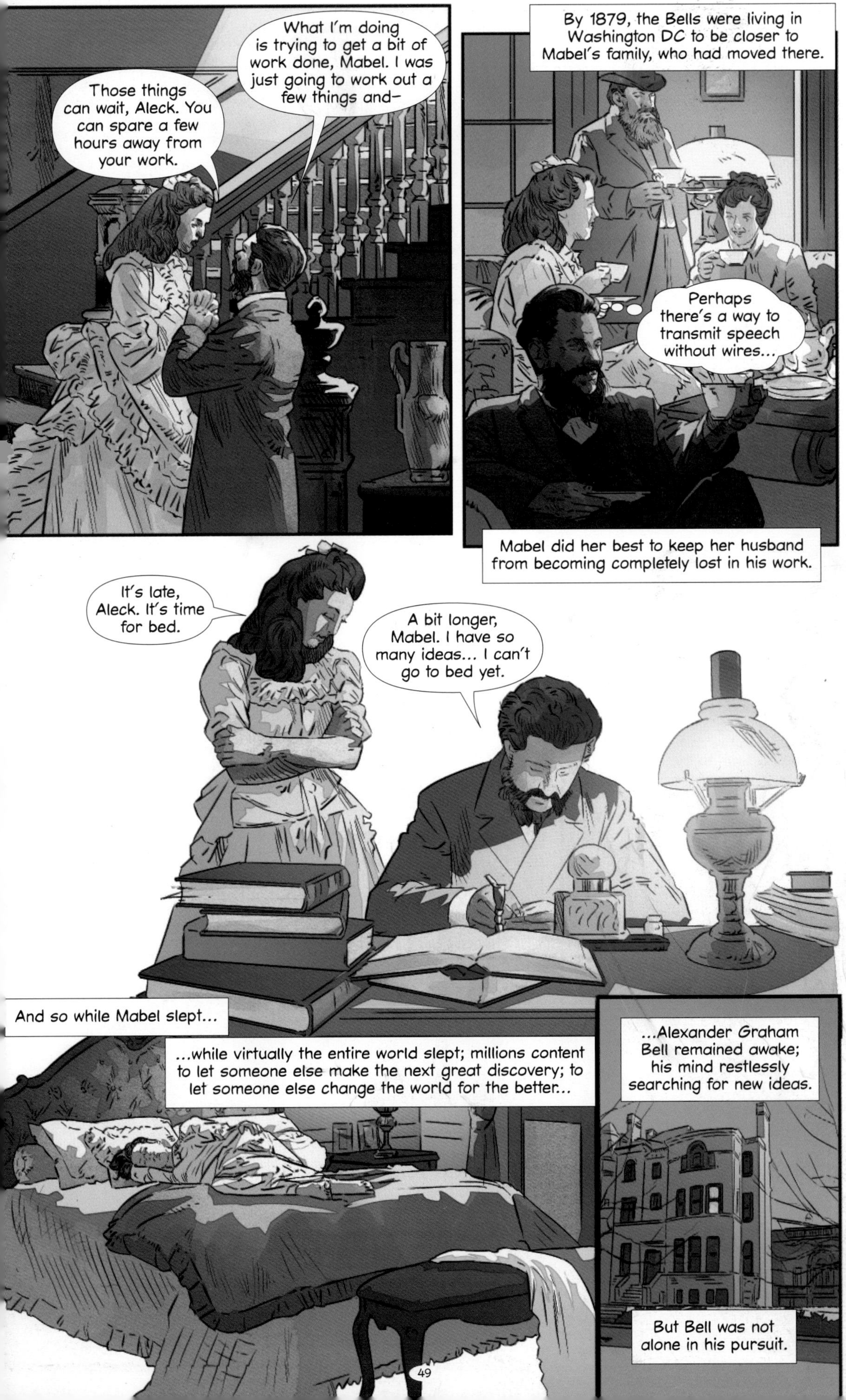
What I'm doing is trying to get a bit of work done, Mabel. I was just going to work out a few things and–
Those things can wait, Aleck. You can spare a few hours away from your work.
By 1879, the Bells were living in Washington DC to be closer to Mabel's family, who had moved there.
Perhaps there's a way to transmit speech without wires...
Mabel did her best to keep her husband from becoming completely lost in his work.
It's late, Aleck. It's time for bed.
A bit longer, Mabel. I have so many ideas... I can't go to bed yet.
And so while Mabel slept...
...while virtually the entire world slept; millions content to let someone else make the next great discovery; to let someone else change the world for the better...
...Alexander Graham Bell remained awake; his mind restlessly searching for new ideas.
But Bell was not alone in his pursuit.

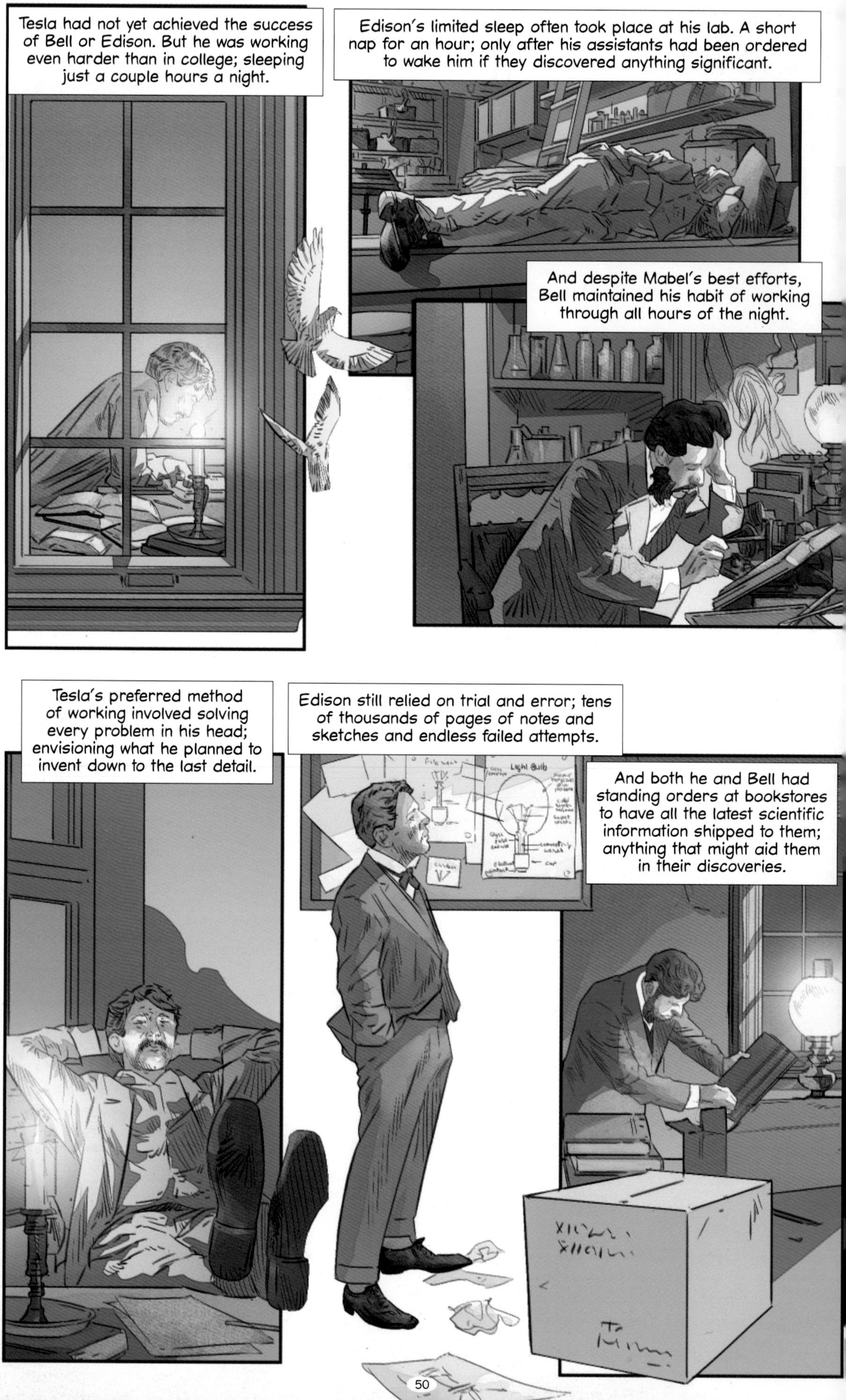
Tesla had not yet achieved the success of Bell or Edison. But he was working even harder than in college; sleeping just a couple hours a night.
Edison's limited sleep often took place at his lab. A short nap for an hour; only after his assistants had been ordered to wake him if they discovered anything significant.
And despite Mabel's best efforts, Bell maintained his habit of working through all hours of the night.
Tesla's preferred method of working involved solving every problem in his head; envisioning what he planned to invent down to the last detail.
Edison still relied on trial and error; tens of thousands of pages of notes and sketches and endless failed attempts.
And both he and Bell had standing orders at bookstores to have all the latest scientific information shipped to them; anything that might aid them in their discoveries.

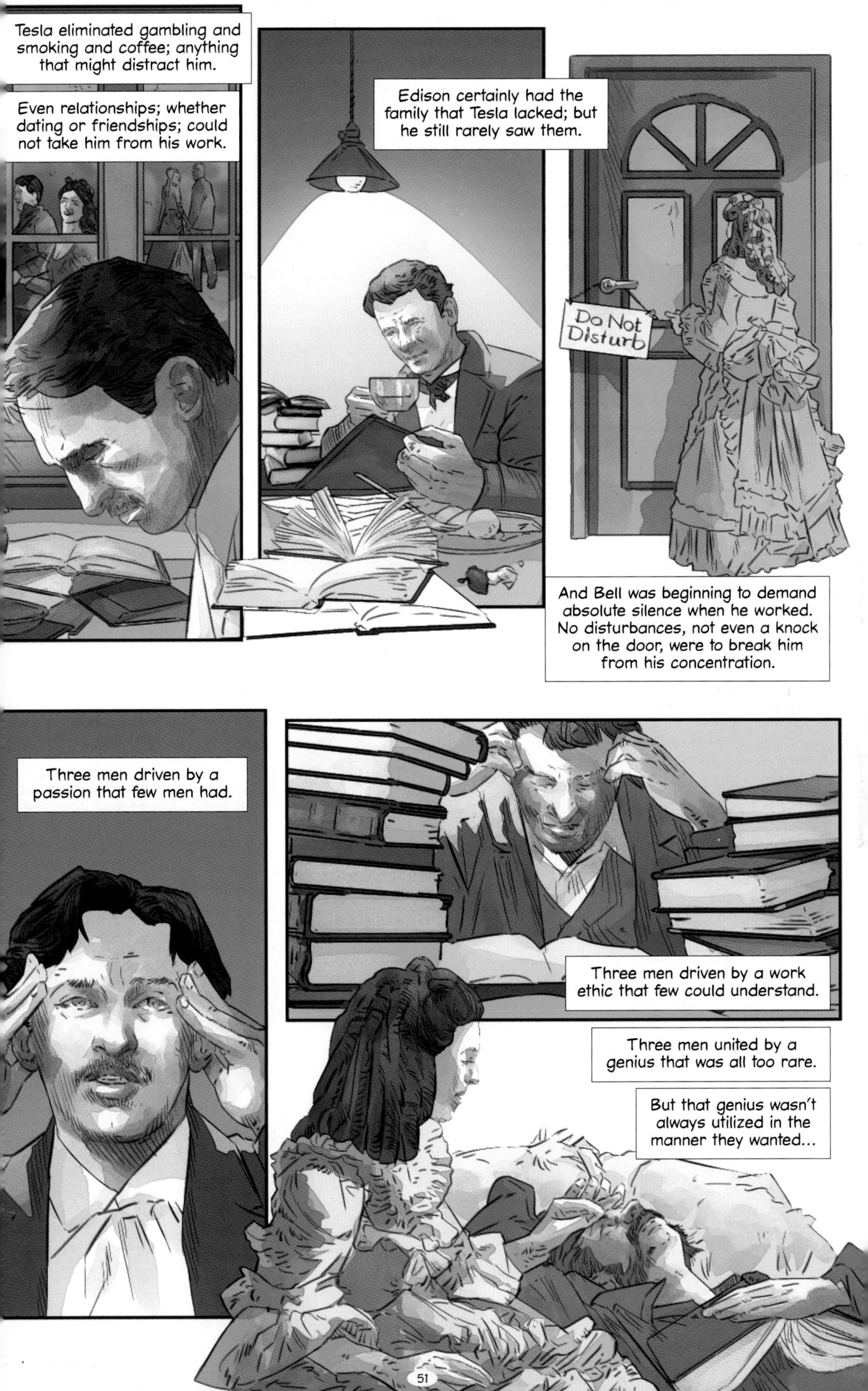
Tesla eliminated gambling and smoking and coffee; anything that might distract him.
Even relationships; whether dating or friendships; could not take him from his work.
Edison certainly had the family that Tesla lacked; but he still rarely saw them.
Do Not Disturb
And Bell was beginning to demand absolute silence when he worked. No disturbances, not even a knock on the door, were to break him from his concentration.
Three men driven by a passion that few men had.
Three men driven by a work ethic that few could understand.
Three men united by a genius that was all too rare.
But that genius wasn't always utilized in the manner they wanted...

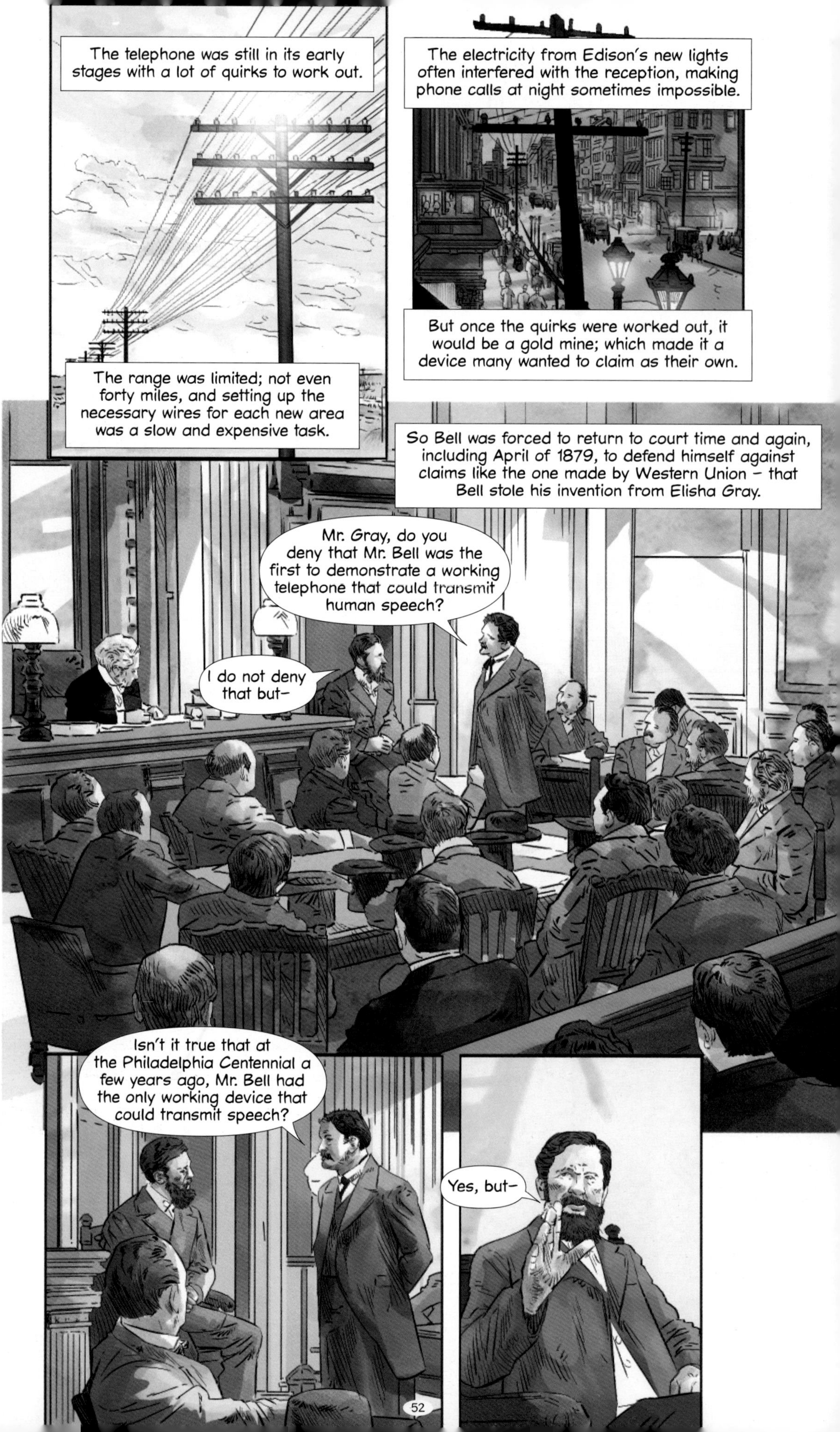
The telephone was still in its early stages with a lot of quirks to work out.
The range was limited; not even forty miles, and setting up the necessary wires for each new area was a slow and expensive task.
The electricity from Edison's new lights often interfered with the reception, making phone calls at night sometimes impossible.
But once the quirks were worked out, it would be a gold mine; which made it a device many wanted to claim as their own.
So Bell was forced to return to court time and again, including April of 1879, to defend himself against claims like the one made by Western Union – that Bell stole his invention from Elisha Gray.
Mr. Gray, do you deny that Mr. Bell was the first to demonstrate a working telephone that could transmit human speech?
I do not deny that but–
Isn't it true that at the Philadelphia Centennial a few years ago, Mr. Bell had the only working device that could transmit speech?
Yes, but–

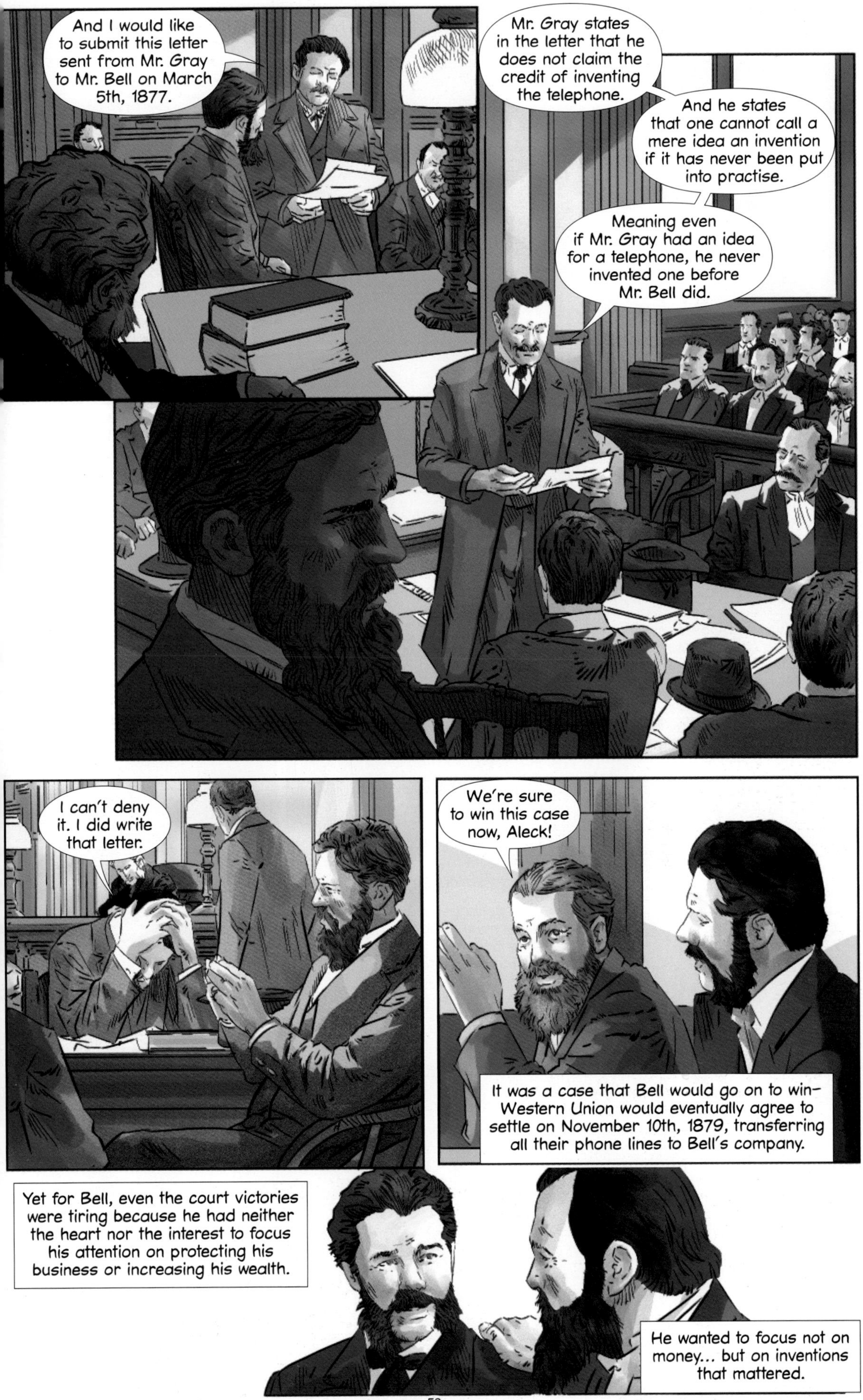

And I would like to submit this letter sent from Mr. Gray to Mr. Bell on March 5th, 1877.
Mr. Gray states in the letter that he does not claim the credit of inventing the telephone.
And he states that one cannot call a mere idea an invention if it has never been put into practise.
Meaning even if Mr. Gray had an idea for a telephone, he never invented one before Mr. Bell did.
I can't deny it. I did write that letter.
We're sure to win this case now, Aleck!
It was a case that Bell would go on to win- Western Union would eventually agree to settle on November 10th, 1879, transferring all their phone lines to Bell's company.
Yet for Bell, even the court victories were tiring because he had neither the heart nor the interest to focus his attention on protecting his business or increasing his wealth.
He wanted to focus not on money... but on inventions that mattered.

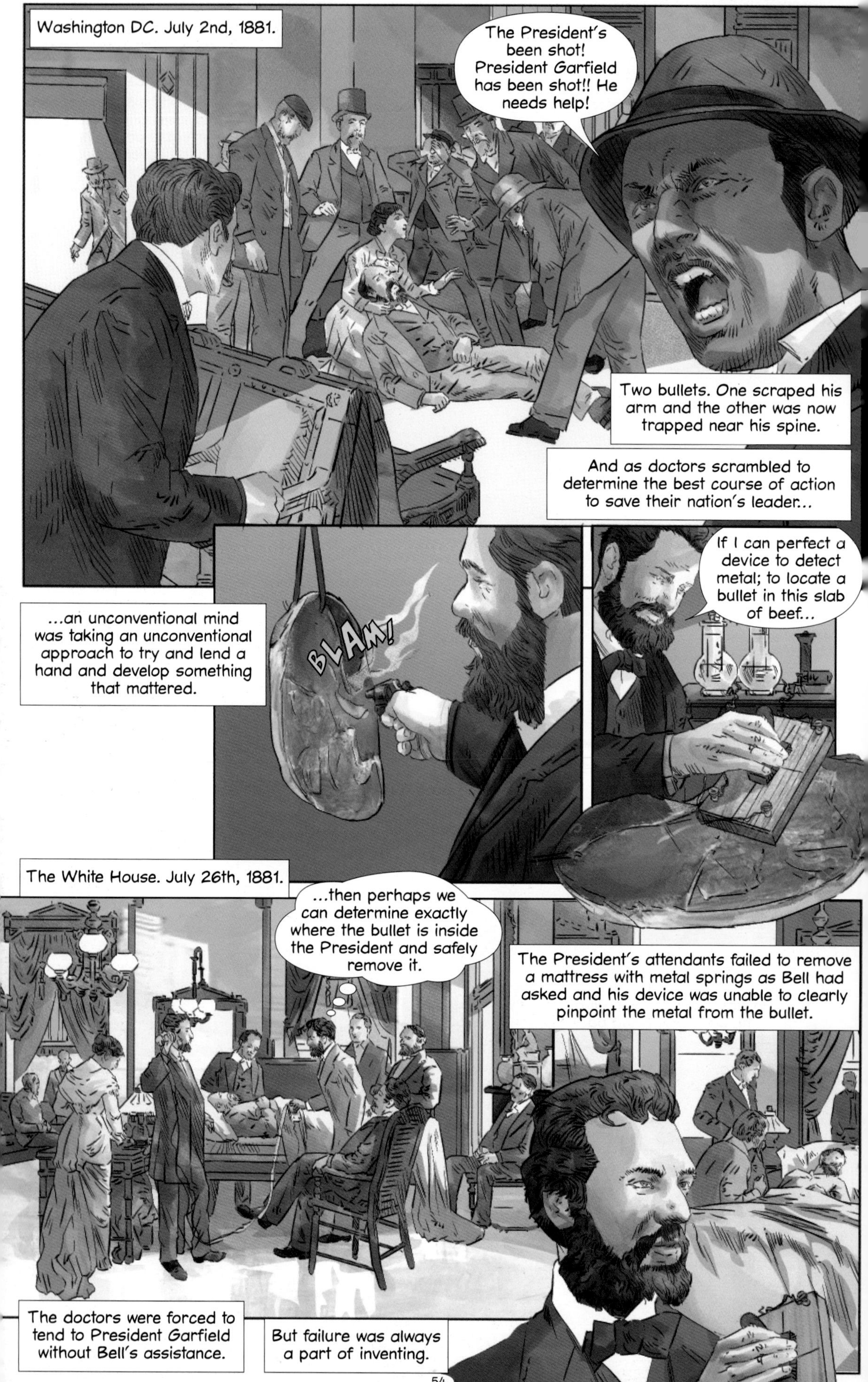
Washington DC. July 2nd, 1881.
The President's been shot! President Garfield has been shot!! He needs help!
Two bullets. One scraped his arm and the other was now trapped near his spine.
And as doctors scrambled to determine the best course of action to save their nation's leader...
...an unconventional mind was taking an unconventional approach to try and lend a hand and develop something that mattered.
BLAM!
If I can perfect a device to detect metal; to locate a bullet in this slab of beef...
The White House. July 26th, 1881.
...then perhaps we can determine exactly where the bullet is inside the President and safely remove it.
The President's attendants failed to remove a mattress with metal springs as Bell had asked and his device was unable to clearly pinpoint the metal from the bullet.
The doctors were forced to tend to President Garfield without Bell's assistance.
But failure was always a part of inventing.

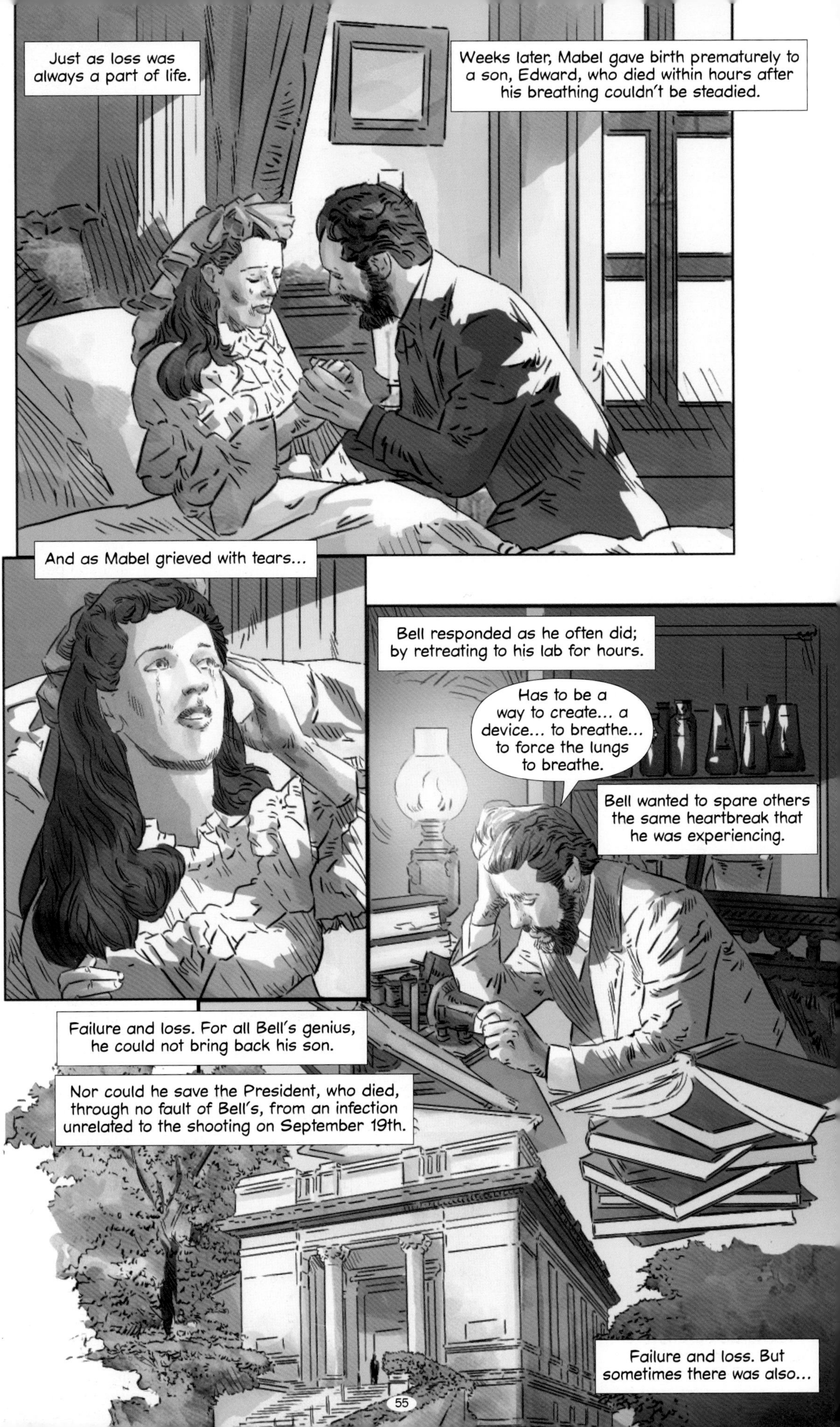
Just as loss was always a part of life.
Weeks later, Mabel gave birth prematurely to a son, Edward, who died within hours after his breathing couldn't be steadied.
And as Mabel grieved with tears...
Bell responded as he often did; by retreating to his lab for hours.
Has to be a way to create... a device... to breathe... to force the lungs to breathe.
Bell wanted to spare others the same heartbreak that he was experiencing.
Failure and loss. For all Bell's genius, he could not bring back his son.
Nor could he save the President, who died, through no fault of Bell's, from an infection unrelated to the shooting on September 19th.
Failure and loss. But sometimes there was also...

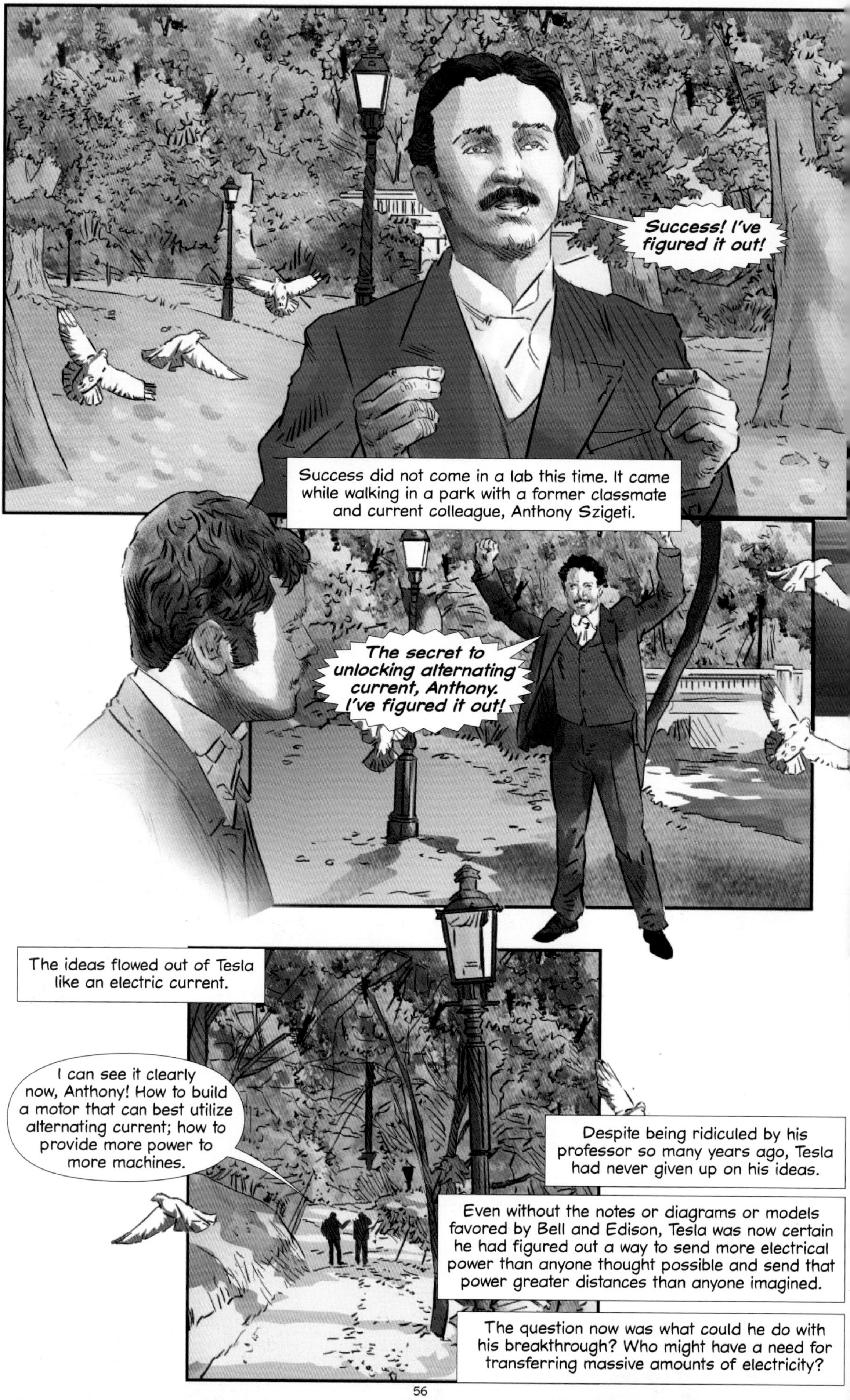
Success! I've figured it out!
Success did not come in a lab this time. It came while walking in a park with a former classmate and current colleague, Anthony Szigeti.
The secret to unlocking alternating current, Anthony. I've figured it out!
The ideas flowed out of Tesla like an electric current.
I can see it clearly now, Anthony! How to build a motor that can best utilize alternating current; how to provide more power to more machines.
Despite being ridiculed by his professor so many years ago, Tesla had never given up on his ideas.
Even without the notes or diagrams or models favored by Bell and Edison, Tesla was now certain he had figured out a way to send more electrical power than anyone thought possible and send that power greater distances than anyone imagined.
The question now was what could he do with his breakthrough? Who might have a need for transferring massive amounts of electricity?

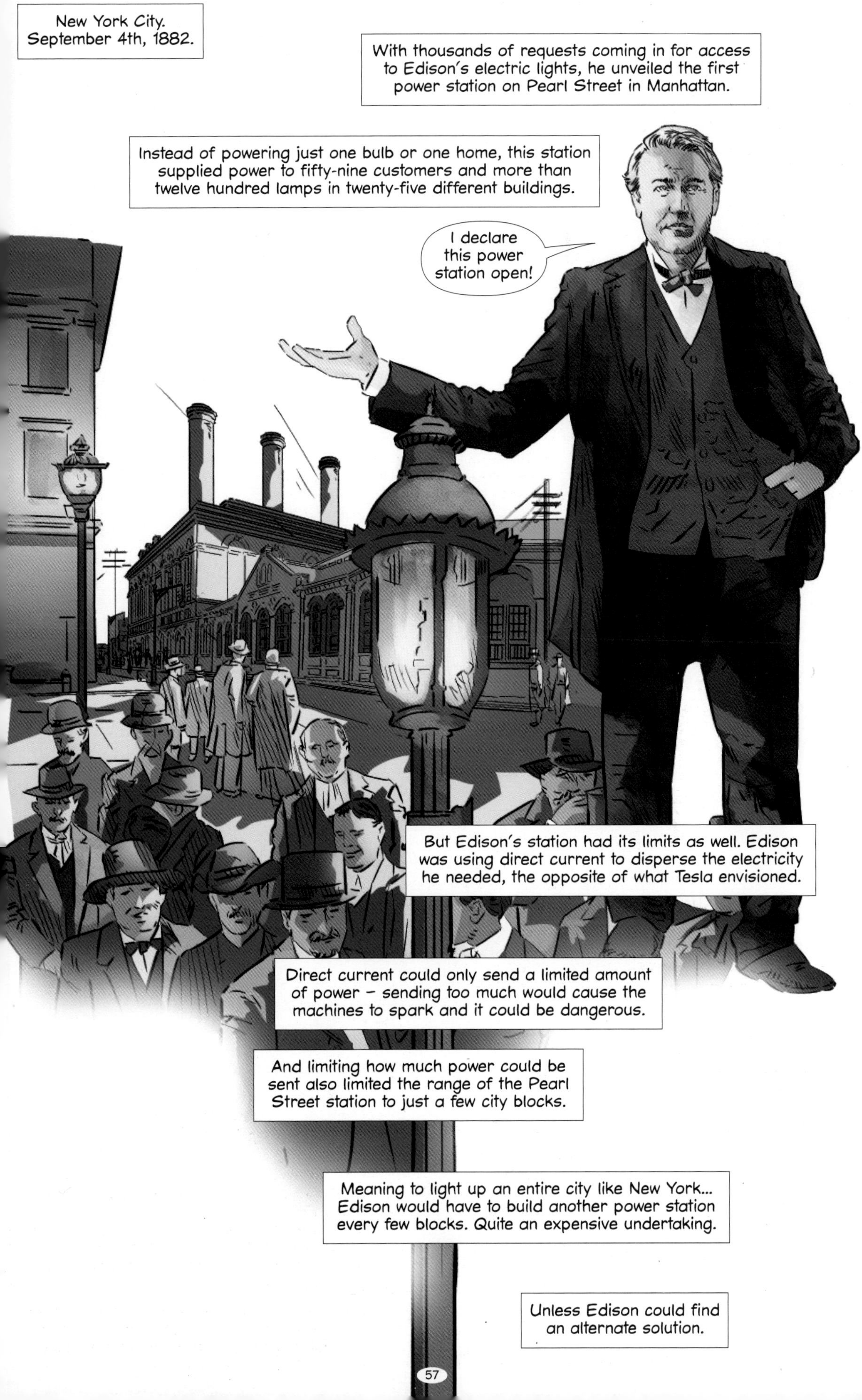

New York City. September 4th, 1882.
With thousands of requests coming in for access to Edison's electric lights, he unveiled the first power station on Pearl Street in Manhattan.
Instead of powering just one bulb or one home, this station supplied power to fifty-nine customers and more than twelve hundred lamps in twenty-five different buildings.
I declare this power station open!
But Edison's station had its limits as well. Edison was using direct current to disperse the electricity he needed, the opposite of what Tesla envisioned.
Direct current could only send a limited amount of power – sending too much would cause the machines to spark and it could be dangerous.
And limiting how much power could be sent also limited the range of the Pearl Street station to just a few city blocks.
Meaning to light up an entire city like New York... Edison would have to build another power station every few blocks. Quite an expensive undertaking.
Unless Edison could find an alternate solution.

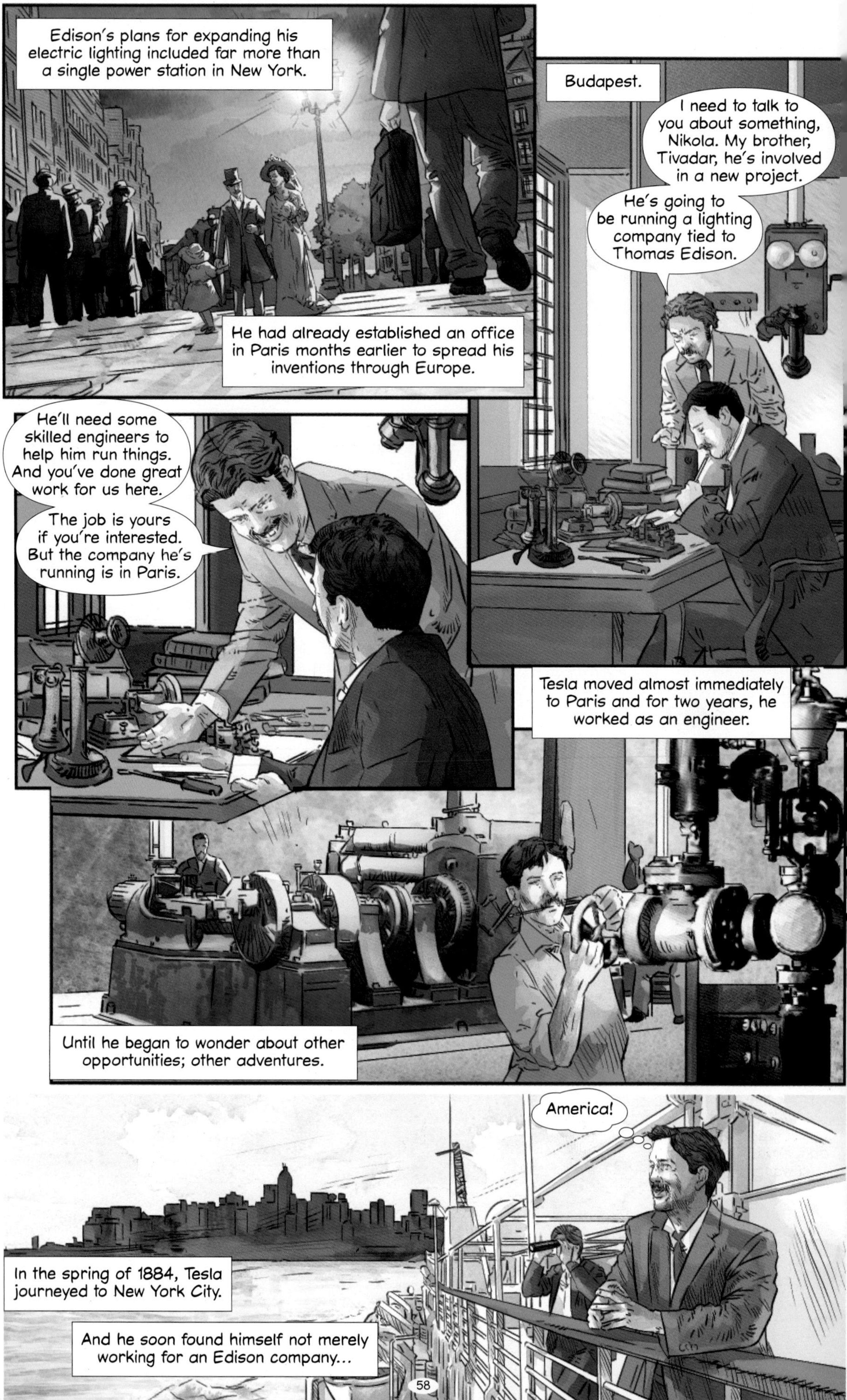
Edison's plans for expanding his electric lighting included far more than a single power station in New York.
He had already established an office in Paris months earlier to spread his inventions through Europe.
Budapest.
I need to talk to you about something, Nikola. My brother, Tivadar, he's involved in a new project.
He's going to be running a lighting company tied to Thomas Edison.
He'll need some skilled engineers to help him run things. And you've done great work for us here.
The job is yours if you're interested. But the company he's running is in Paris.
Tesla moved almost immediately to Paris and for two years, he worked as an engineer.
Until he began to wonder about other opportunities; other adventures.
America!
In the spring of 1884, Tesla journeyed to New York City.
And he soon found himself not merely working for an Edison company...

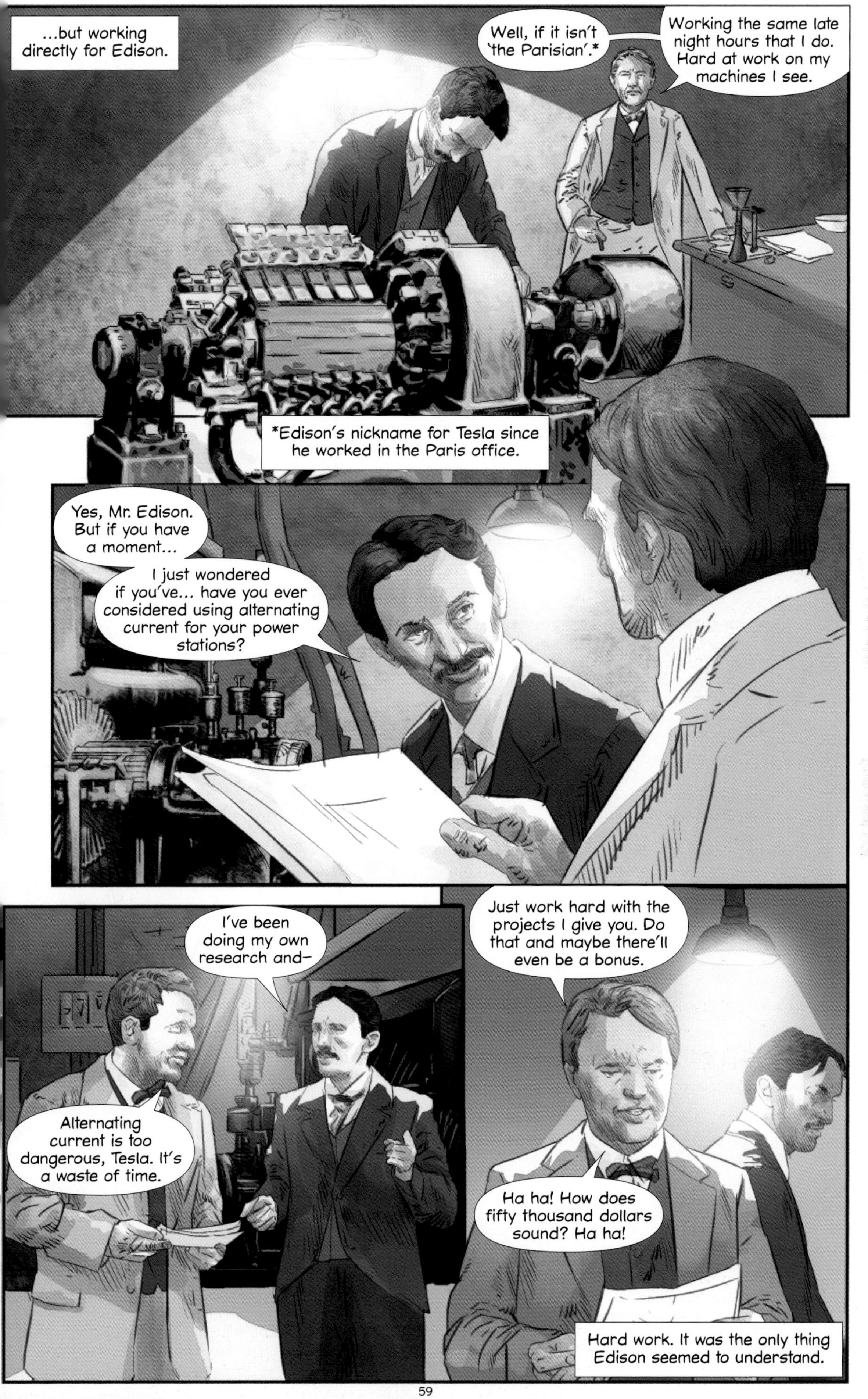
...but working directly for Edison.
Well, if it isn't 'the Parisian'.*
Working the same late night hours that I do. Hard at work on my machines I see.
*Edison's nickname for Tesla since he worked in the Paris office.
Yes, Mr. Edison. But if you have a moment...
I just wondered if you've... have you ever considered using alternating current for your power stations?
I've been doing my own research and–
Alternating current is too dangerous, Tesla. It's a waste of time.
Just work hard with the projects I give you. Do that and maybe there'll even be a bonus.
Ha ha! How does fifty thousand dollars sound? Ha ha!
Hard work. It was the only thing Edison seemed to understand.

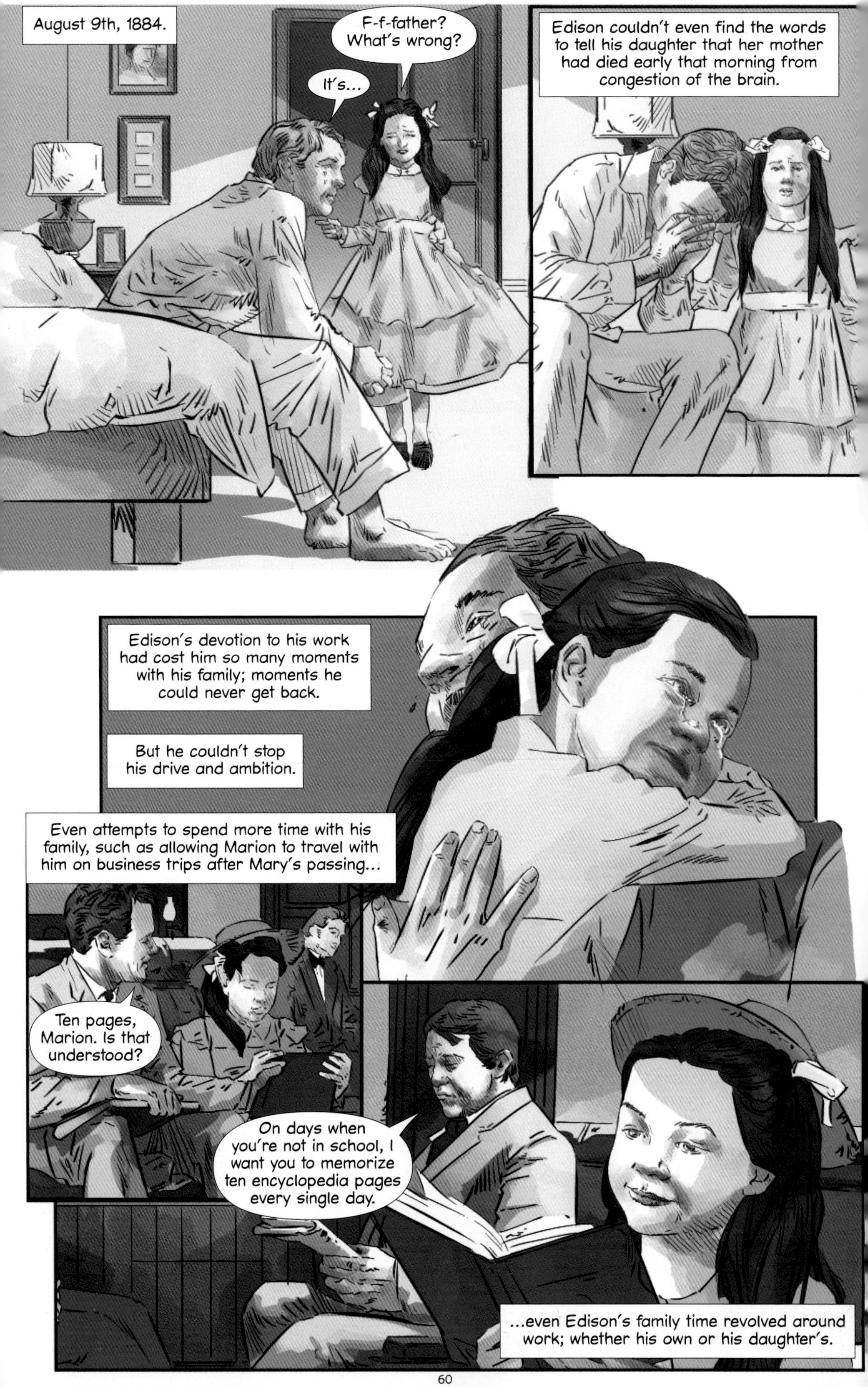
August 9th, 1884.
F-f-father? What's wrong?
It's...
Edison couldn't even find the words to tell his daughter that her mother had died early that morning from congestion of the brain.
Edison's devotion to his work had cost him so many moments with his family; moments he could never get back.
But he couldn't stop his drive and ambition.
Even attempts to spend more time with his family, such as allowing Marion to travel with him on business trips after Mary's passing...
Ten pages, Marion. Is that understood?
On days when you're not in school, I want you to memorize ten encyclopedia pages every single day.
...even Edison's family time revolved around work; whether his own or his daughter's.

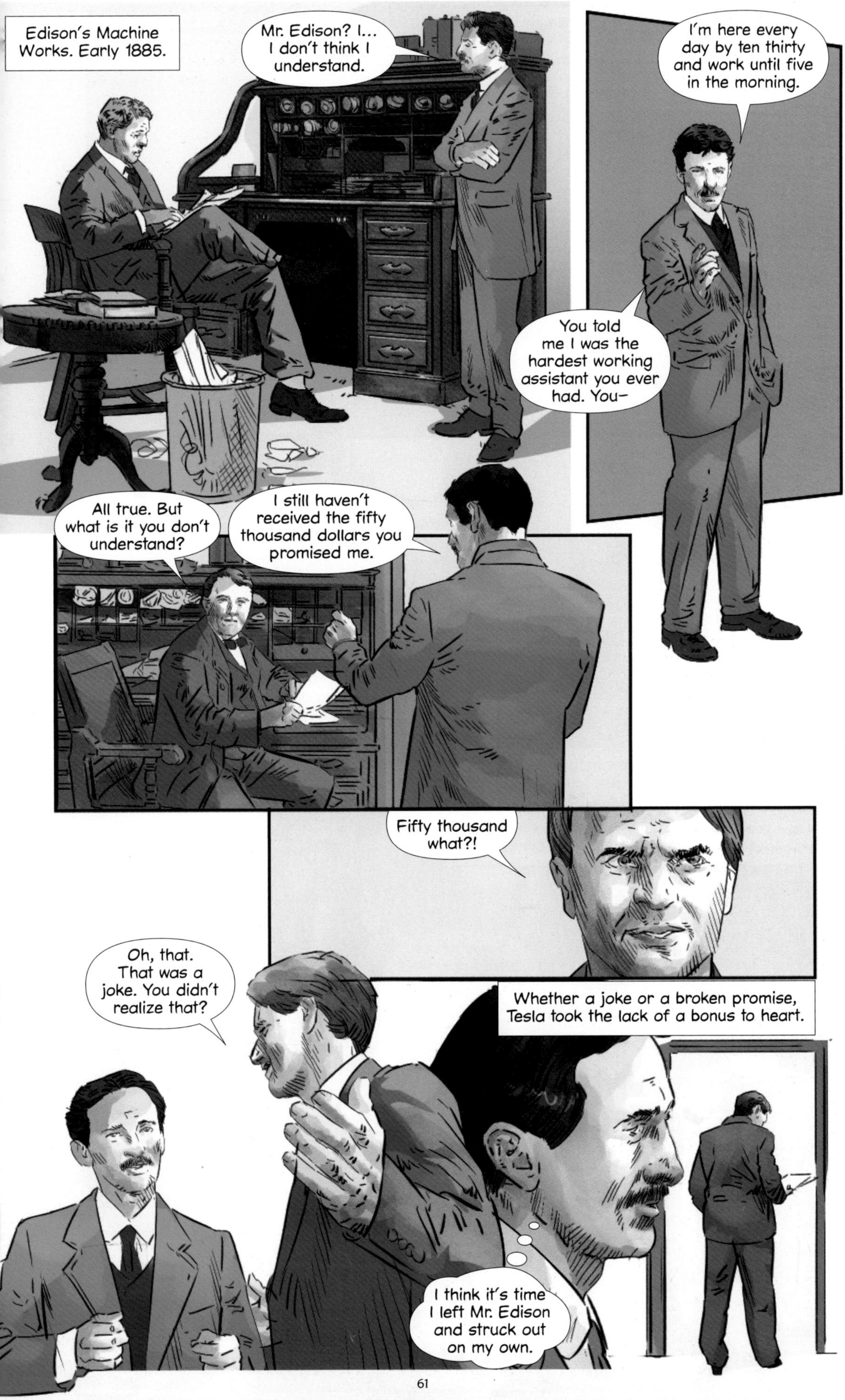
Edison's Machine Works. Early 1885.
Mr. Edison? I... I don't think I understand.
I'm here every day by ten thirty and work until five in the morning.
You told me I was the hardest working assistant you ever had. You–
All true. But what is it you don't understand?
I still haven't received the fifty thousand dollars you promised me.
Fifty thousand what?!
Oh, that. That was a joke. You didn't realize that?
Whether a joke or a broken promise, Tesla took the lack of a bonus to heart.
I think it's time I left Mr. Edison and struck out on my own.

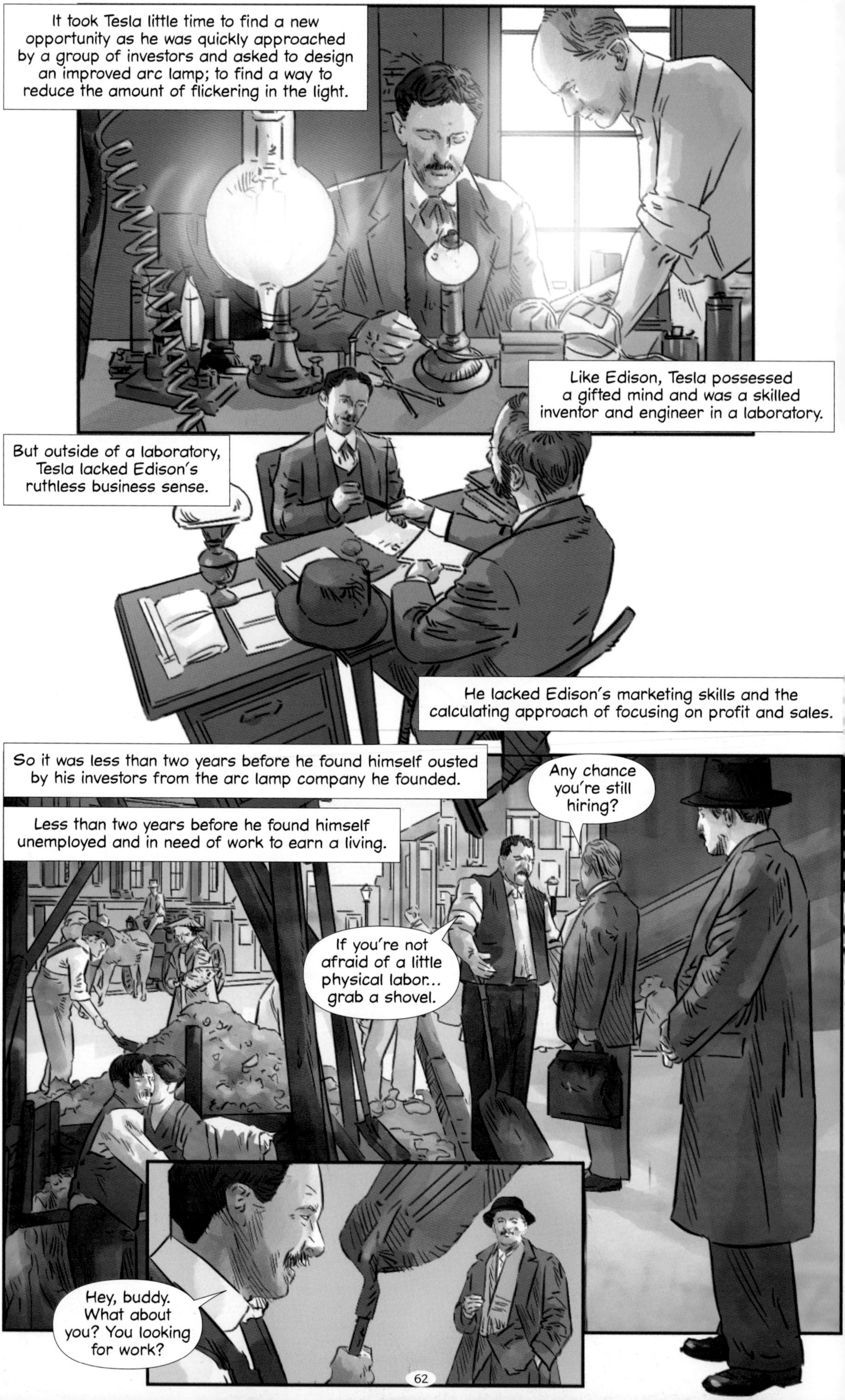
It took Tesla little time to find a new opportunity as he was quickly approached by a group of investors and asked to design an improved arc lamp; to find a way to reduce the amount of flickering in the light.
Like Edison, Tesla possessed a gifted mind and was a skilled inventor and engineer in a laboratory.
But outside of a laboratory, Tesla lacked Edison's ruthless business sense.
He lacked Edison's marketing skills and the calculating approach of focusing on profit and sales.
So it was less than two years before he found himself ousted by his investors from the arc lamp company he founded.
Less than two years before he found himself unemployed and in need of work to earn a living.
Any chance you're still hiring?
If you're not afraid of a little physical labor... grab a shovel.
Hey, buddy. What about you? You looking for work?

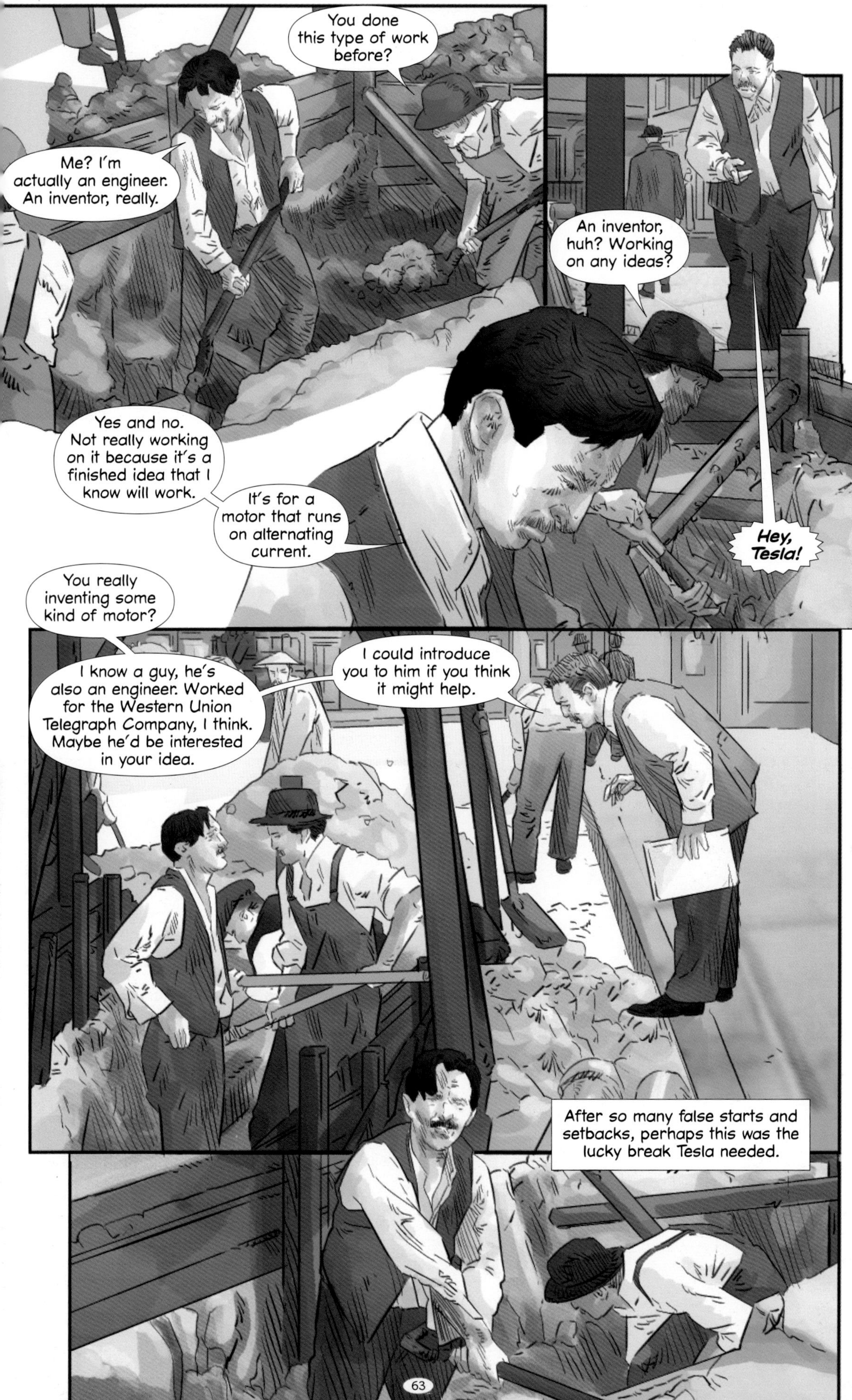
You done this type of work before?
Me? I'm actually an engineer. An inventor, really.
An inventor, huh? Working on any ideas?
Yes and no. Not really working on it because it's a finished idea that I know will work.
It's for a motor that runs on alternating current.
Hey, Tesla!
You really inventing some kind of motor?
I know a guy, he's also an engineer. Worked for the Western Union Telegraph Company, I think. Maybe he'd be interested in your idea.
I could introduce you to him if you think it might help.
After so many false starts and setbacks, perhaps this was the lucky break Tesla needed.

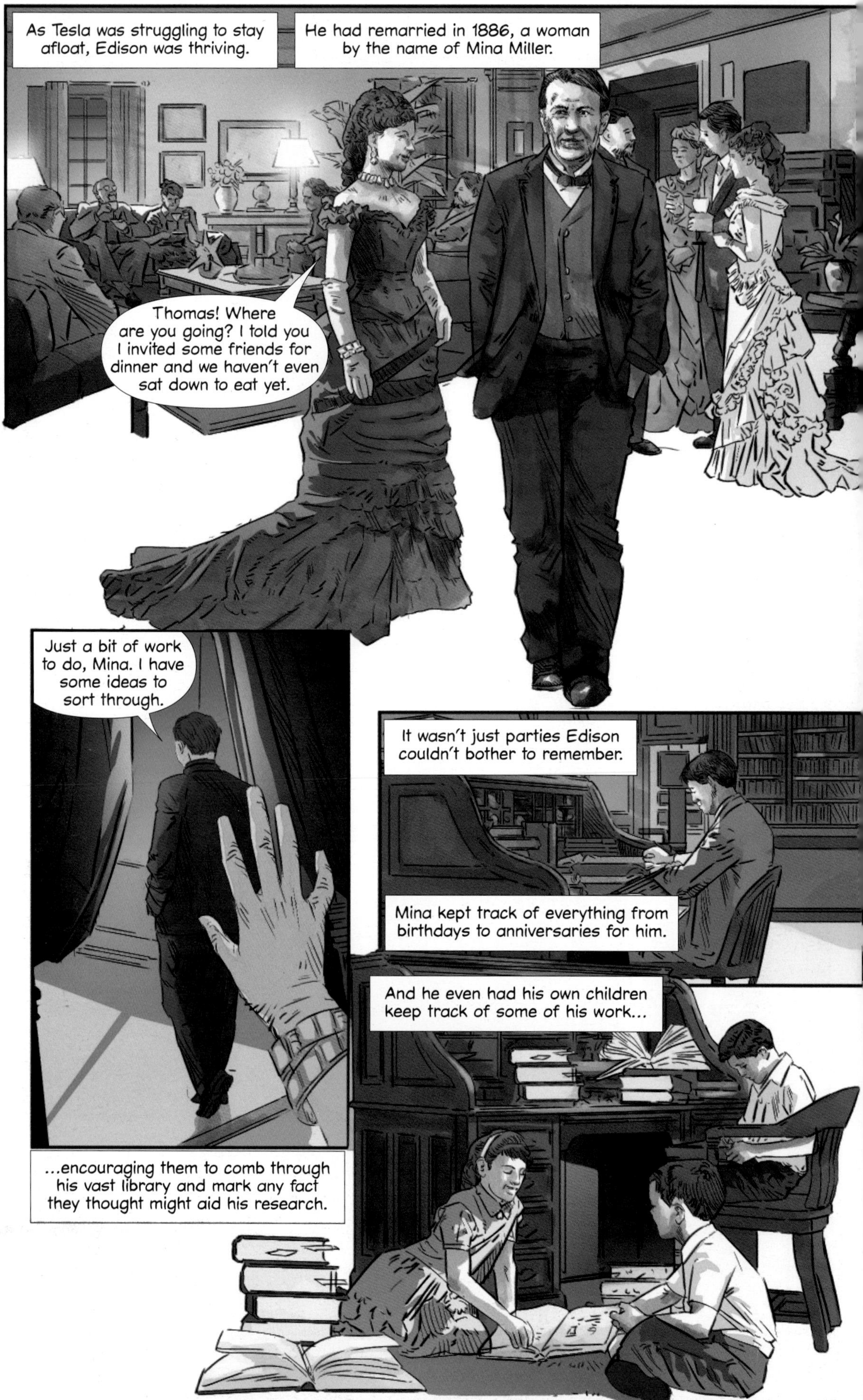

As Tesla was struggling to stay afloat, Edison was thriving.
He had remarried in 1886, a woman by the name of Mina Miller.
Thomas! Where are you going? I told you I invited some friends for dinner and we haven't even sat down to eat yet.
Just a bit of work to do, Mina. I have some ideas to sort through.
It wasn't just parties Edison couldn't bother to remember.
Mina kept track of everything from birthdays to anniversaries for him.
And he even had his own children keep track of some of his work...
...encouraging them to comb through his vast library and mark any fact they thought might aid his research.

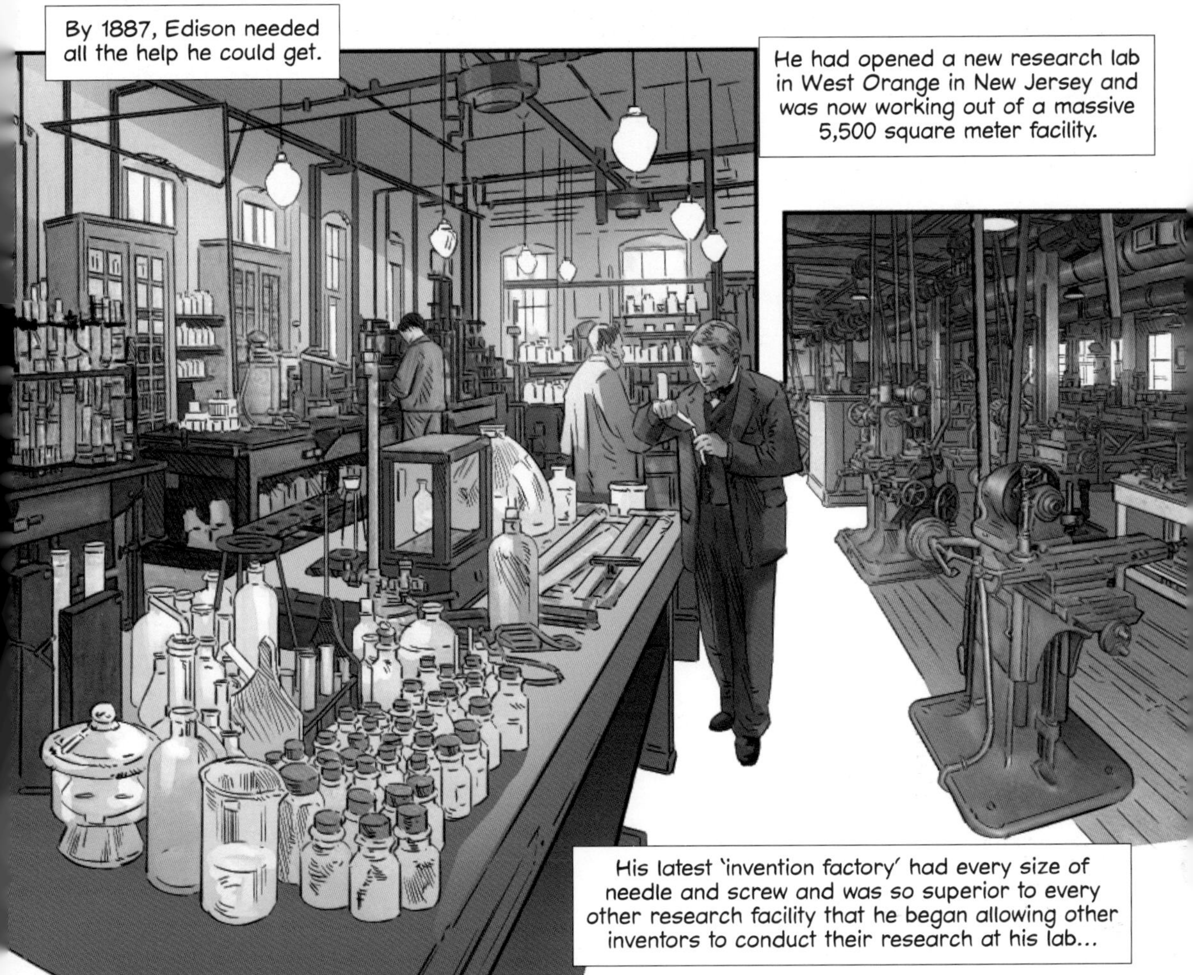
By 1887, Edison needed all the help he could get.
He had opened a new research lab in West Orange in New Jersey and was now working out of a massive 5,500 square meter facility.
His latest 'invention factory' had every size of needle and screw and was so superior to every other research facility that he began allowing other inventors to conduct their research at his lab...

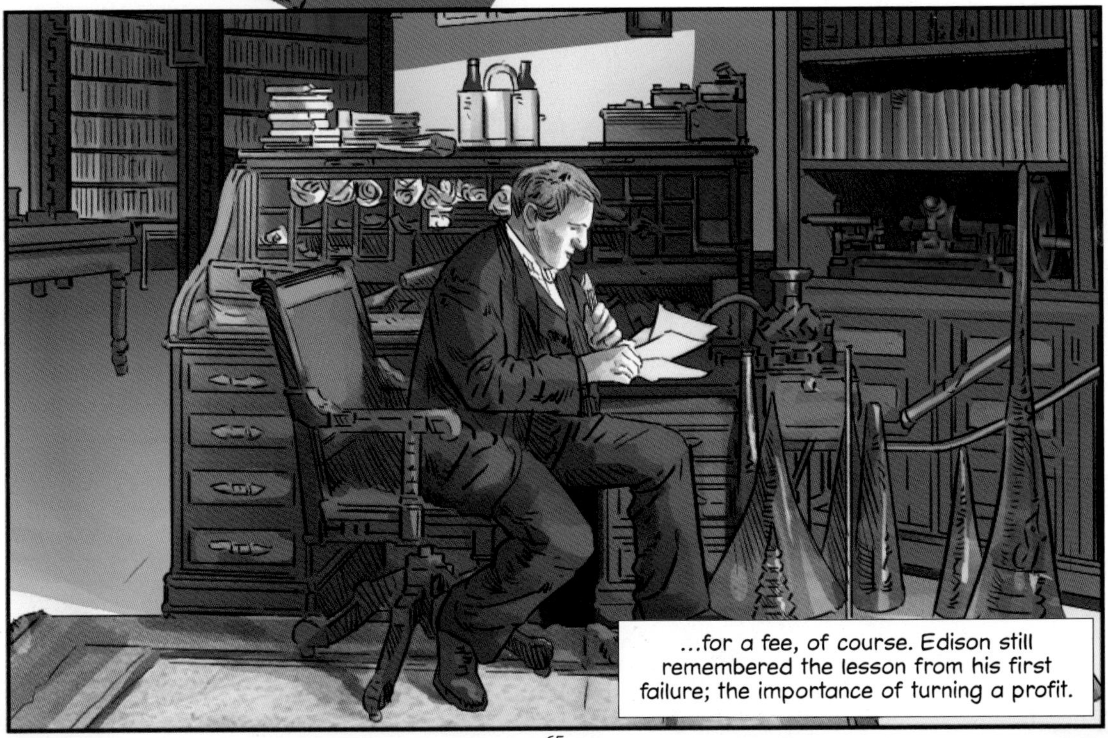
...for a fee, of course. Edison still remembered the lesson from his first failure; the importance of turning a profit.

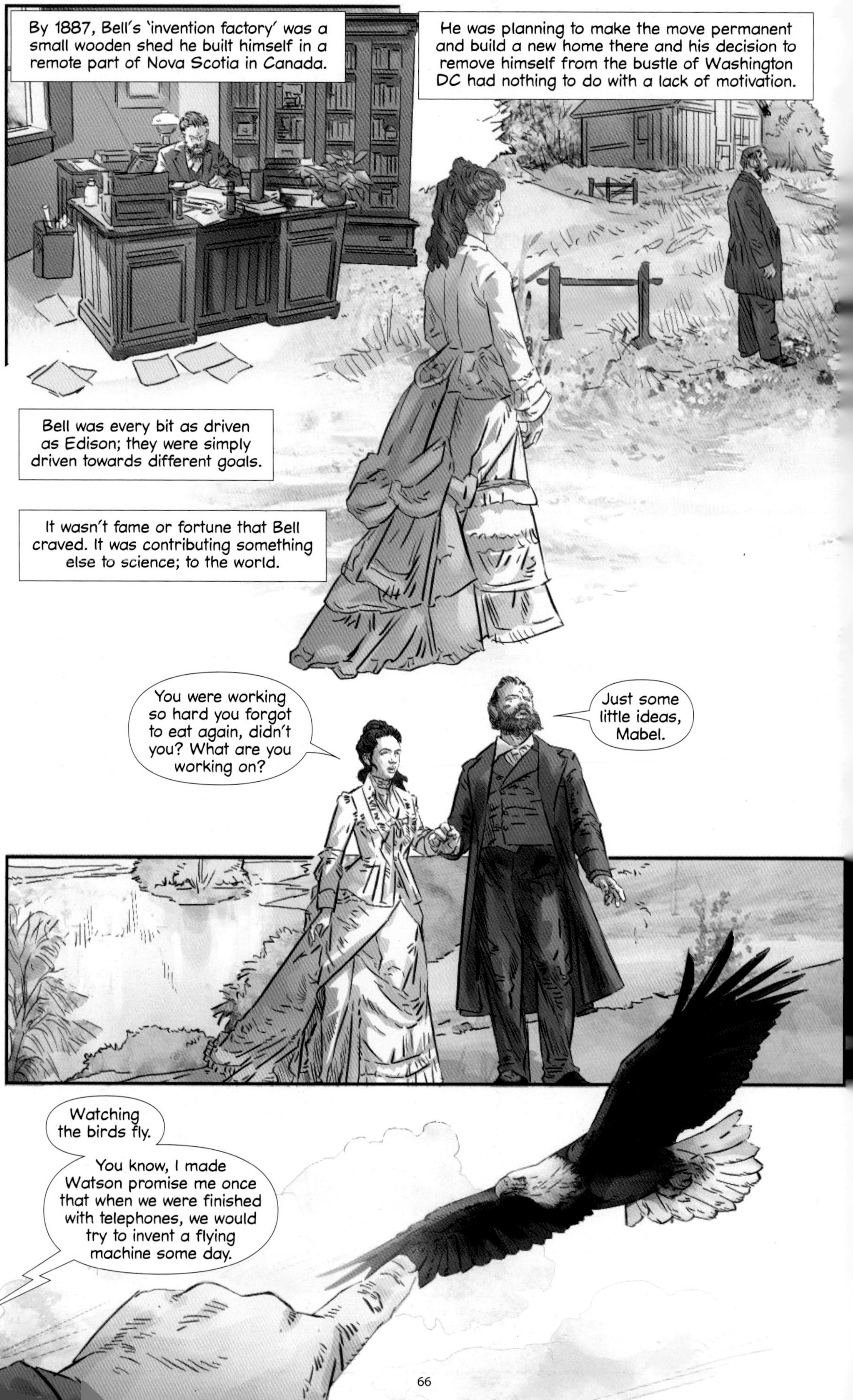
By 1887, Bell's 'invention factory' was a small wooden shed he built himself in a remote part of Nova Scotia in Canada.
He was planning to make the move permanent and build a new home there and his decision to remove himself from the bustle of Washington DC had nothing to do with a lack of motivation.
Bell was every bit as driven as Edison; they were simply driven towards different goals.
It wasn't fame or fortune that Bell craved. It was contributing something else to science; to the world.
You were working so hard you forgot to eat again, didn't you? What are you working on?
Just some little ideas, Mabel.
Watching the birds fly.
You know, I made Watson promise me once that when we were finished with telephones, we would try to invent a flying machine some day.

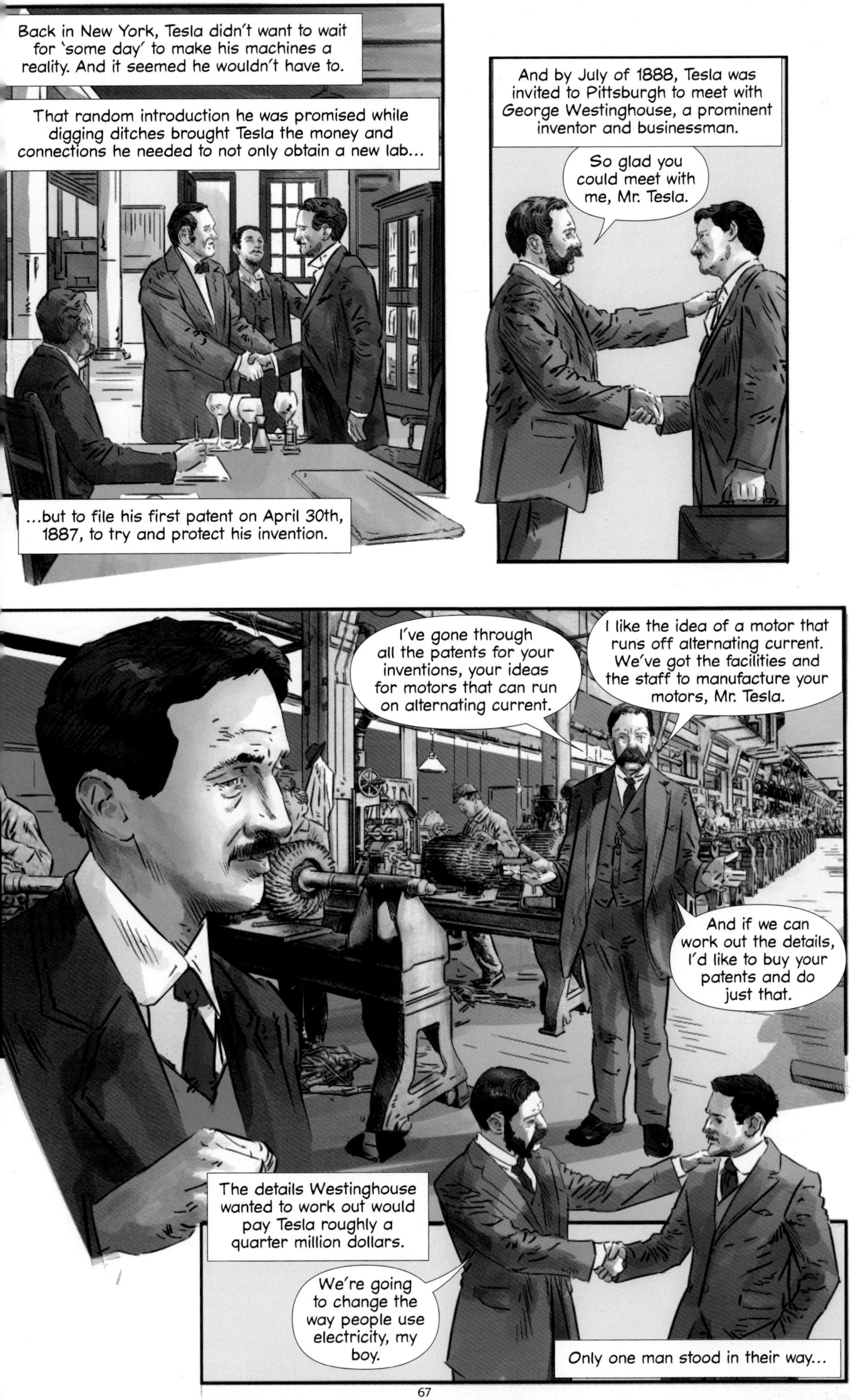
Back in New York, Tesla didn't want to wait for 'some day' to make his machines a reality. And it seemed he wouldn't have to.
That random introduction he was promised while digging ditches brought Tesla the money and connections he needed to not only obtain a new lab...
...but to file his first patent on April 30th, 1887, to try and protect his invention.
And by July of 1888, Tesla was invited to Pittsburgh to meet with George Westinghouse, a prominent inventor and businessman.
So glad you could meet with me, Mr. Tesla.
I've gone through all the patents for your inventions, your ideas for motors that can run on alternating current.
I like the idea of a motor that runs off alternating current. We've got the facilities and the staff to manufacture your motors, Mr. Tesla.
And if we can work out the details, I'd like to buy your patents and do just that.
The details Westinghouse wanted to work out would pay Tesla roughly a quarter million dollars.
We're going to change the way people use electricity, my boy.
Only one man stood in their way...

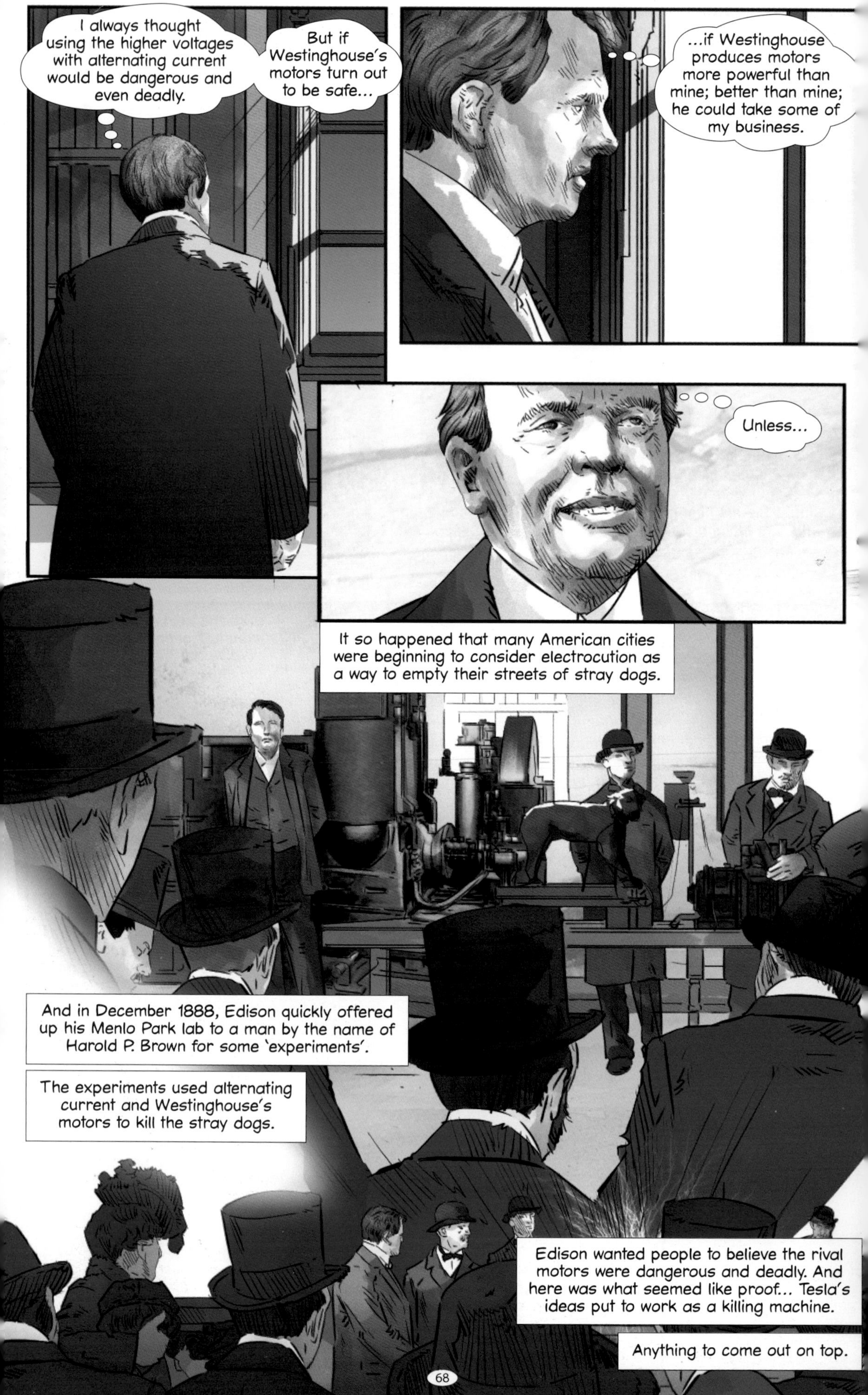
I always thought using the higher voltages with alternating current would be dangerous and even deadly.
But if Westinghouse's motors turn out to be safe...
...if Westinghouse produces motors more powerful than mine; better than mine; he could take some of my business.
Unless...
It so happened that many American cities were beginning to consider electrocution as a way to empty their streets of stray dogs.
And in December 1888, Edison quickly offered up his Menlo Park lab to a man by the name of Harold P. Brown for some 'experiments'.
The experiments used alternating current and Westinghouse's motors to kill the stray dogs.
Edison wanted people to believe the rival motors were dangerous and deadly. And here was what seemed like proof... Tesla's ideas put to work as a killing machine.
Anything to come out on top.

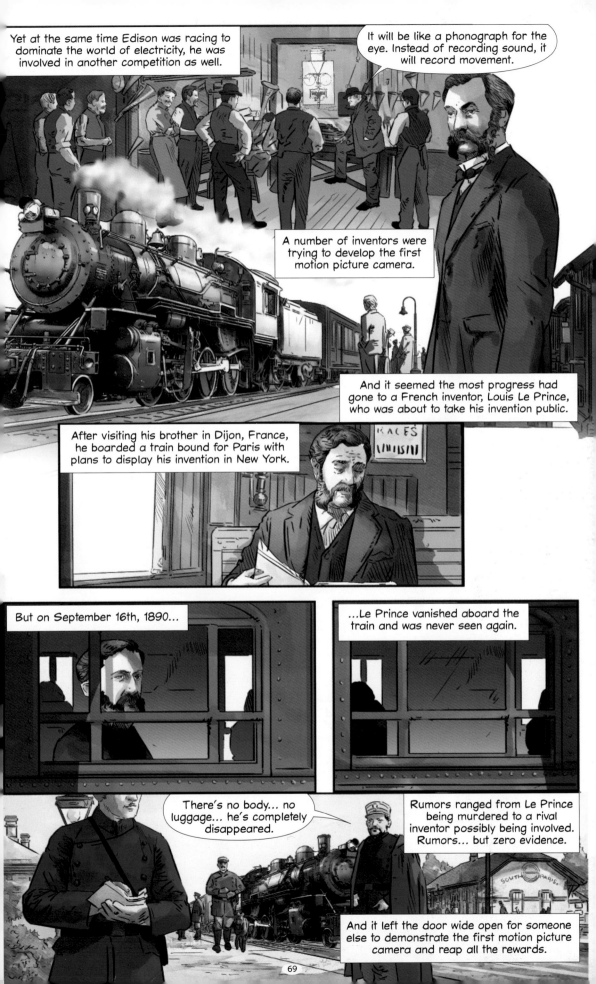

Yet at the same time Edison was racing to dominate the world of electricity, he was involved in another competition as well.

It will be like a phonograph for the eye. Instead of recording sound, it will record movement.

A number of inventors were trying to develop the first motion picture camera.

And it seemed the most progress had gone to a French inventor, Louis Le Prince, who was about to take his invention public.

After visiting his brother in Dijon, France, he boarded a train bound for Paris with plans to display his invention in New York.

But on September 16th, 1890...

...Le Prince vanished aboard the train and was never seen again.

There's no body... no luggage... he's completely disappeared.

Rumors ranged from Le Prince being murdered to a rival inventor possibly being involved. Rumors... but zero evidence.

And it left the door wide open for someone else to demonstrate the first motion picture camera and reap all the rewards.

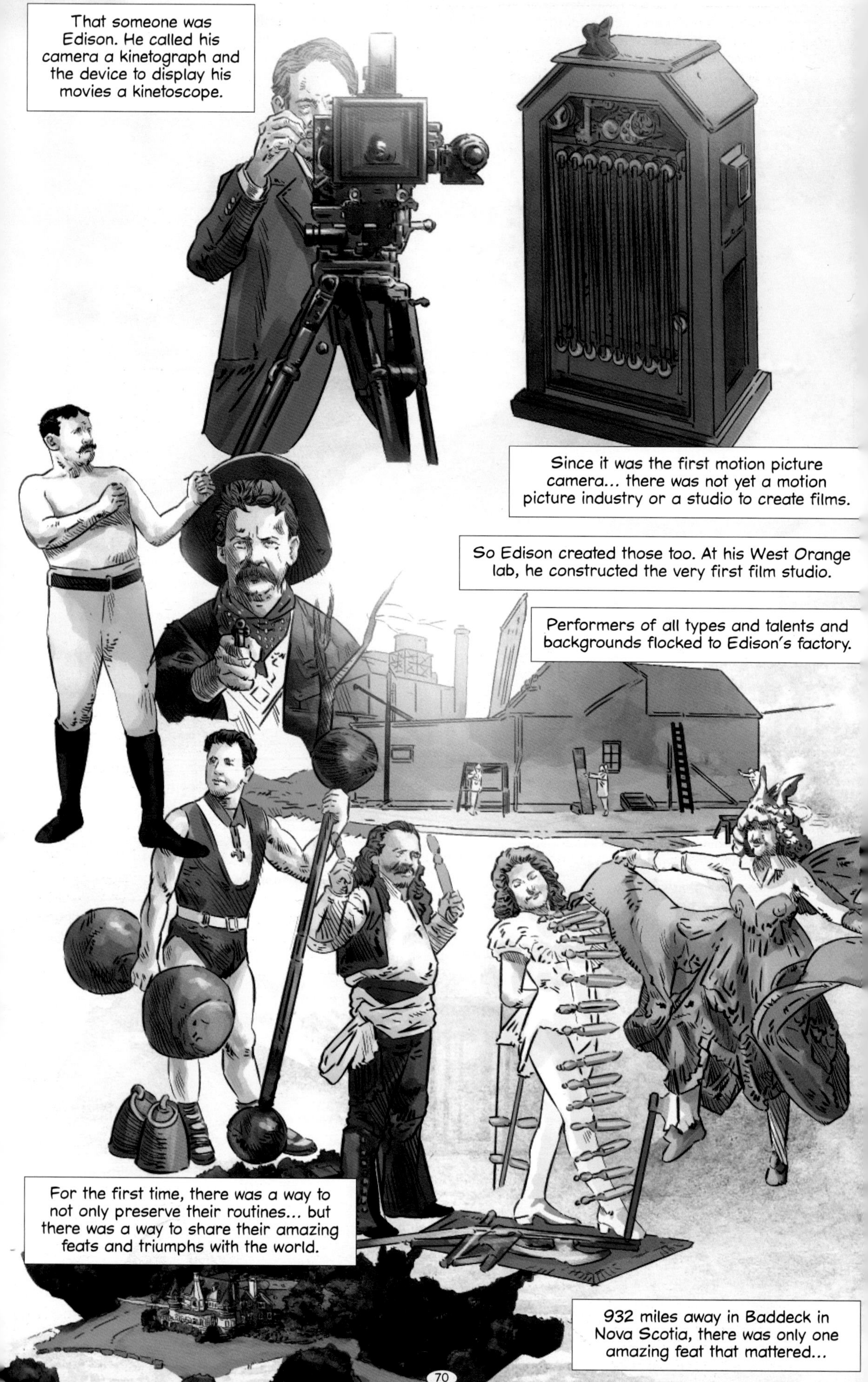
That someone was Edison. He called his camera a kinetograph and the device to display his movies a kinetoscope.
Since it was the first motion picture camera... there was not yet a motion picture industry or a studio to create films.
So Edison created those too. At his West Orange lab, he constructed the very first film studio.
Performers of all types and talents and backgrounds flocked to Edison's factory.
For the first time, there was a way to not only preserve their routines... but there was a way to share their amazing feats and triumphs with the world.
932 miles away in Baddeck in Nova Scotia, there was only one amazing feat that mattered...

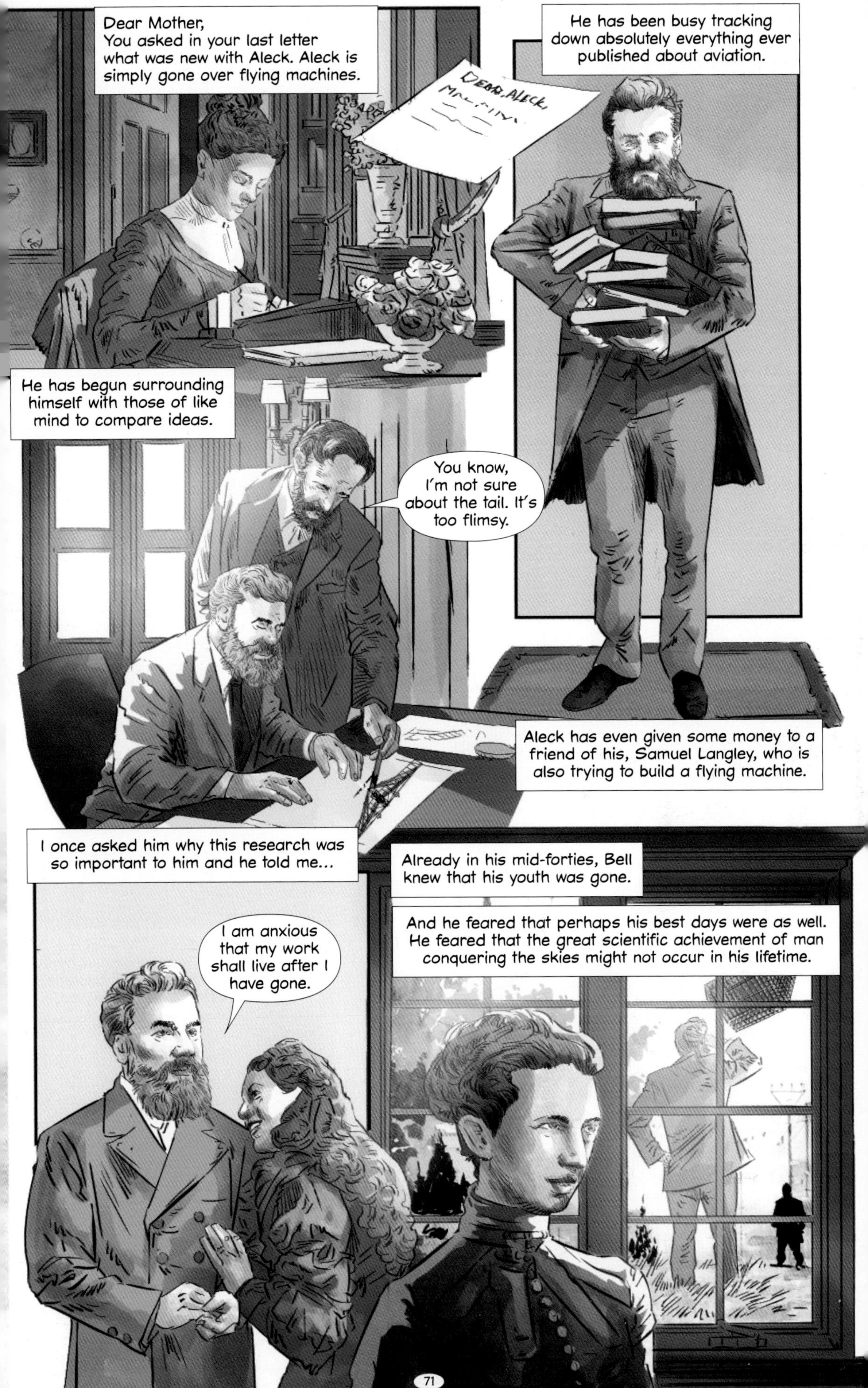

Dear Mother,
You asked in your last letter what was new with Aleck. Aleck is simply gone over flying machines.
He has been busy tracking down absolutely everything ever published about aviation.
He has begun surrounding himself with those of like mind to compare ideas.
You know, I'm not sure about the tail. It's too flimsy.
Aleck has even given some money to a friend of his, Samuel Langley, who is also trying to build a flying machine.
I once asked him why this research was so important to him and he told me...
I am anxious that my work shall live after I have gone.
Already in his mid-forties, Bell knew that his youth was gone.
And he feared that perhaps his best days were as well. He feared that the great scientific achievement of man conquering the skies might not occur in his lifetime.

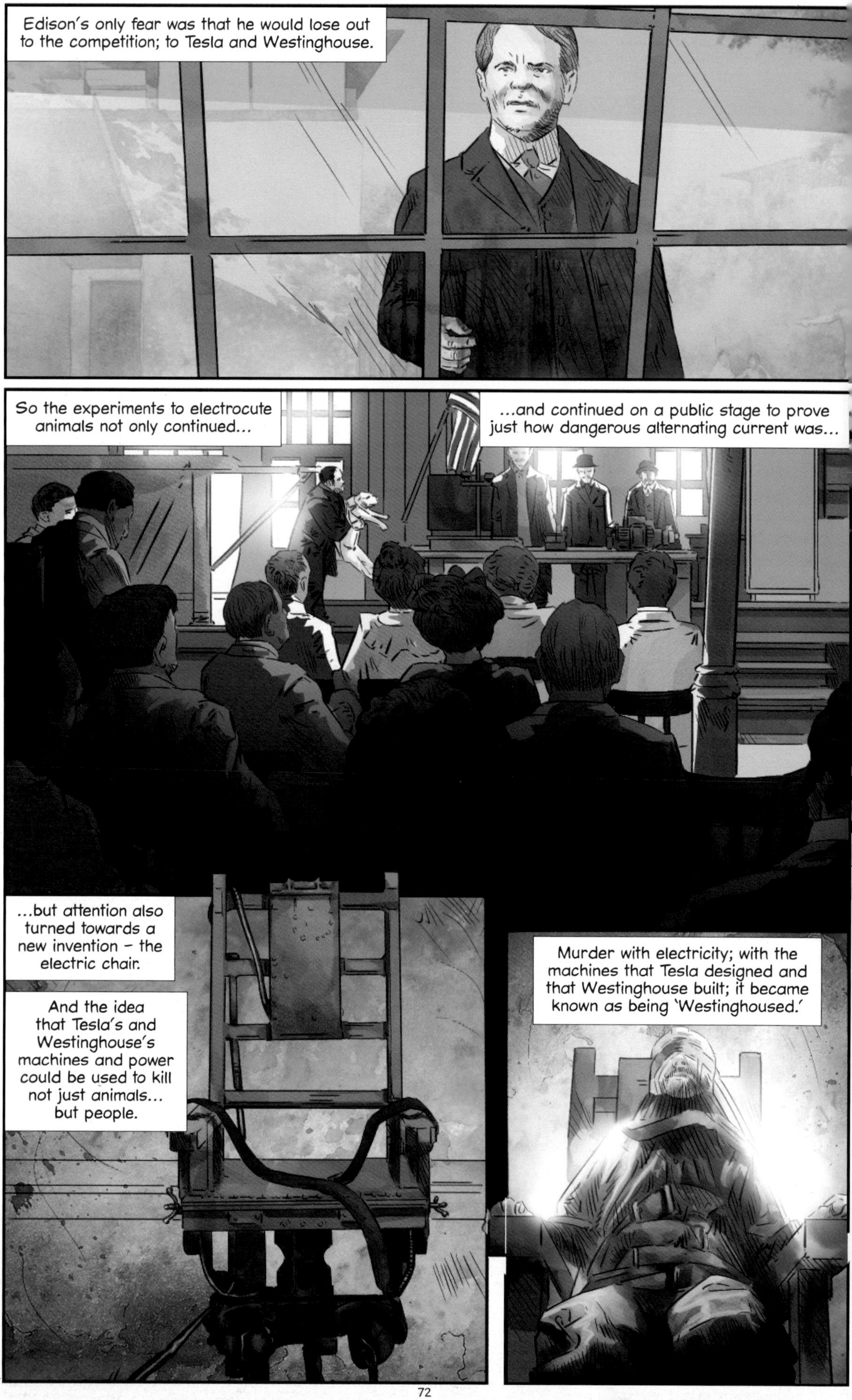
Edison's only fear was that he would lose out to the competition; to Tesla and Westinghouse.
So the experiments to electrocute animals not only continued...
...and continued on a public stage to prove just how dangerous alternating current was...
...but attention also turned towards a new invention – the electric chair.
And the idea that Tesla's and Westinghouse's machines and power could be used to kill not just animals... but people.
Murder with electricity; with the machines that Tesla designed and that Westinghouse built; it became known as being 'Westinghoused.'

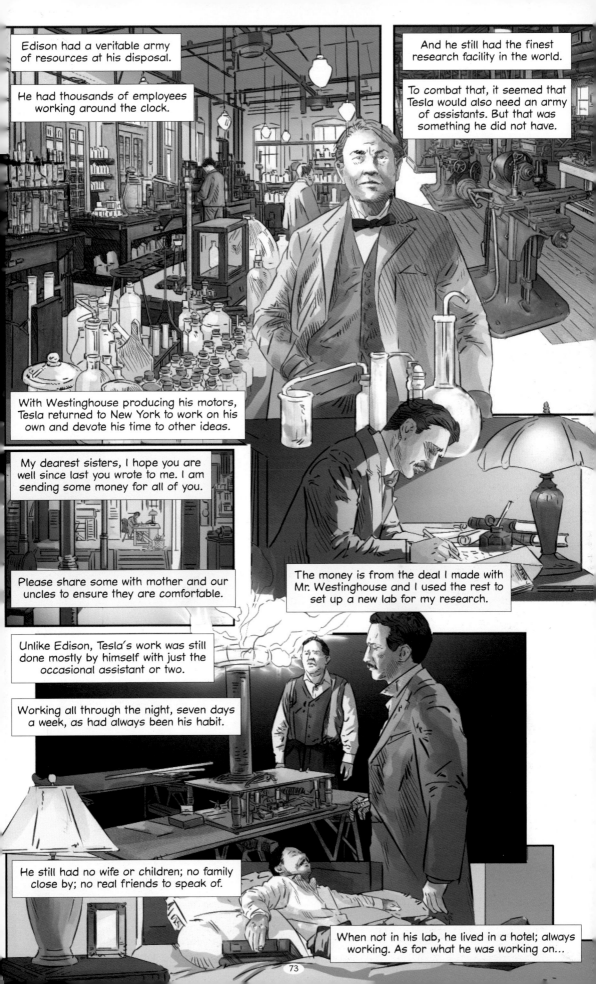

Edison had a veritable army of resources at his disposal.

He had thousands of employees working around the clock.

And he still had the finest research facility in the world.

To combat that, it seemed that Tesla would also need an army of assistants. But that was something he did not have.

With Westinghouse producing his motors, Tesla returned to New York to work on his own and devote his time to other ideas.

My dearest sisters, I hope you are well since last you wrote to me. I am sending some money for all of you.

Please share some with mother and our uncles to ensure they are comfortable.

The money is from the deal I made with Mr. Westinghouse and I used the rest to set up a new lab for my research.

Unlike Edison, Tesla's work was still done mostly by himself with just the occasional assistant or two.

Working all through the night, seven days a week, as had always been his habit.

He still had no wife or children; no family close by; no real friends to speak of.

When not in his lab, he lived in a hotel; always working. As for what he was working on...

73

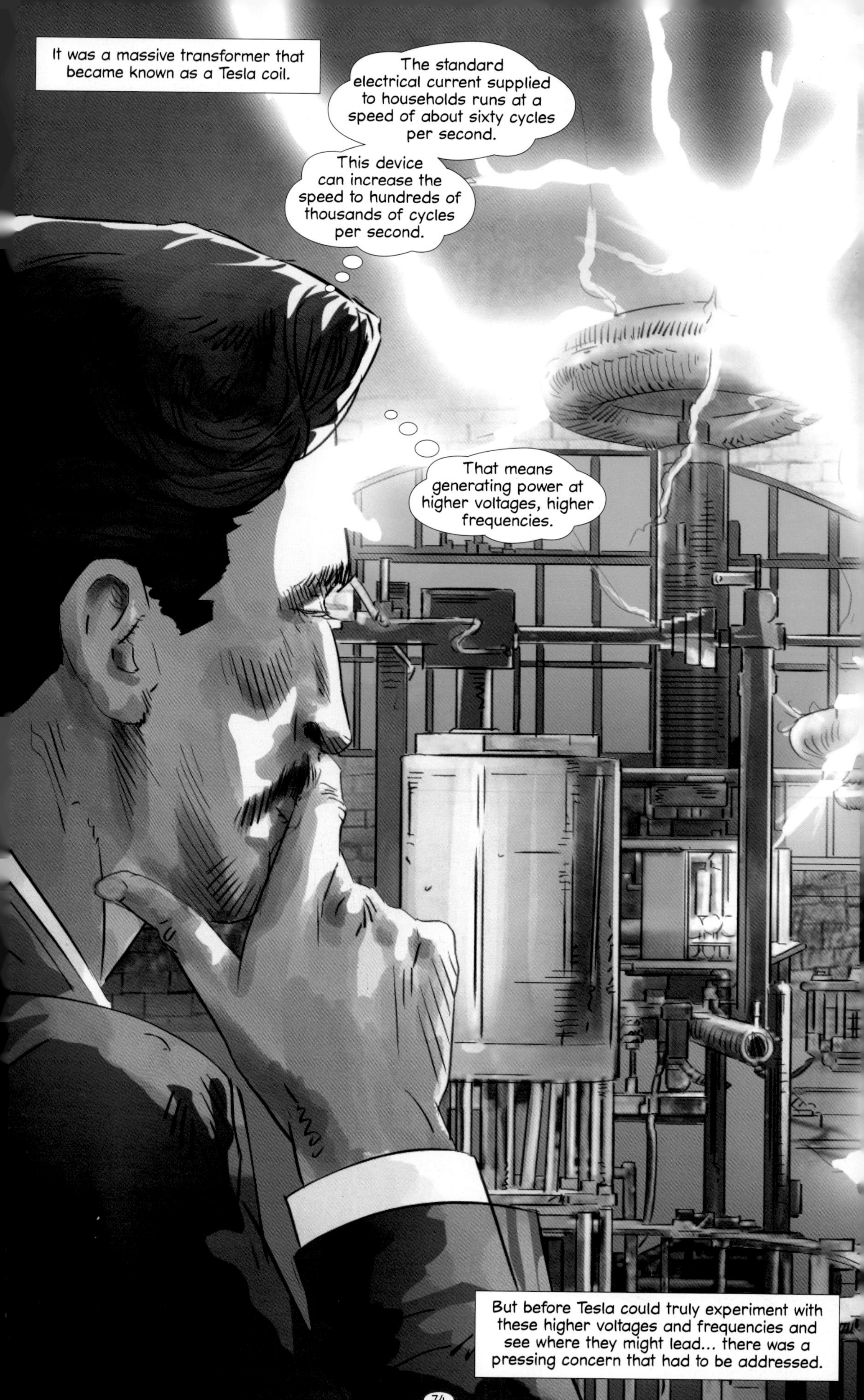
It was a massive transformer that became known as a Tesla coil.
The standard electrical current supplied to households runs at a speed of about sixty cycles per second.
This device can increase the speed to hundreds of thousands of cycles per second.
That means generating power at higher voltages, higher frequencies.
But before Tesla could truly experiment with these higher voltages and frequencies and see where they might lead... there was a pressing concern that had to be addressed.

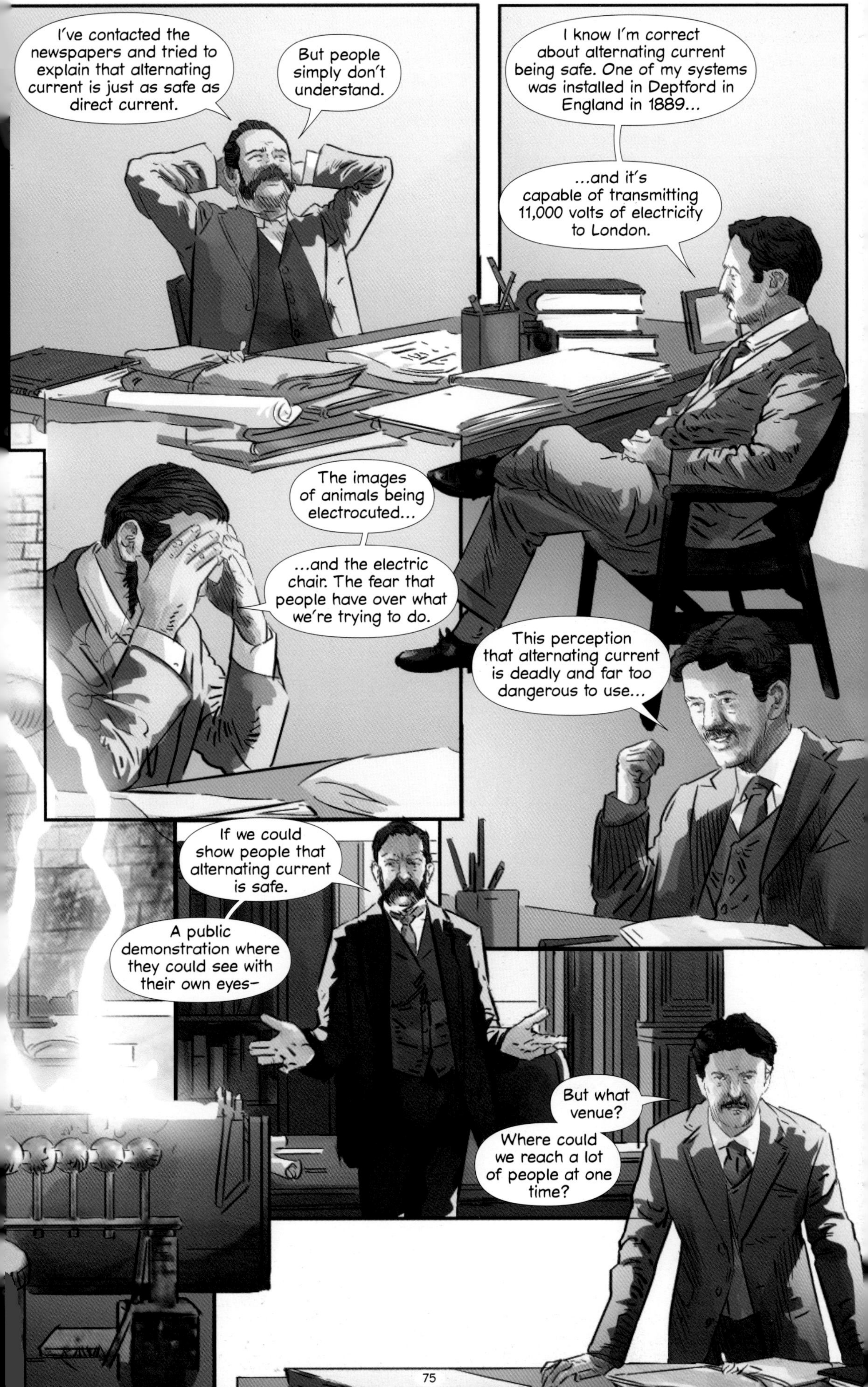
I've contacted the newspapers and tried to explain that alternating current is just as safe as direct current.
But people simply don't understand.
I know I'm correct about alternating current being safe. One of my systems was installed in Deptford in England in 1889...
...and it's capable of transmitting 11,000 volts of electricity to London.
The images of animals being electrocuted...
...and the electric chair. The fear that people have over what we're trying to do.
This perception that alternating current is deadly and far too dangerous to use...
If we could show people that alternating current is safe.
A public demonstration where they could see with their own eyes–
But what venue?
Where could we reach a lot of people at one time?

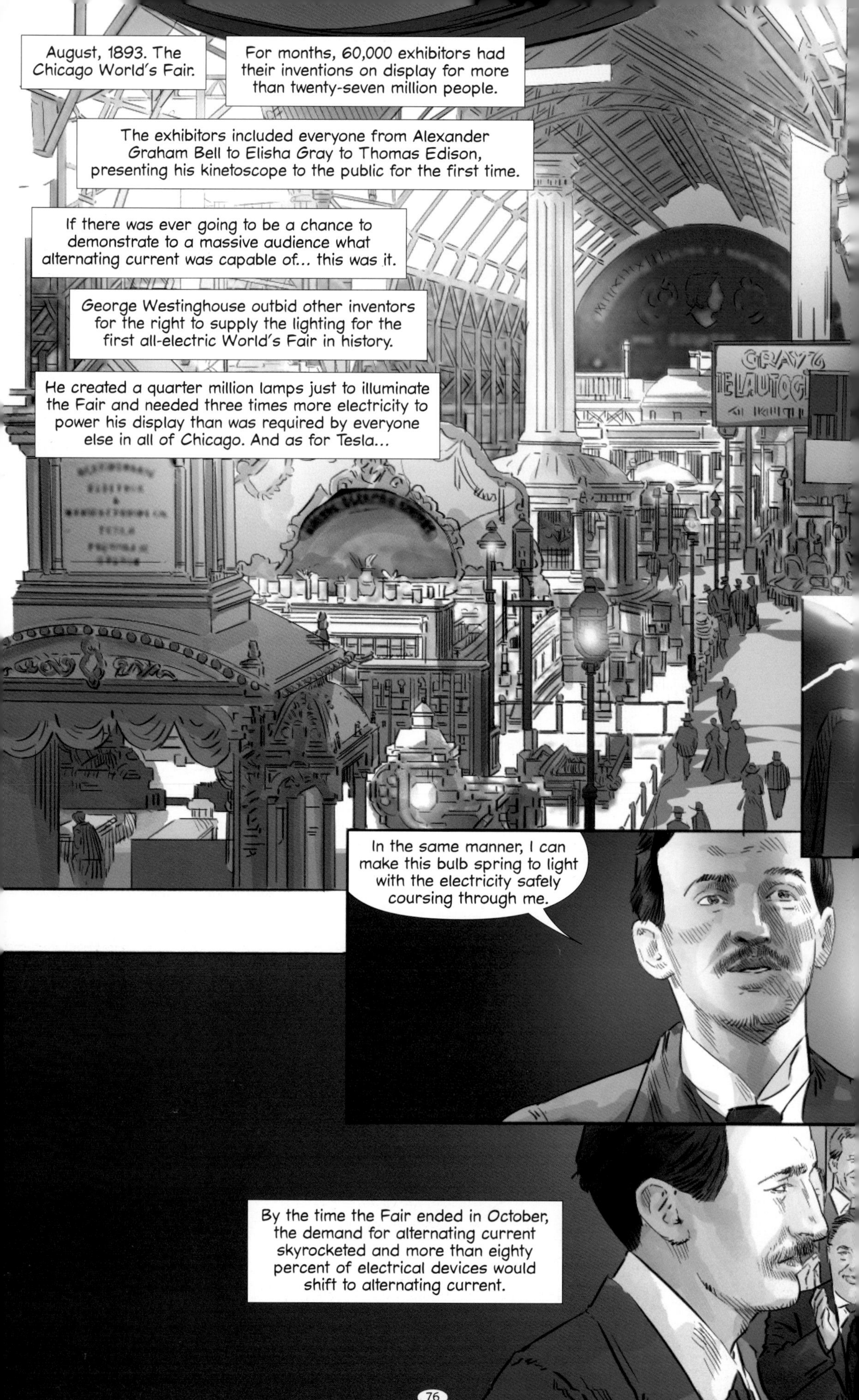
August, 1893. The Chicago World's Fair.
For months, 60,000 exhibitors had their inventions on display for more than twenty-seven million people.
The exhibitors included everyone from Alexander Graham Bell to Elisha Gray to Thomas Edison, presenting his kinetoscope to the public for the first time.
If there was ever going to be a chance to demonstrate to a massive audience what alternating current was capable of... this was it.
George Westinghouse outbid other inventors for the right to supply the lighting for the first all-electric World's Fair in history.
He created a quarter million lamps just to illuminate the Fair and needed three times more electricity to power his display than was required by everyone else in all of Chicago. And as for Tesla...
In the same manner, I can make this bulb spring to light with the electricity safely coursing through me.
By the time the Fair ended in October, the demand for alternating current skyrocketed and more than eighty percent of electrical devices would shift to alternating current.

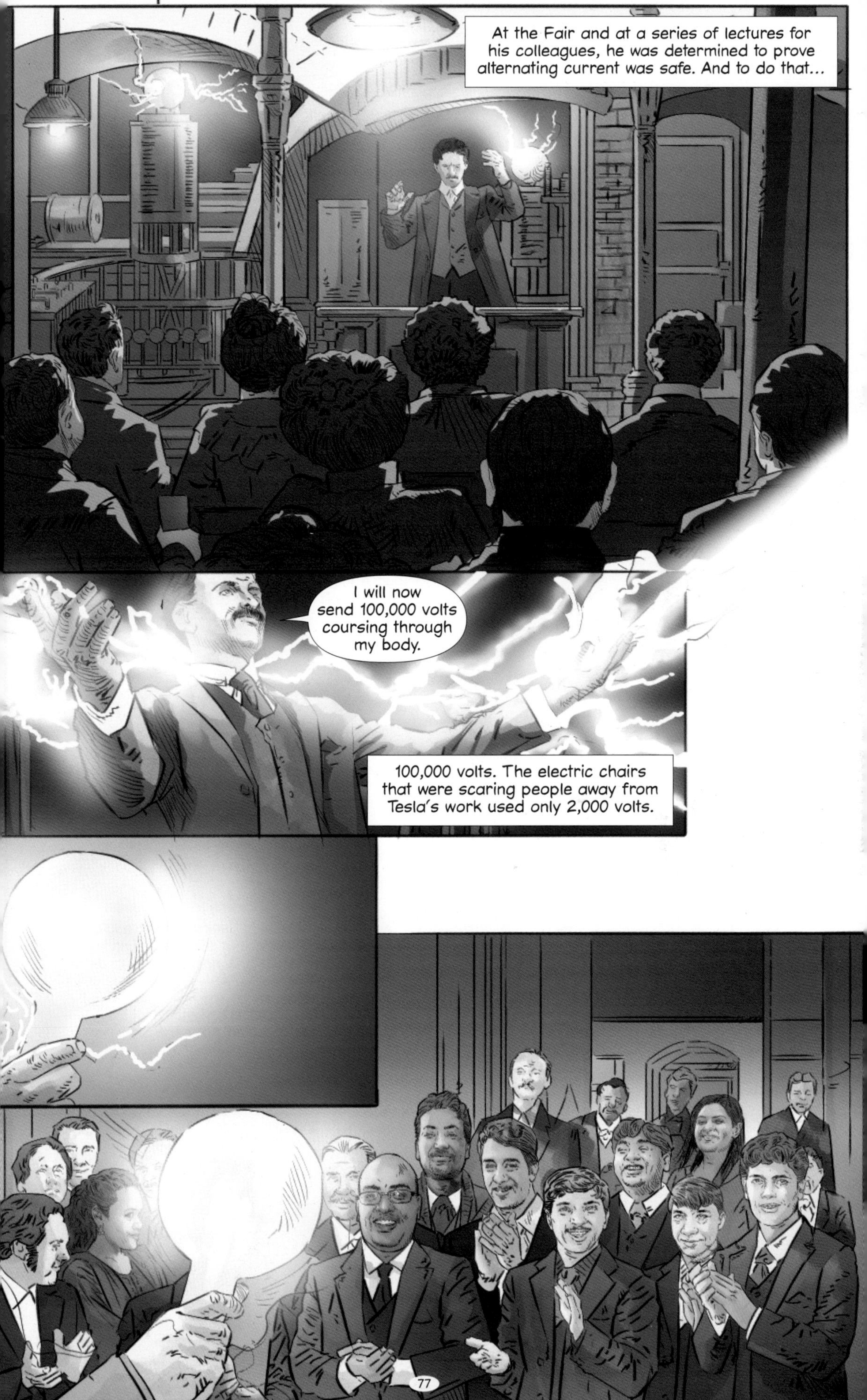
At the Fair and at a series of lectures for his colleagues, he was determined to prove alternating current was safe. And to do that...
I will now send 100,000 volts coursing through my body.
100,000 volts. The electric chairs that were scaring people away from Tesla's work used only 2,000 volts.

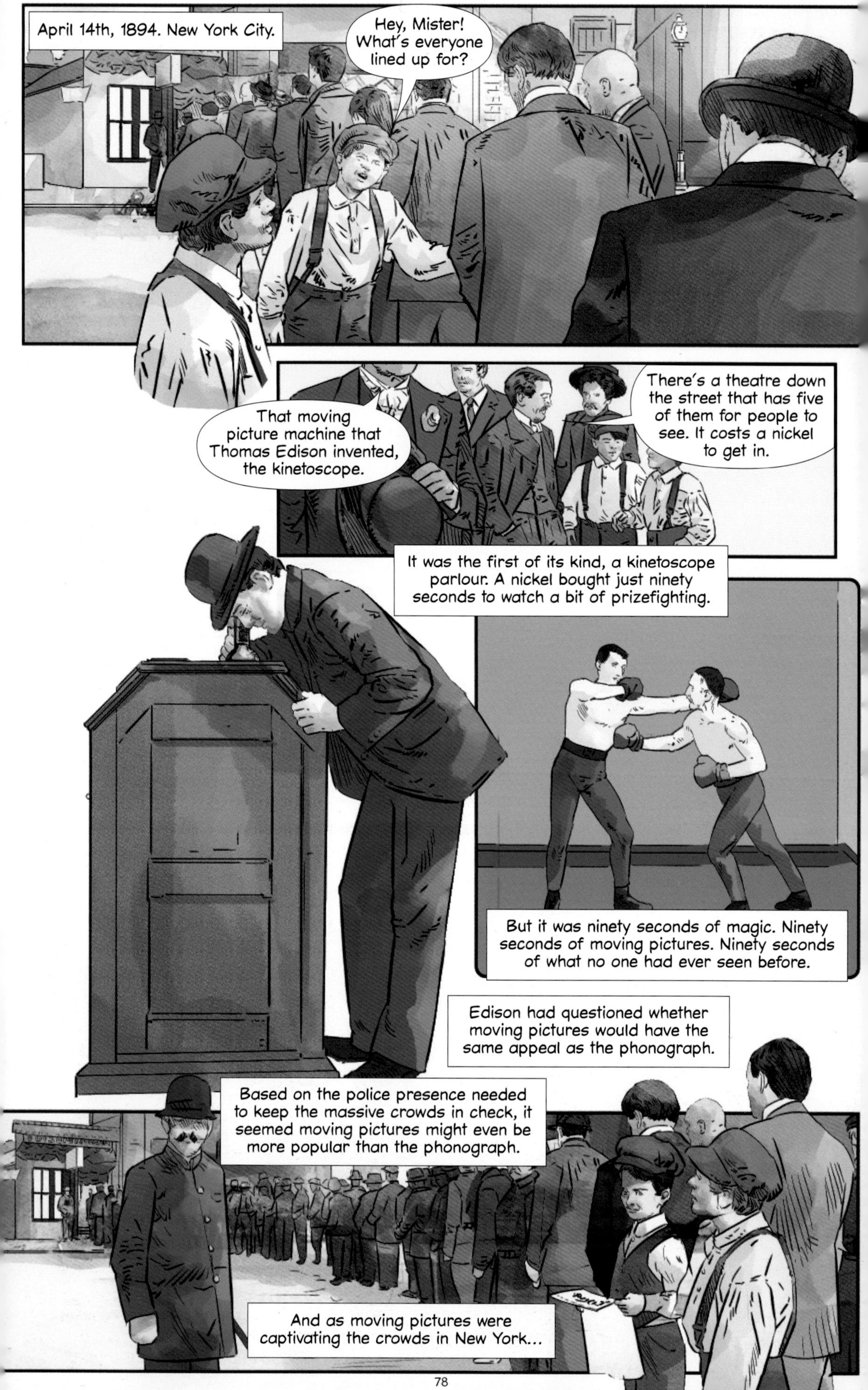
April 14th, 1894. New York City.
Hey, Mister! What's everyone lined up for?
That moving picture machine that Thomas Edison invented, the kinetoscope.
There's a theatre down the street that has five of them for people to see. It costs a nickel to get in.
It was the first of its kind, a kinetoscope parlour. A nickel bought just ninety seconds to watch a bit of prizefighting.
But it was ninety seconds of magic. Ninety seconds of moving pictures. Ninety seconds of what no one had ever seen before.
Edison had questioned whether moving pictures would have the same appeal as the phonograph.
Based on the police presence needed to keep the massive crowds in check, it seemed moving pictures might even be more popular than the phonograph.
And as moving pictures were captivating the crowds in New York...

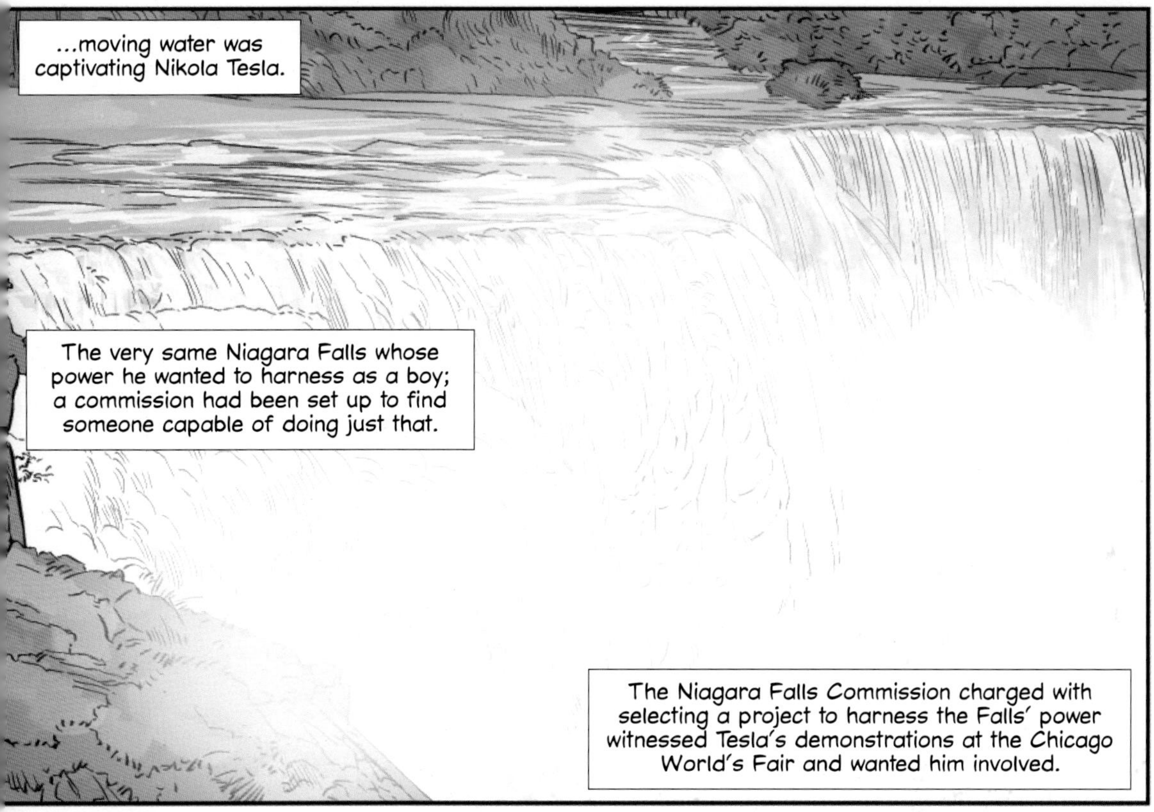
...moving water was captivating Nikola Tesla.
The very same Niagara Falls whose power he wanted to harness as a boy; a commission had been set up to find someone capable of doing just that.
The Niagara Falls Commission charged with selecting a project to harness the Falls' power witnessed Tesla's demonstrations at the Chicago World's Fair and wanted him involved.

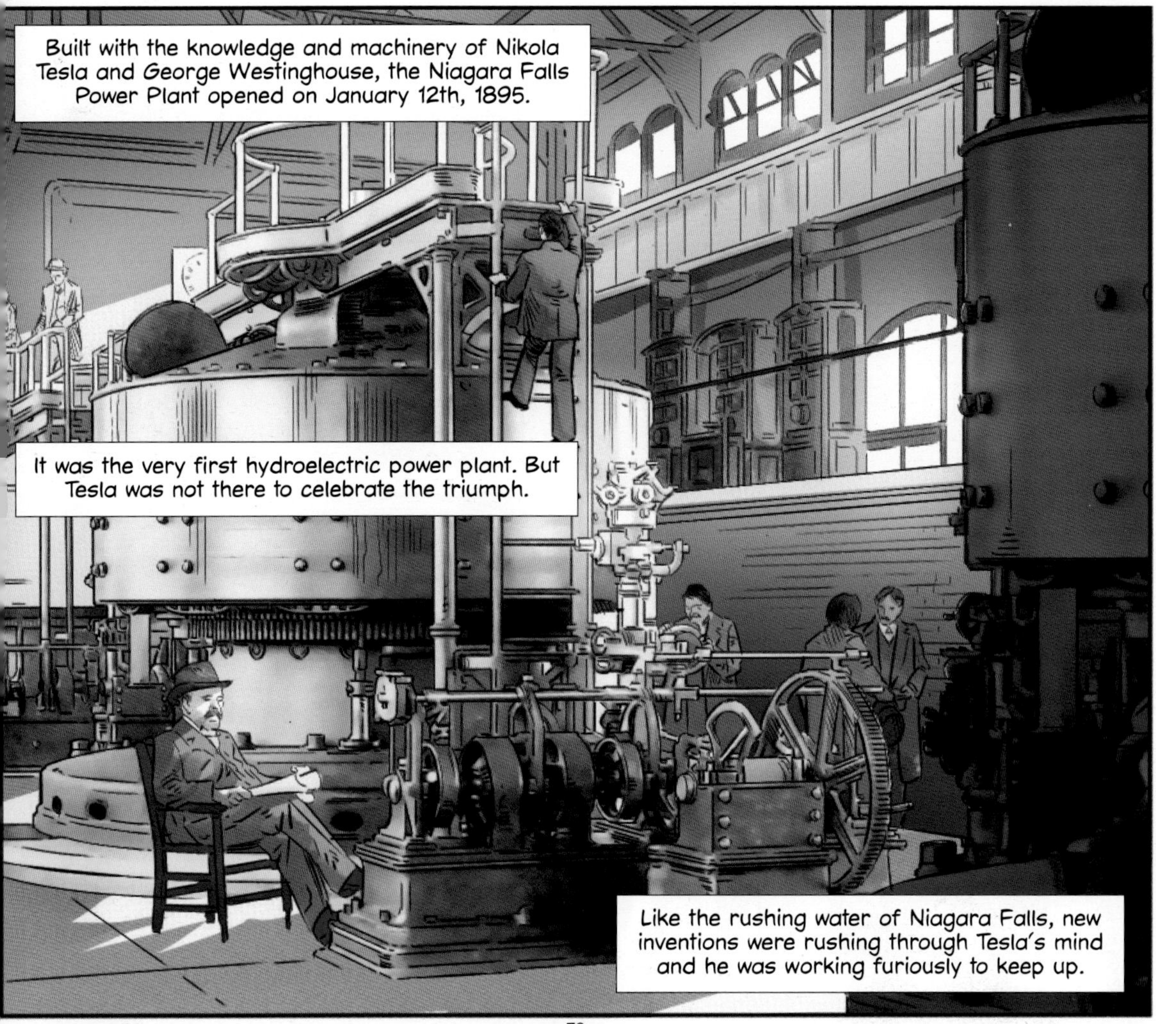
Built with the knowledge and machinery of Nikola Tesla and George Westinghouse, the Niagara Falls Power Plant opened on January 12th, 1895.
It was the very first hydroelectric power plant. But Tesla was not there to celebrate the triumph.
Like the rushing water of Niagara Falls, new inventions were rushing through Tesla's mind and he was working furiously to keep up.

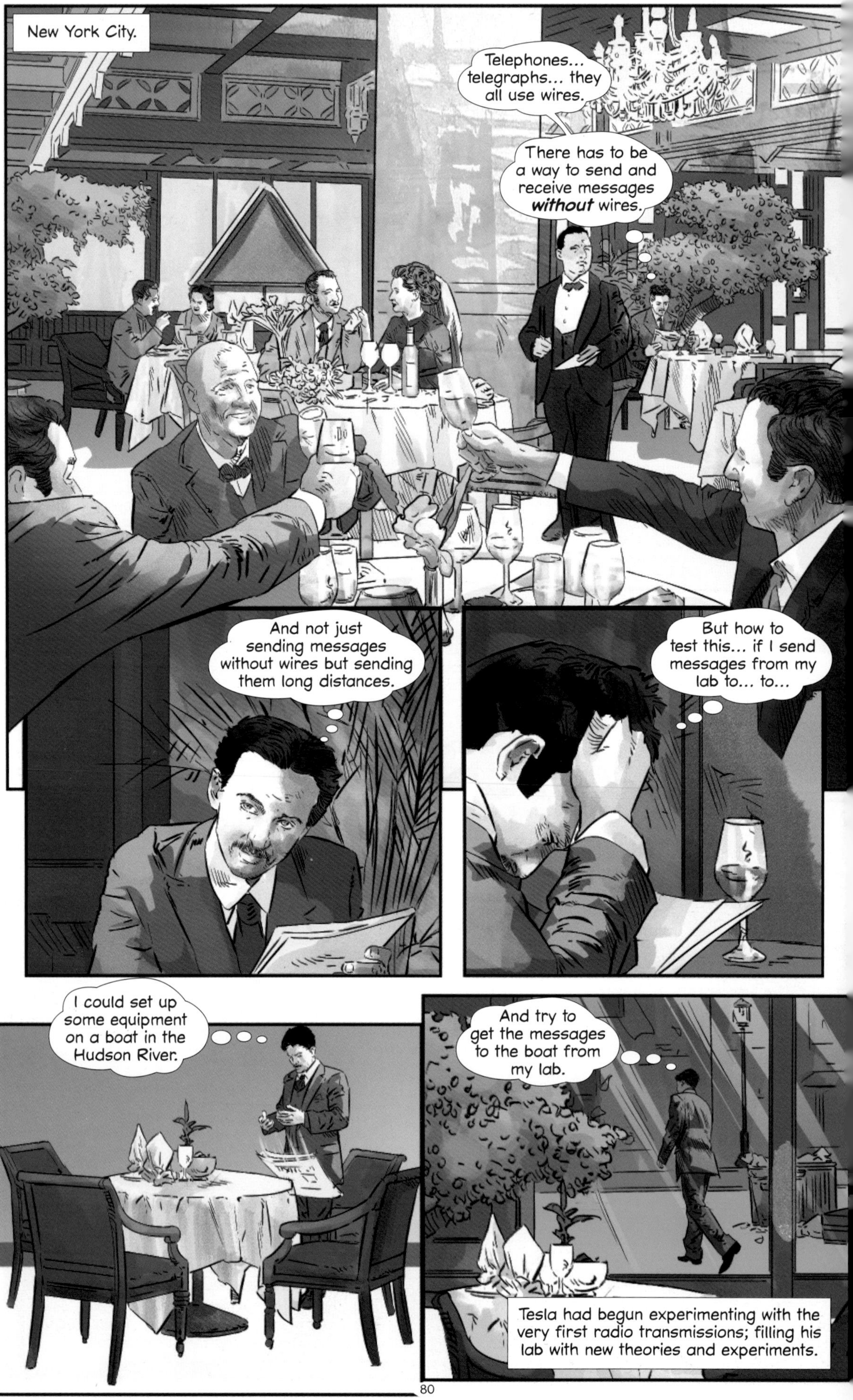
New York City.
Telephones... telegraphs... they all use wires.
There has to be a way to send and receive messages *without* wires.
And not just sending messages without wires but sending them long distances.
But how to test this... if I send messages from my lab to... to...
I could set up some equipment on a boat in the Hudson River.
And try to get the messages to the boat from my lab.
Tesla had begun experimenting with the very first radio transmissions; filling his lab with new theories and experiments.

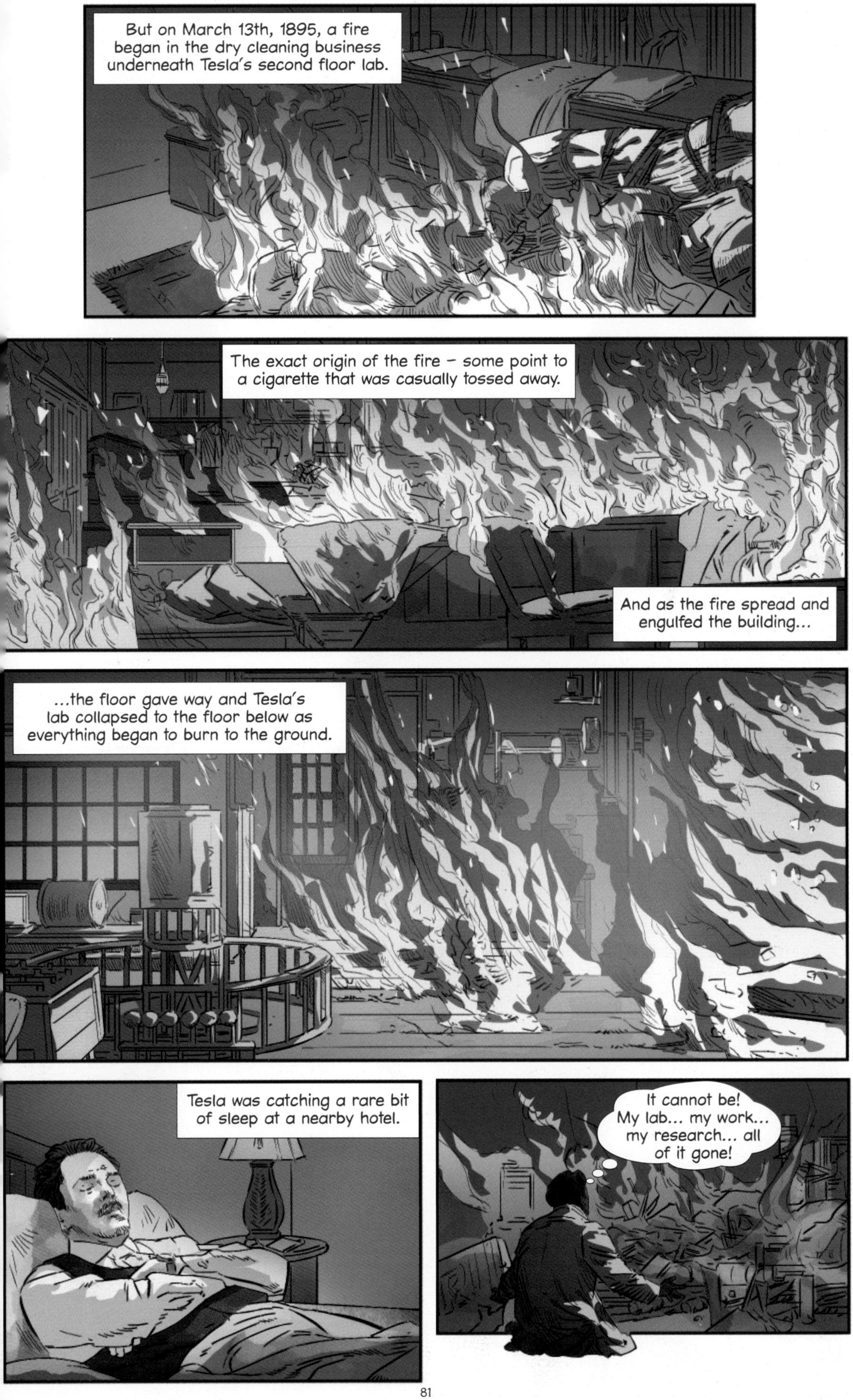
But on March 13th, 1895, a fire began in the dry cleaning business underneath Tesla's second floor lab.
The exact origin of the fire – some point to a cigarette that was casually tossed away.
And as the fire spread and engulfed the building...
...the floor gave way and Tesla's lab collapsed to the floor below as everything began to burn to the ground.
Tesla was catching a rare bit of sleep at a nearby hotel.
It cannot be! My lab... my work... my research... all of it gone!

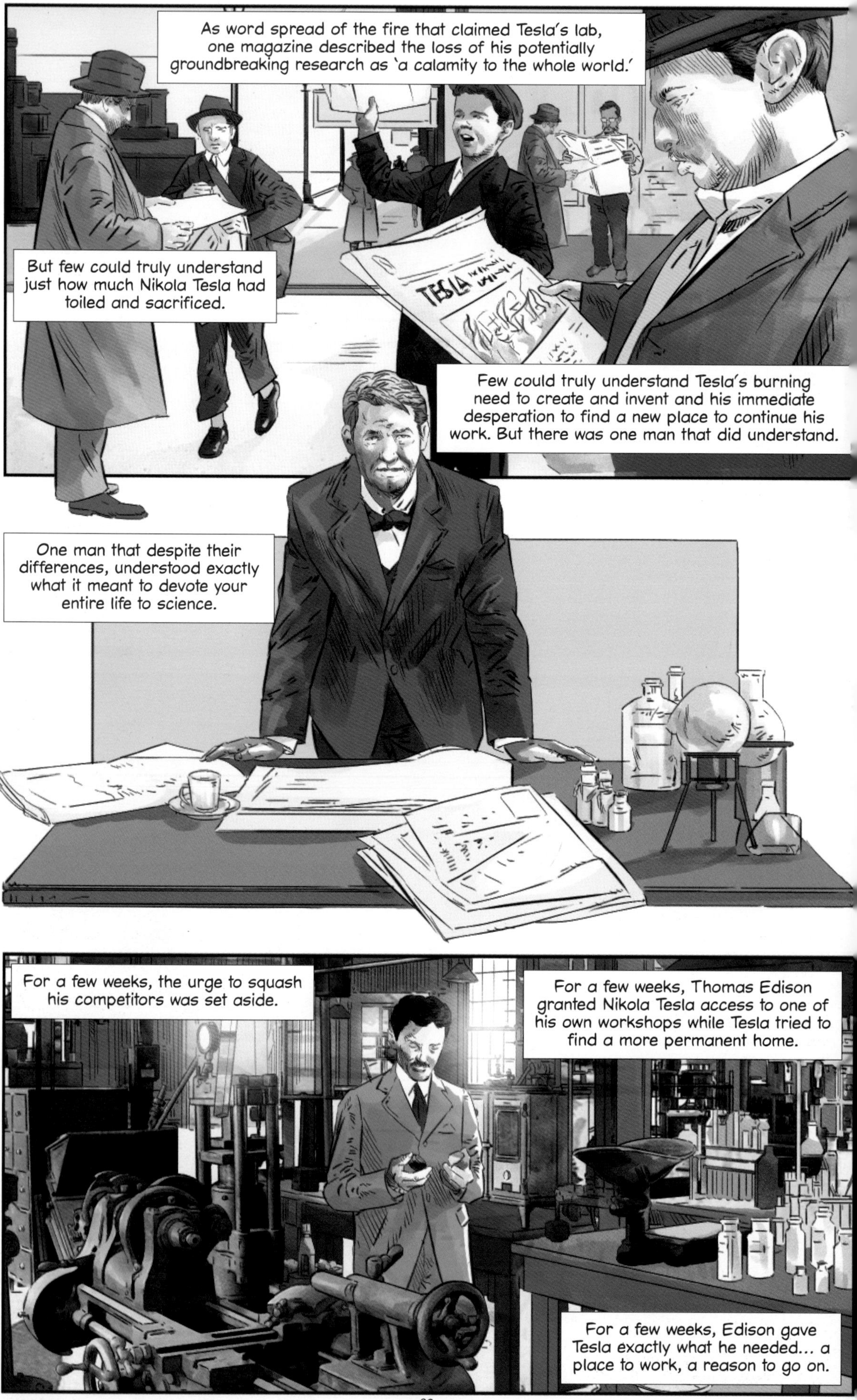
As word spread of the fire that claimed Tesla's lab, one magazine described the loss of his potentially groundbreaking research as 'a calamity to the whole world.'
But few could truly understand just how much Nikola Tesla had toiled and sacrificed.
TESLA
Few could truly understand Tesla's burning need to create and invent and his immediate desperation to find a new place to continue his work. But there was one man that did understand.
One man that despite their differences, understood exactly what it meant to devote your entire life to science.
For a few weeks, the urge to squash his competitors was set aside.
For a few weeks, Thomas Edison granted Nikola Tesla access to one of his own workshops while Tesla tried to find a more permanent home.
For a few weeks, Edison gave Tesla exactly what he needed... a place to work, a reason to go on.

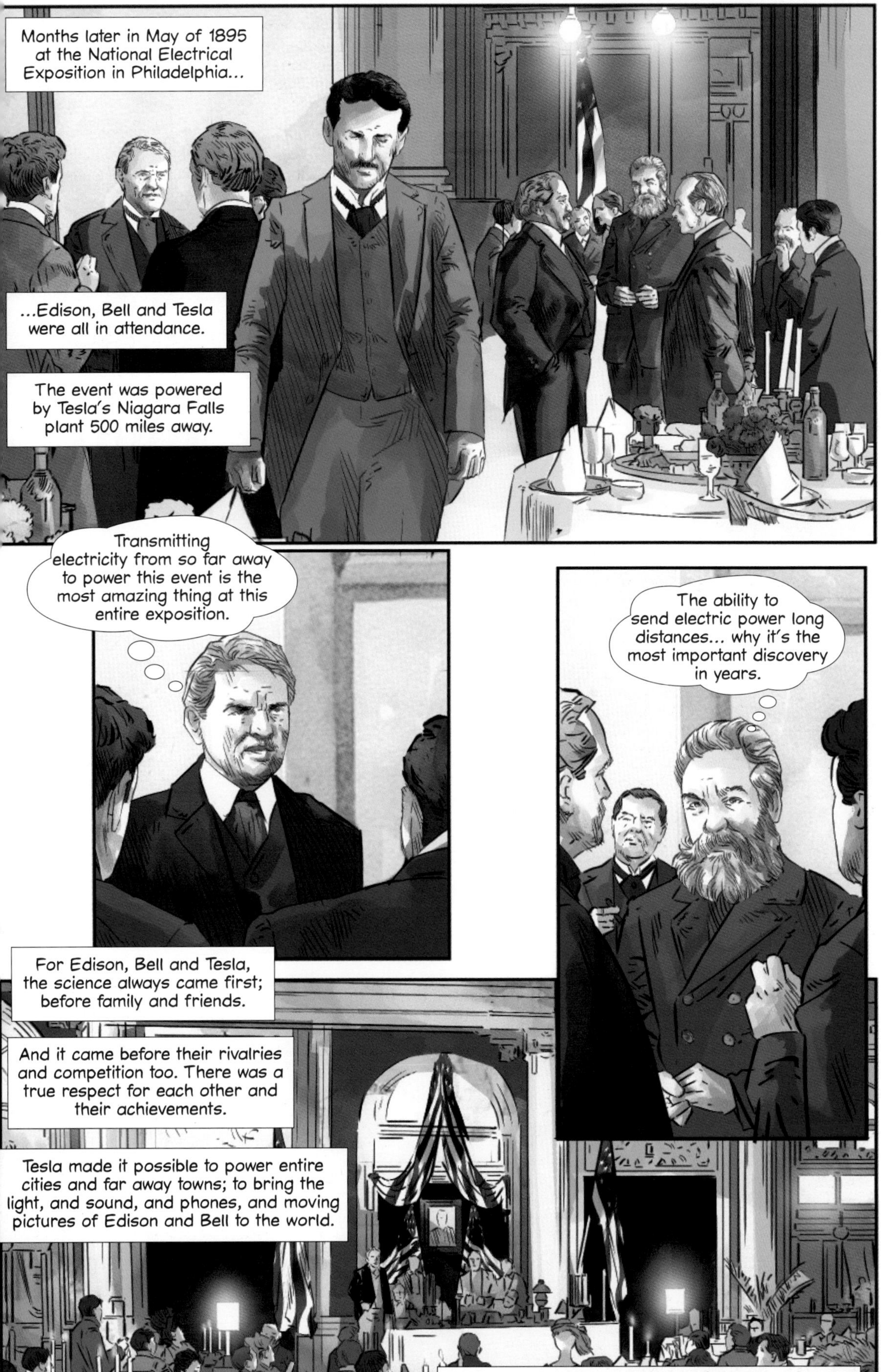
Months later in May of 1895 at the National Electrical Exposition in Philadelphia...
...Edison, Bell and Tesla were all in attendance.
The event was powered by Tesla's Niagara Falls plant 500 miles away.
Transmitting electricity from so far away to power this event is the most amazing thing at this entire exposition.
The ability to send electric power long distances... why it's the most important discovery in years.
For Edison, Bell and Tesla, the science always came first; before family and friends.
And it came before their rivalries and competition too. There was a true respect for each other and their achievements.
Tesla made it possible to power entire cities and far away towns; to bring the light, and sound, and phones, and moving pictures of Edison and Bell to the world.
All three men had achieved unthinkable greatness. But even that was not enough for them.

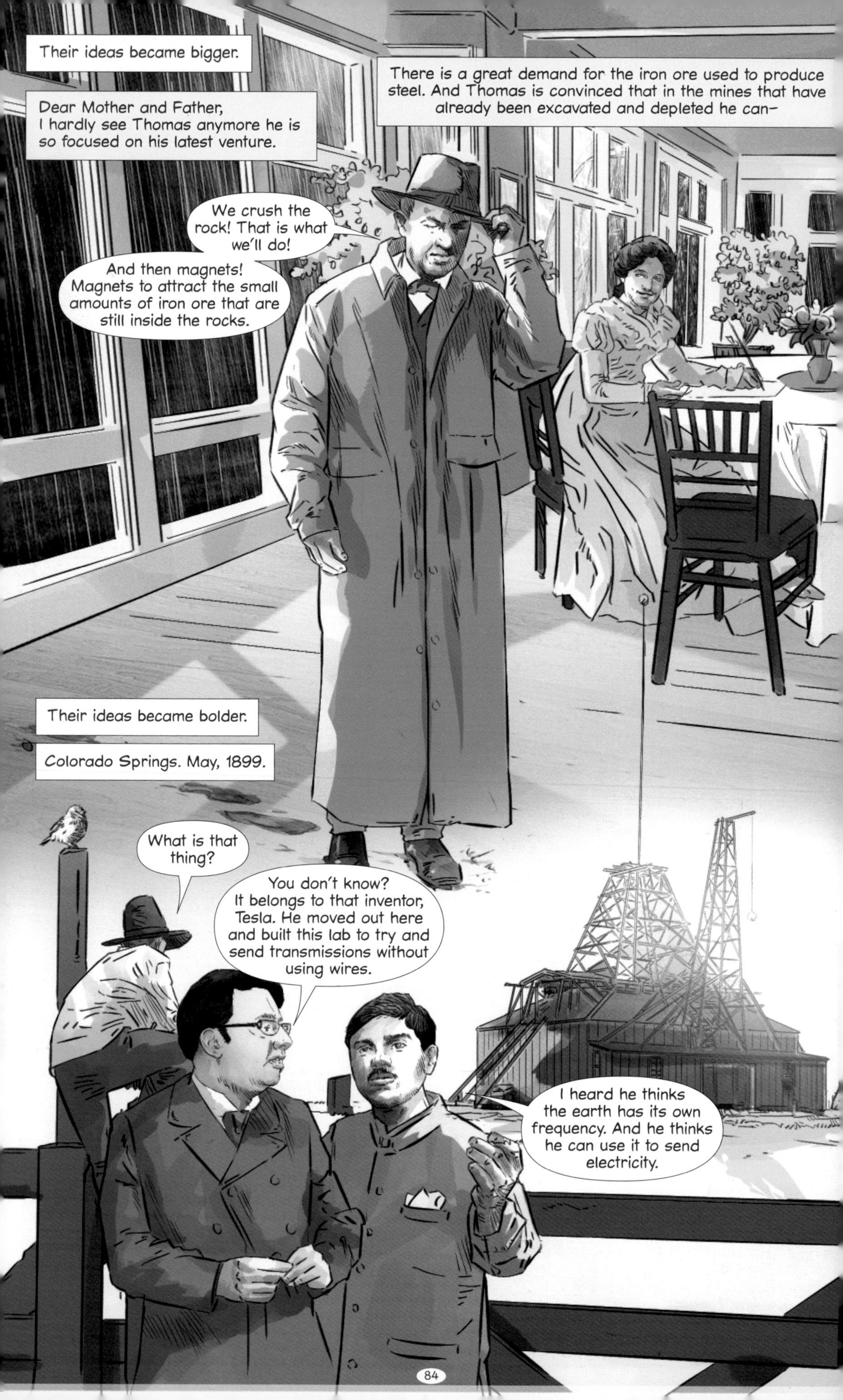
Their ideas became bigger.
Dear Mother and Father, I hardly see Thomas anymore he is so focused on his latest venture.
There is a great demand for the iron ore used to produce steel. And Thomas is convinced that in the mines that have already been excavated and depleted he can–
We crush the rock! That is what we'll do!
And then magnets! Magnets to attract the small amounts of iron ore that are still inside the rocks.
Their ideas became bolder.
Colorado Springs. May, 1899.
What is that thing?
You don't know? It belongs to that inventor, Tesla. He moved out here and built this lab to try and send transmissions without using wires.
I heard he thinks the earth has its own frequency. And he thinks he can use it to send electricity.

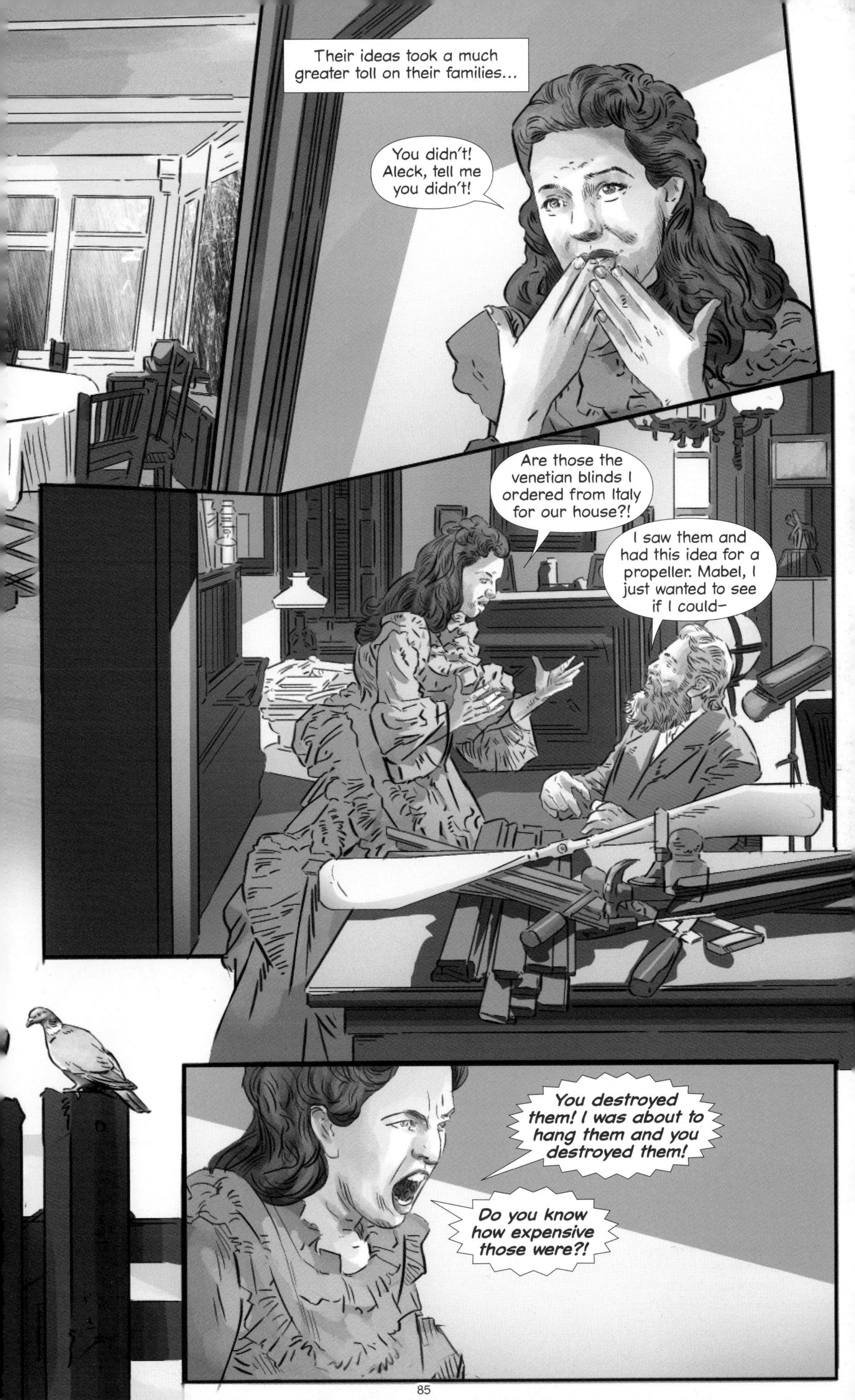
Their ideas took a much greater toll on their families...
You didn't! Aleck, tell me you didn't!
Are those the venetian blinds I ordered from Italy for our house?!
I saw them and had this idea for a propeller. Mabel, I just wanted to see if I could–
You destroyed them! I was about to hang them and you destroyed them!
Do you know how expensive those were?!

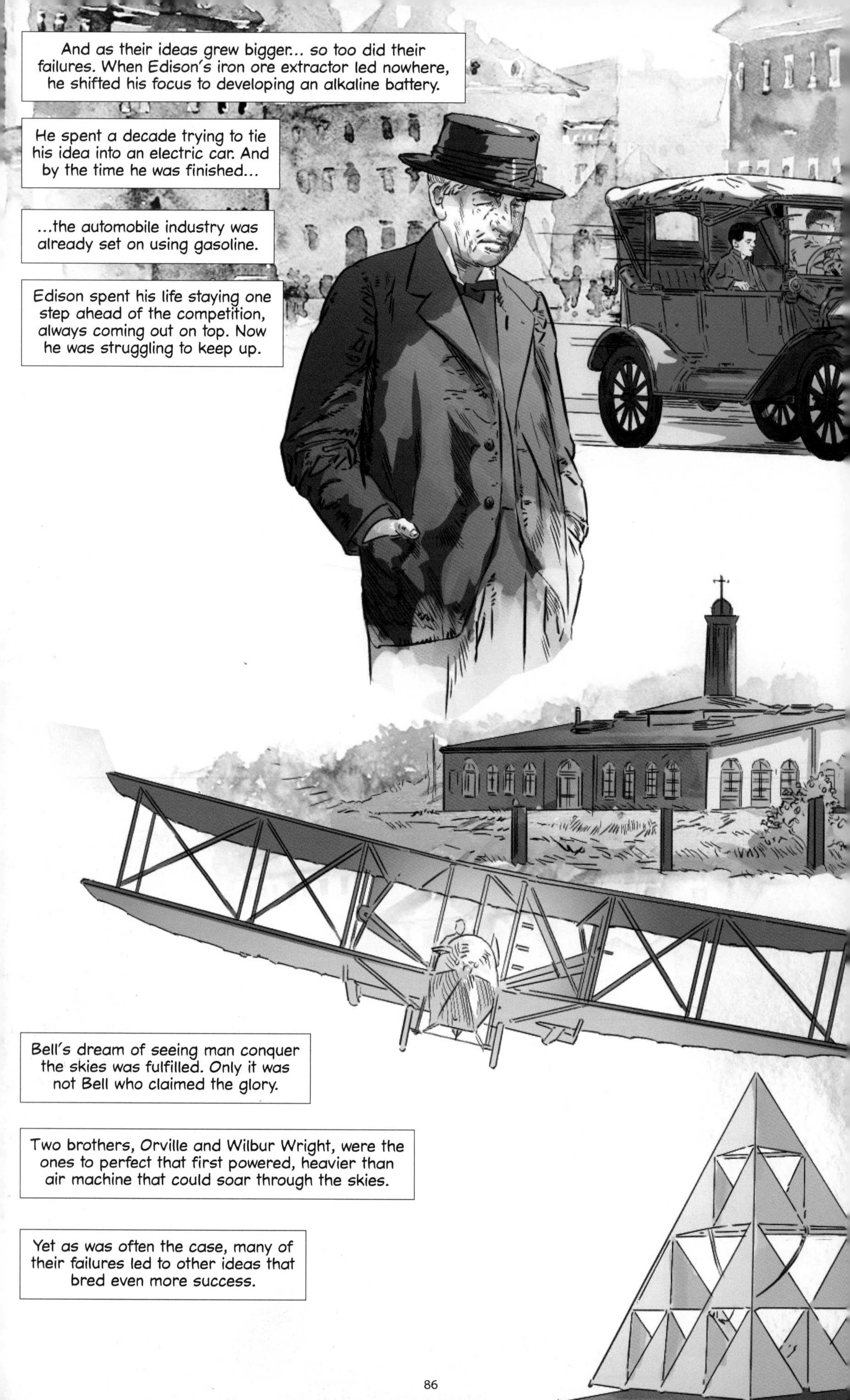
And as their ideas grew bigger... so too did their failures. When Edison's iron ore extractor led nowhere, he shifted his focus to developing an alkaline battery.
He spent a decade trying to tie his idea into an electric car. And by the time he was finished...
...the automobile industry was already set on using gasoline.
Edison spent his life staying one step ahead of the competition, always coming out on top. Now he was struggling to keep up.
Bell's dream of seeing man conquer the skies was fulfilled. Only it was not Bell who claimed the glory.
Two brothers, Orville and Wilbur Wright, were the ones to perfect that first powered, heavier than air machine that could soar through the skies.
Yet as was often the case, many of their failures led to other ideas that bred even more success.

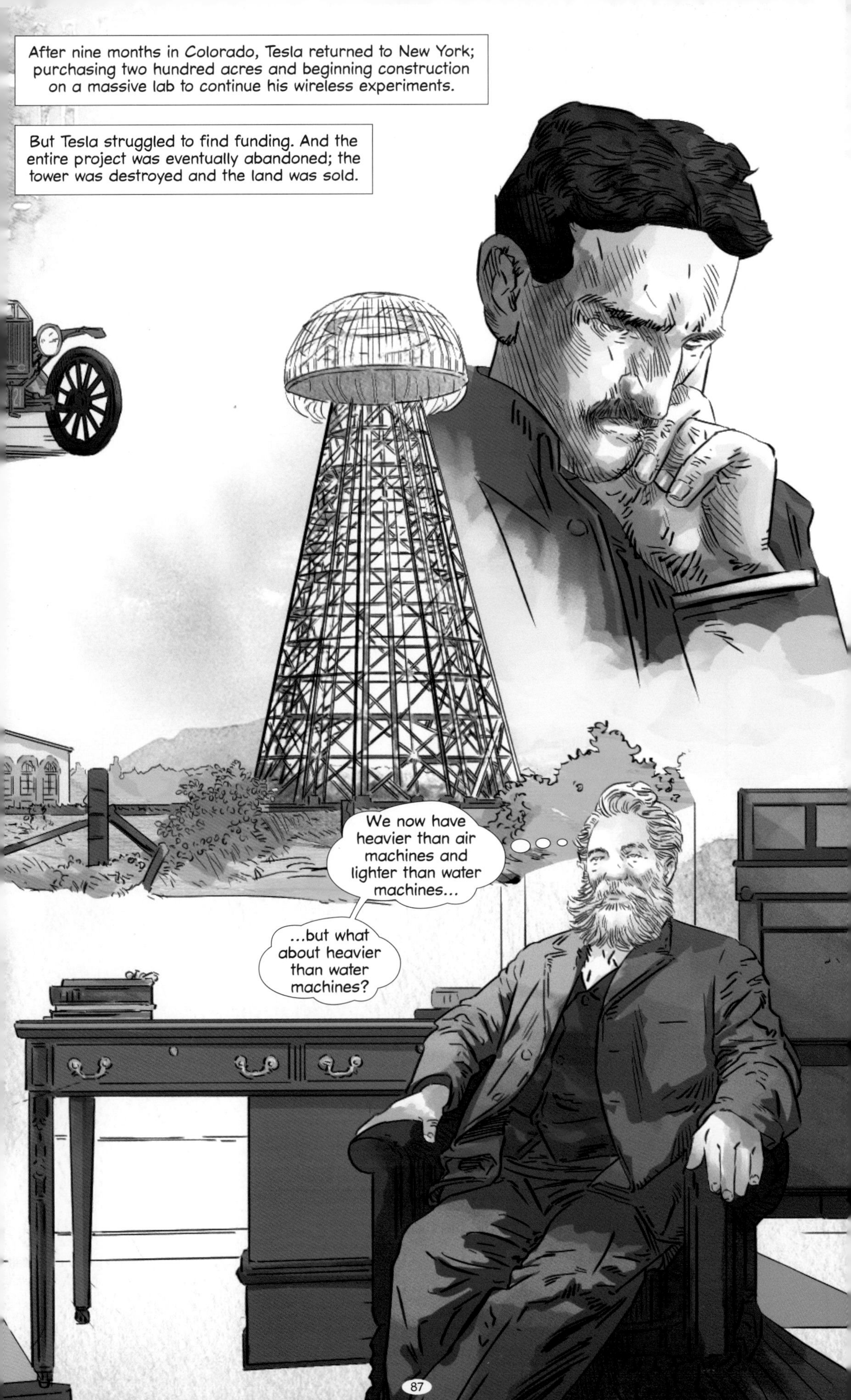
After nine months in Colorado, Tesla returned to New York; purchasing two hundred acres and beginning construction on a massive lab to continue his wireless experiments.
But Tesla struggled to find funding. And the entire project was eventually abandoned; the tower was destroyed and the land was sold.
We now have heavier than air machines and lighter than water machines...
...but what about heavier than water machines?

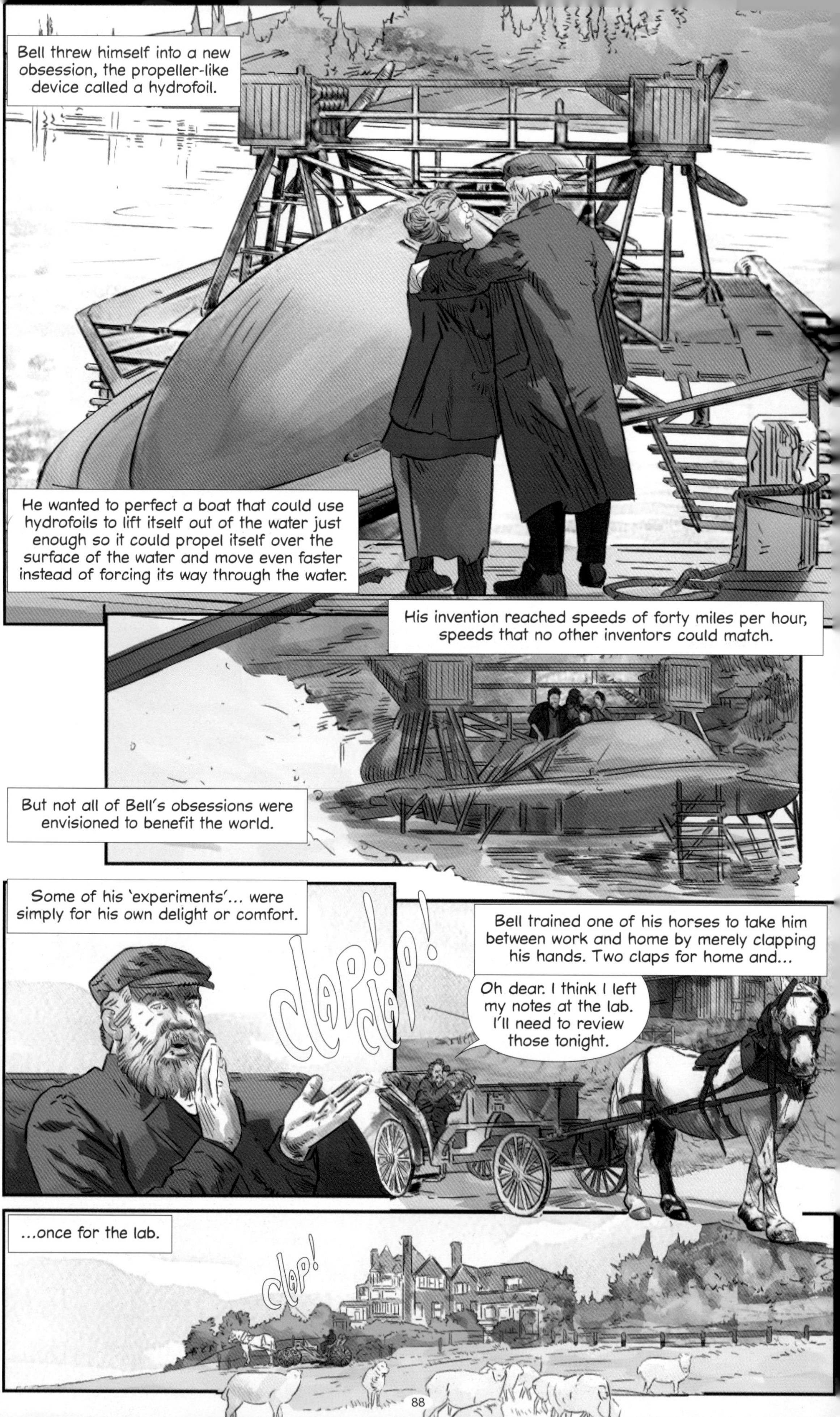

Bell threw himself into a new obsession, the propeller-like device called a hydrofoil.
He wanted to perfect a boat that could use hydrofoils to lift itself out of the water just enough so it could propel itself over the surface of the water and move even faster instead of forcing its way through the water.
His invention reached speeds of forty miles per hour, speeds that no other inventors could match.
But not all of Bell's obsessions were envisioned to benefit the world.
Some of his 'experiments'... were simply for his own delight or comfort.
clap! clap!
Bell trained one of his horses to take him between work and home by merely clapping his hands. Two claps for home and...
Oh dear. I think I left my notes at the lab. I'll need to review those tonight.
...once for the lab.
clap!

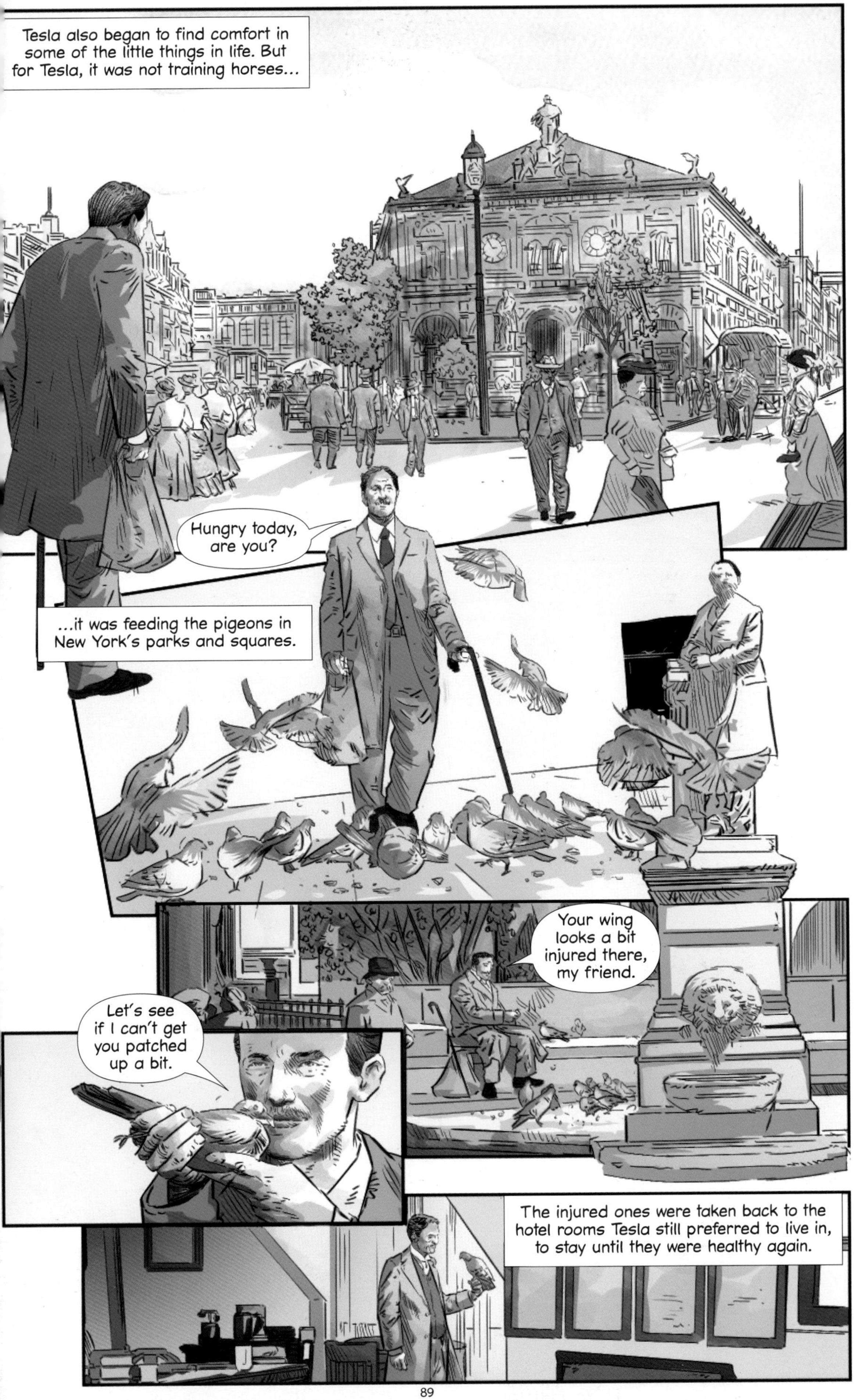

Tesla also began to find comfort in some of the little things in life. But for Tesla, it was not training horses...
Hungry today, are you?
...it was feeding the pigeons in New York's parks and squares.
Your wing looks a bit injured there, my friend.
Let's see if I can't get you patched up a bit.
The injured ones were taken back to the hotel rooms Tesla still preferred to live in, to stay until they were healthy again.

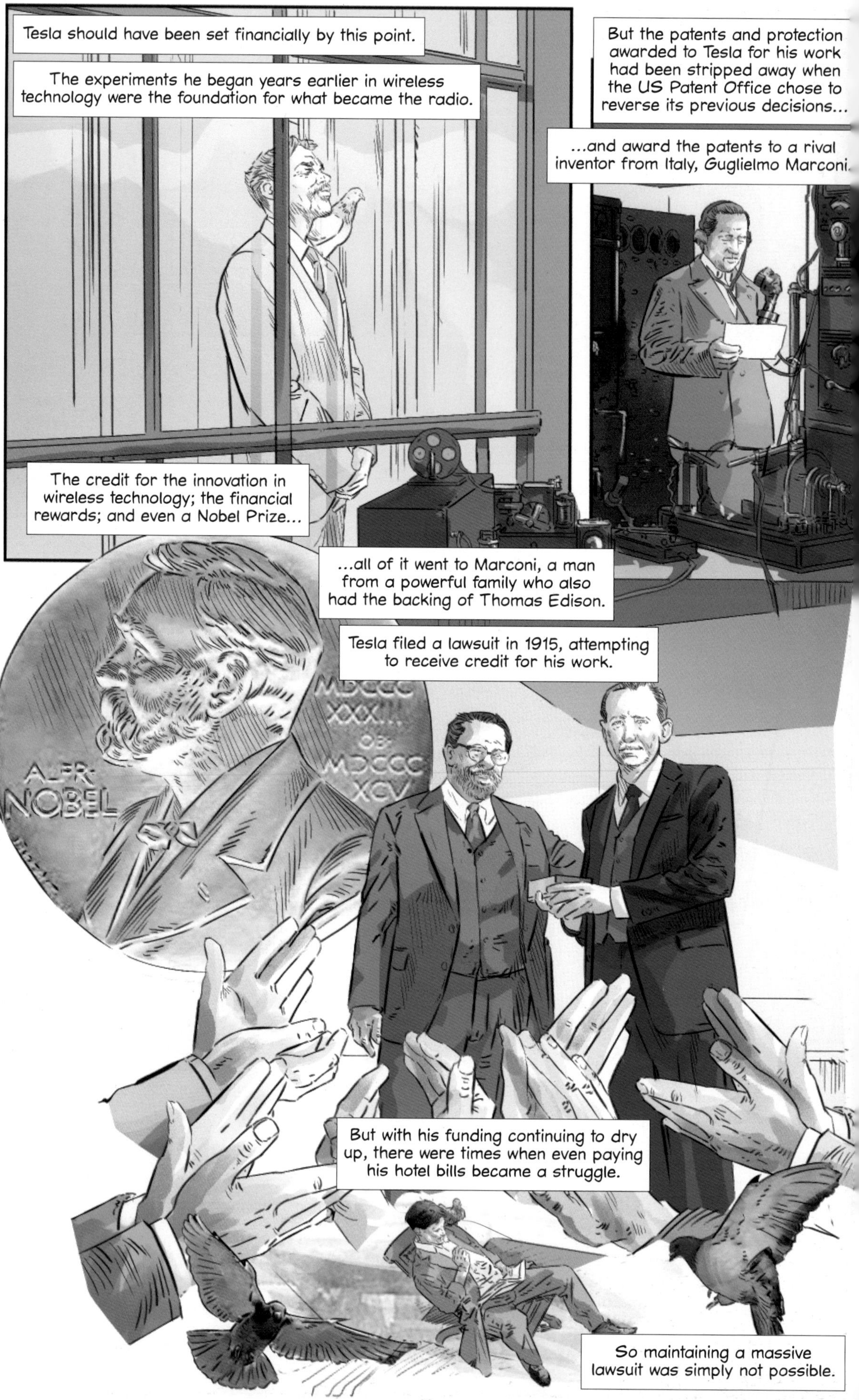
Tesla should have been set financially by this point.
The experiments he began years earlier in wireless technology were the foundation for what became the radio.
But the patents and protection awarded to Tesla for his work had been stripped away when the US Patent Office chose to reverse its previous decisions...
...and award the patents to a rival inventor from Italy, Guglielmo Marconi.
The credit for the innovation in wireless technology; the financial rewards; and even a Nobel Prize...
...all of it went to Marconi, a man from a powerful family who also had the backing of Thomas Edison.
Tesla filed a lawsuit in 1915, attempting to receive credit for his work.
ALFR. NOBEL
MDCCC XXXIII OB. MDCCC XCVI
But with his funding continuing to dry up, there were times when even paying his hotel bills became a struggle.
So maintaining a massive lawsuit was simply not possible.

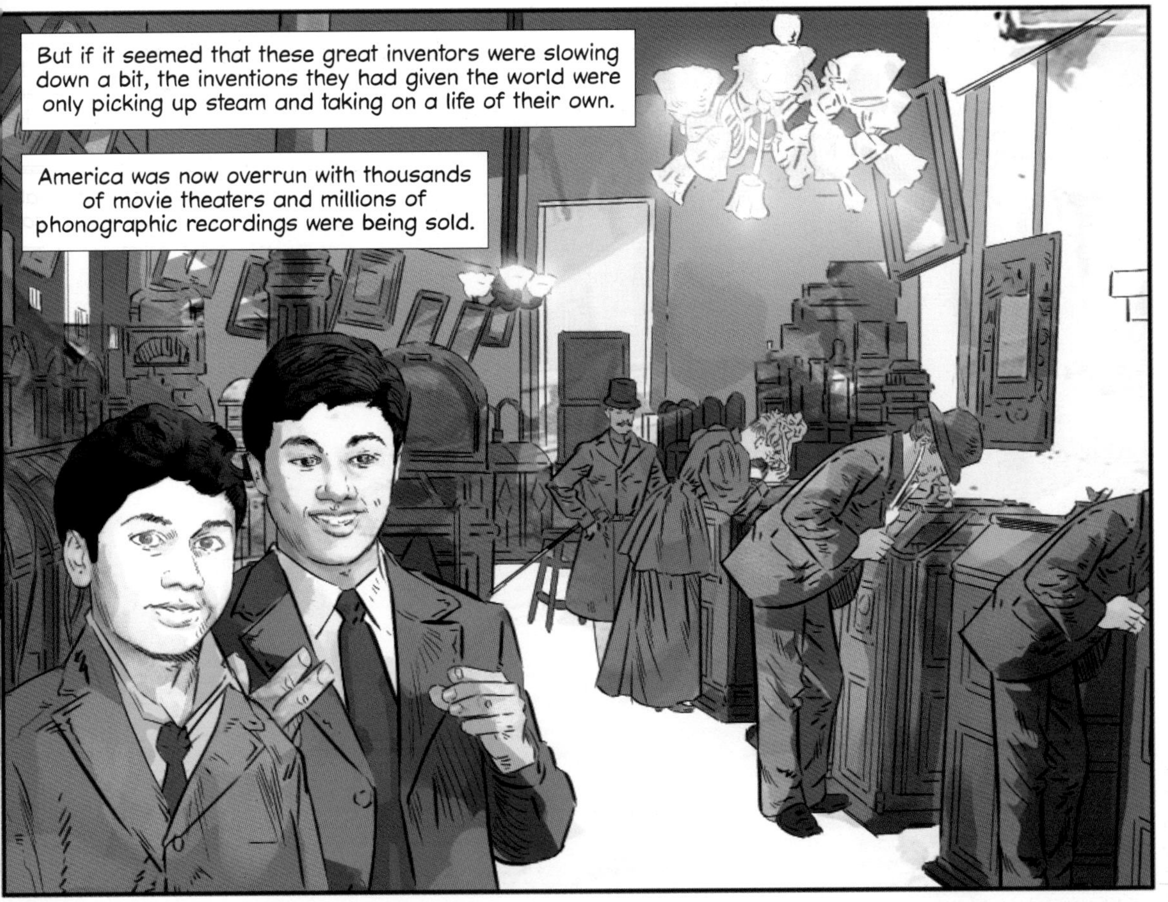
But if it seemed that these great inventors were slowing down a bit, the inventions they had given the world were only picking up steam and taking on a life of their own.
America was now overrun with thousands of movie theaters and millions of phonographic recordings were being sold.

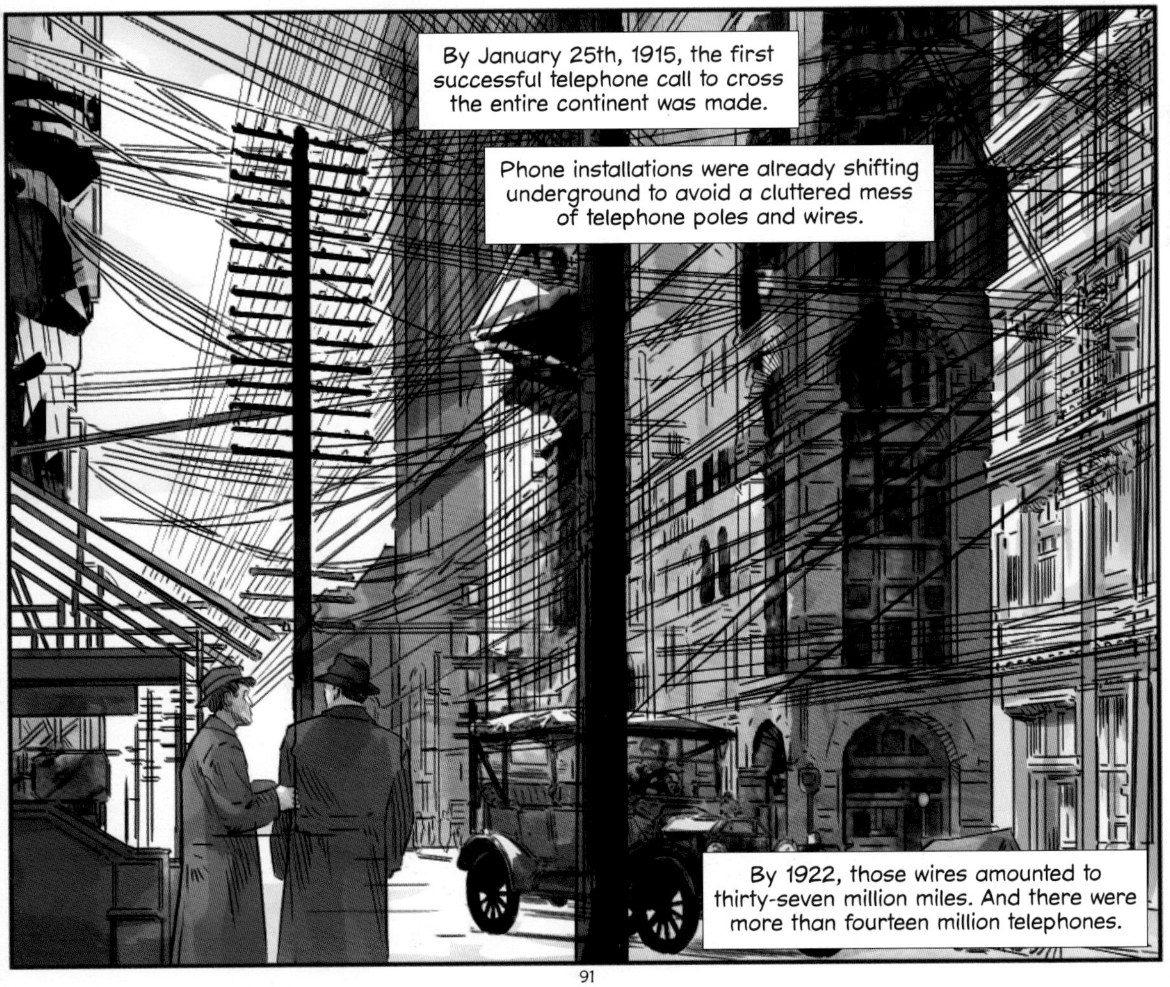
By January 25th, 1915, the first successful telephone call to cross the entire continent was made.
Phone installations were already shifting underground to avoid a cluttered mess of telephone poles and wires.
By 1922, those wires amounted to thirty-seven million miles. And there were more than fourteen million telephones.

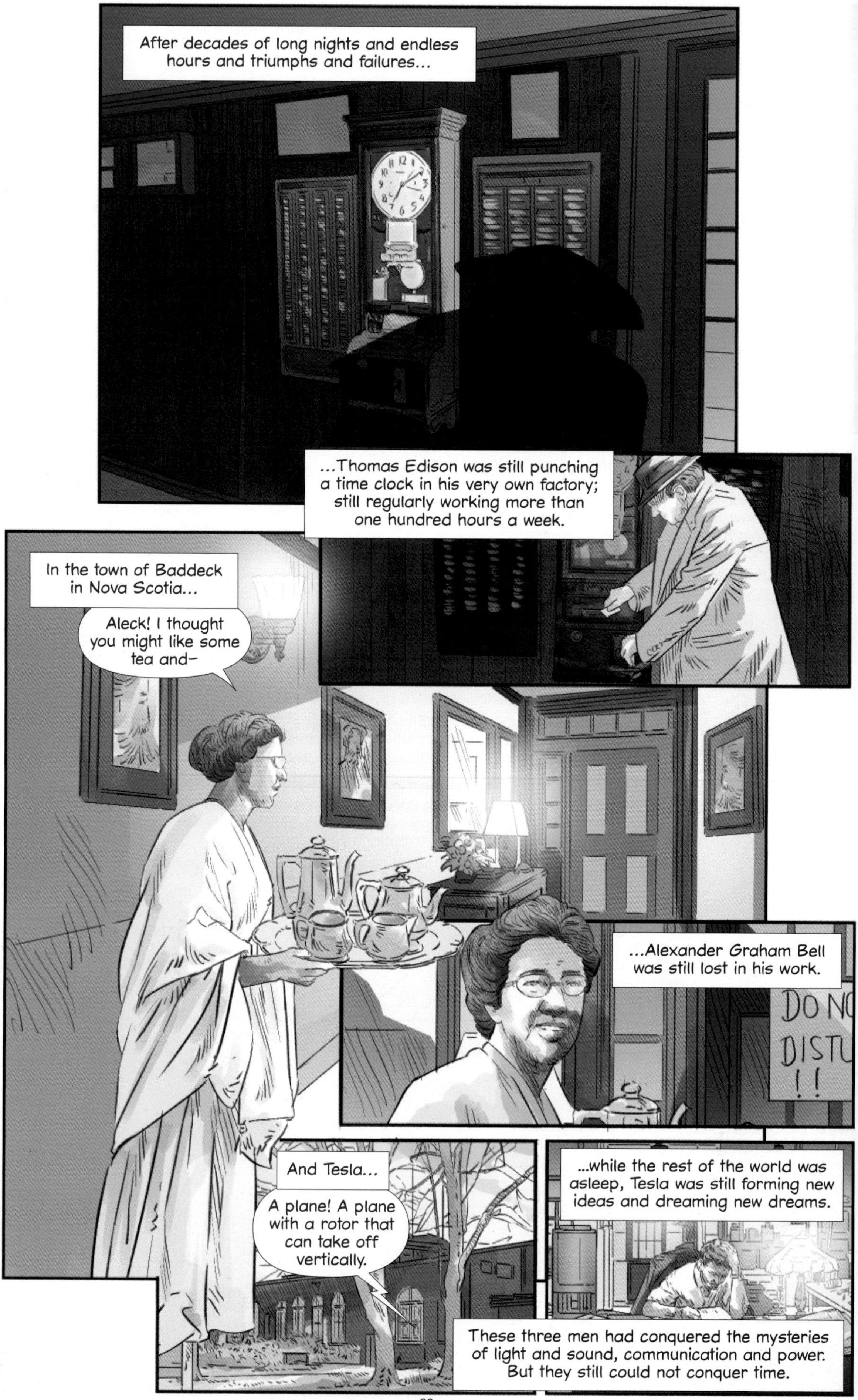
After decades of long nights and endless hours and triumphs and failures...
...Thomas Edison was still punching a time clock in his very own factory; still regularly working more than one hundred hours a week.
In the town of Baddeck in Nova Scotia...
Aleck! I thought you might like some tea and–
...Alexander Graham Bell was still lost in his work.
DO NO
DISTU
!!
And Tesla...
A plane! A plane with a rotor that can take off vertically.
...while the rest of the world was asleep, Tesla was still forming new ideas and dreaming new dreams.
These three men had conquered the mysteries of light and sound, communication and power. But they still could not conquer time.

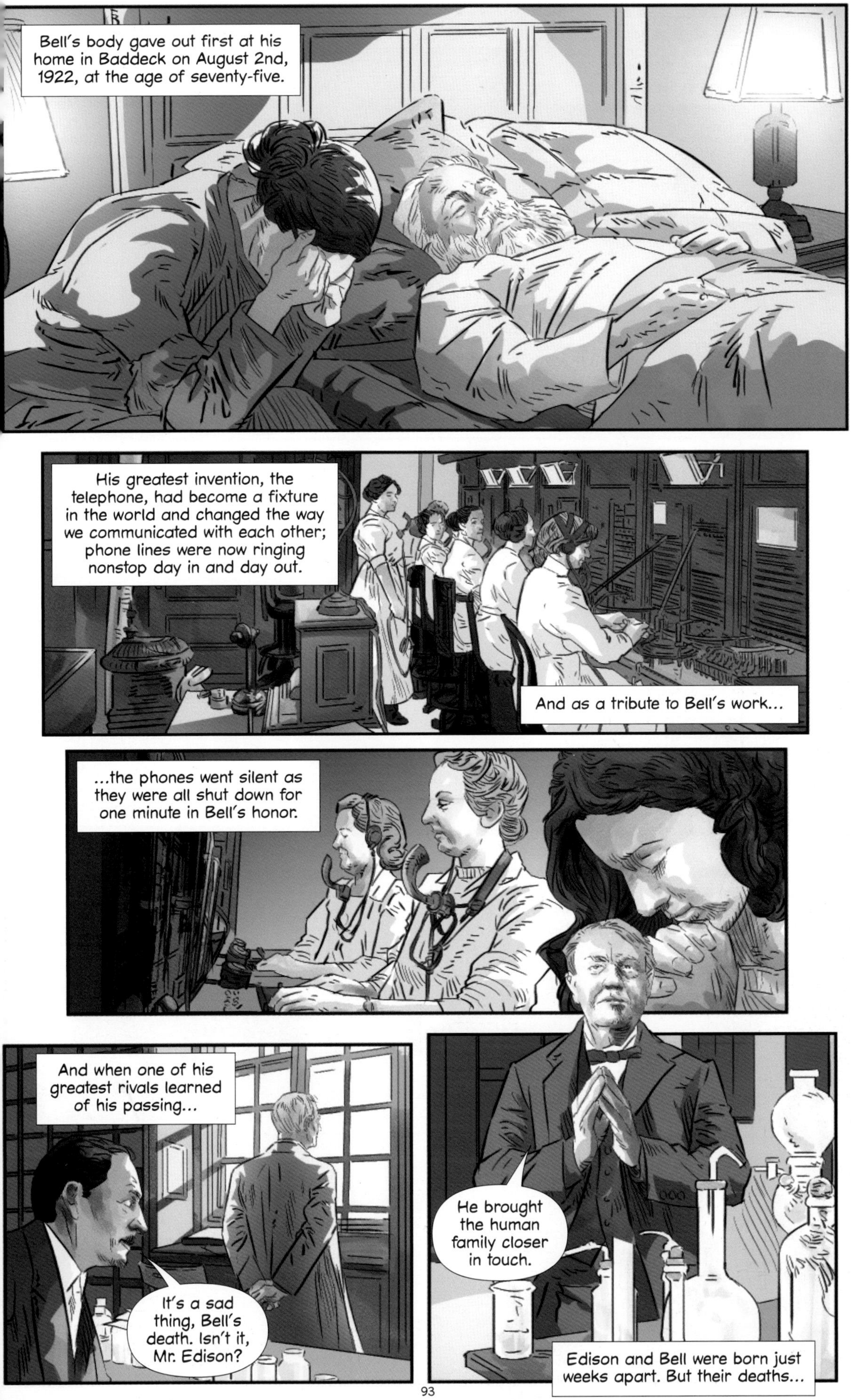
Bell's body gave out first at his home in Baddeck on August 2nd, 1922, at the age of seventy-five.
His greatest invention, the telephone, had become a fixture in the world and changed the way we communicated with each other; phone lines were now ringing nonstop day in and day out.
And as a tribute to Bell's work...
...the phones went silent as they were all shut down for one minute in Bell's honor.
And when one of his greatest rivals learned of his passing...
It's a sad thing, Bell's death. Isn't it, Mr. Edison?
He brought the human family closer in touch.
Edison and Bell were born just weeks apart. But their deaths...

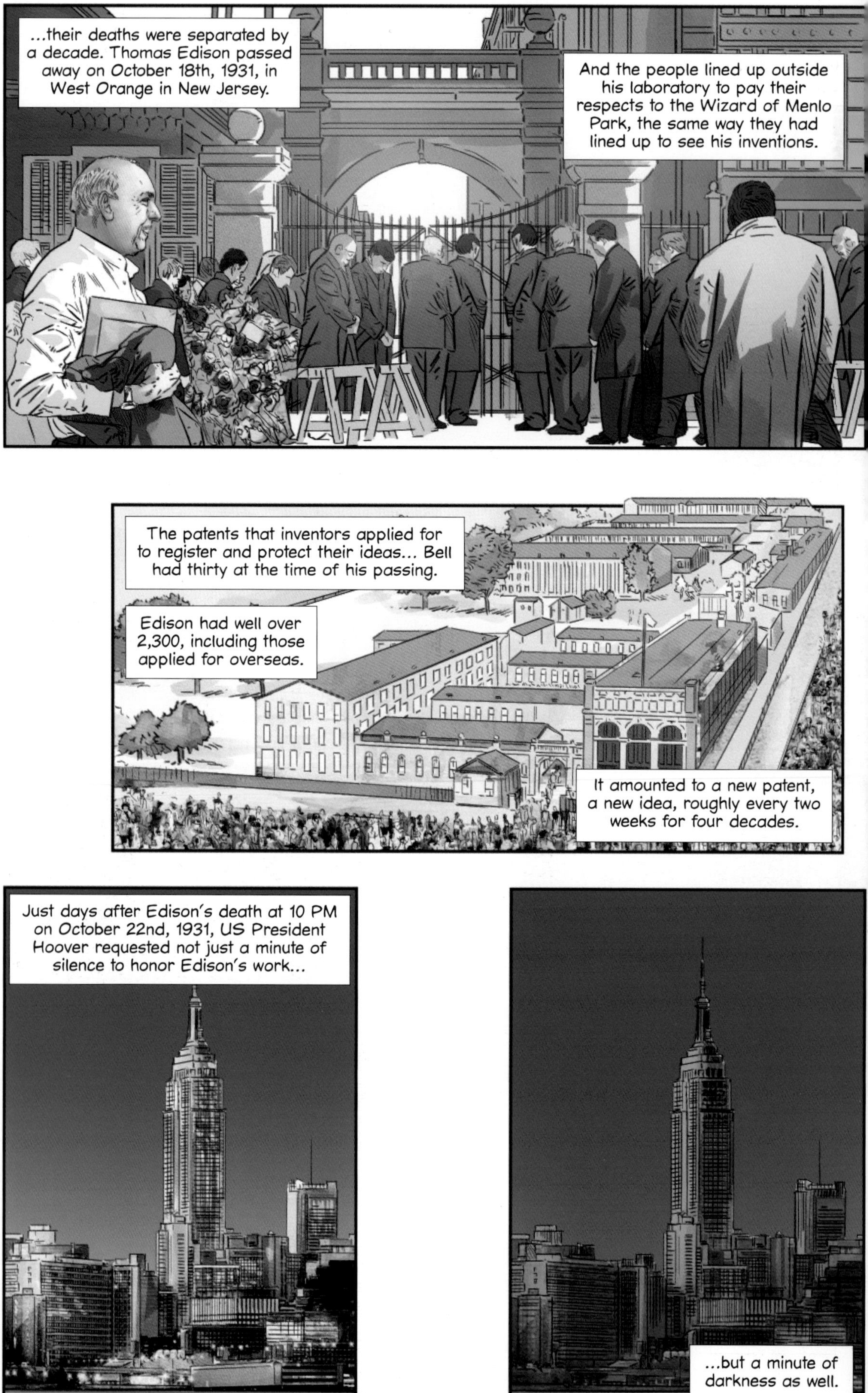
...their deaths were separated by a decade. Thomas Edison passed away on October 18th, 1931, in West Orange in New Jersey.
And the people lined up outside his laboratory to pay their respects to the Wizard of Menlo Park, the same way they had lined up to see his inventions.
The patents that inventors applied for to register and protect their ideas... Bell had thirty at the time of his passing.
Edison had well over 2,300, including those applied for overseas.
It amounted to a new patent, a new idea, roughly every two weeks for four decades.
Just days after Edison's death at 10 PM on October 22nd, 1931, US President Hoover requested not just a minute of silence to honor Edison's work...
...but a minute of darkness as well.

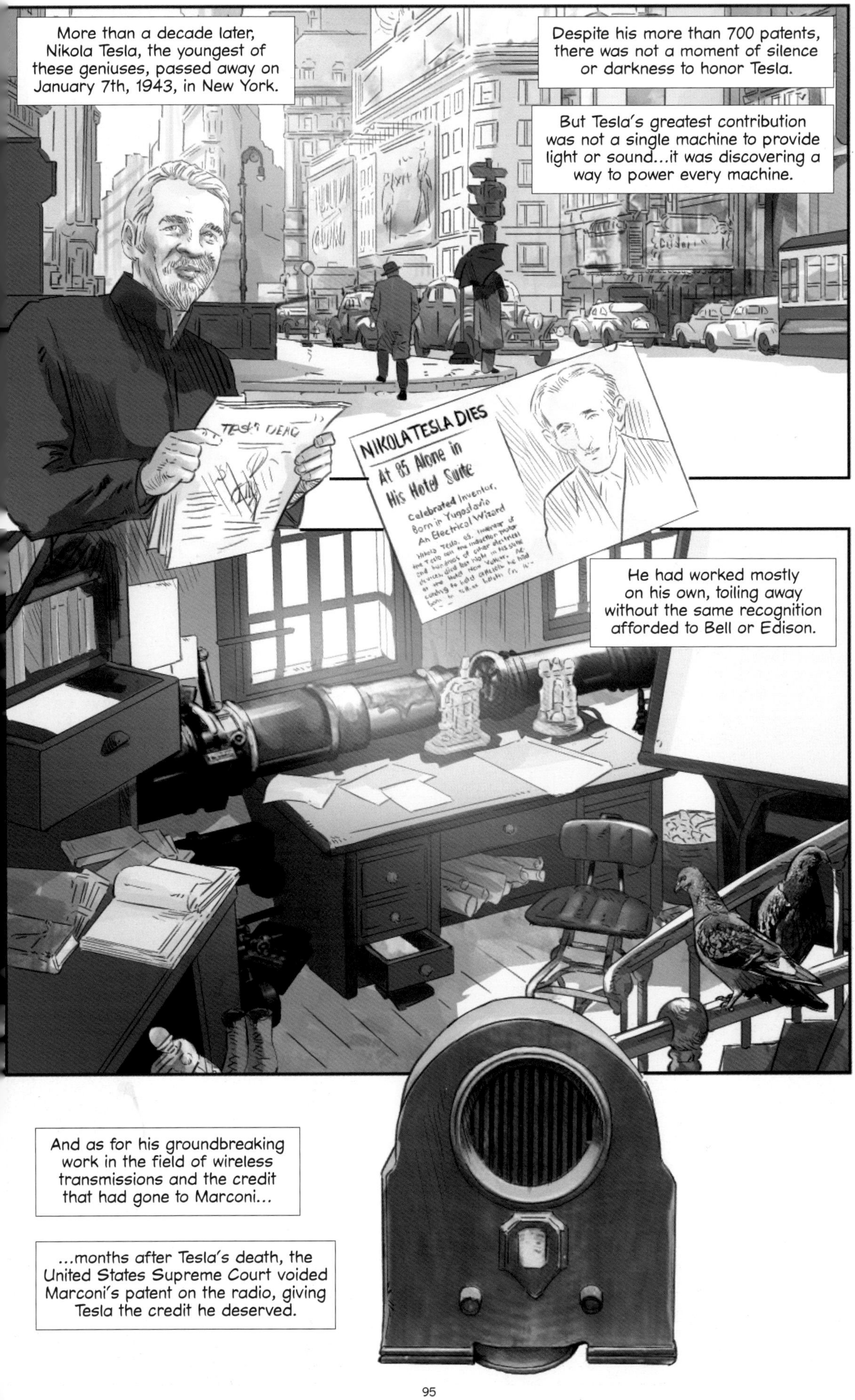
More than a decade later, Nikola Tesla, the youngest of these geniuses, passed away on January 7th, 1943, in New York.
Despite his more than 700 patents, there was not a moment of silence or darkness to honor Tesla.
But Tesla's greatest contribution was not a single machine to provide light or sound...it was discovering a way to power every machine.
NIKOLA TESLA DIES
At 85 Alone in His Hotel Suite
Celebrated Inventor, Born in Yugoslavia An Electrical Wizard
He had worked mostly on his own, toiling away without the same recognition afforded to Bell or Edison.
And as for his groundbreaking work in the field of wireless transmissions and the credit that had gone to Marconi...
...months after Tesla's death, the United States Supreme Court voided Marconi's patent on the radio, giving Tesla the credit he deserved.

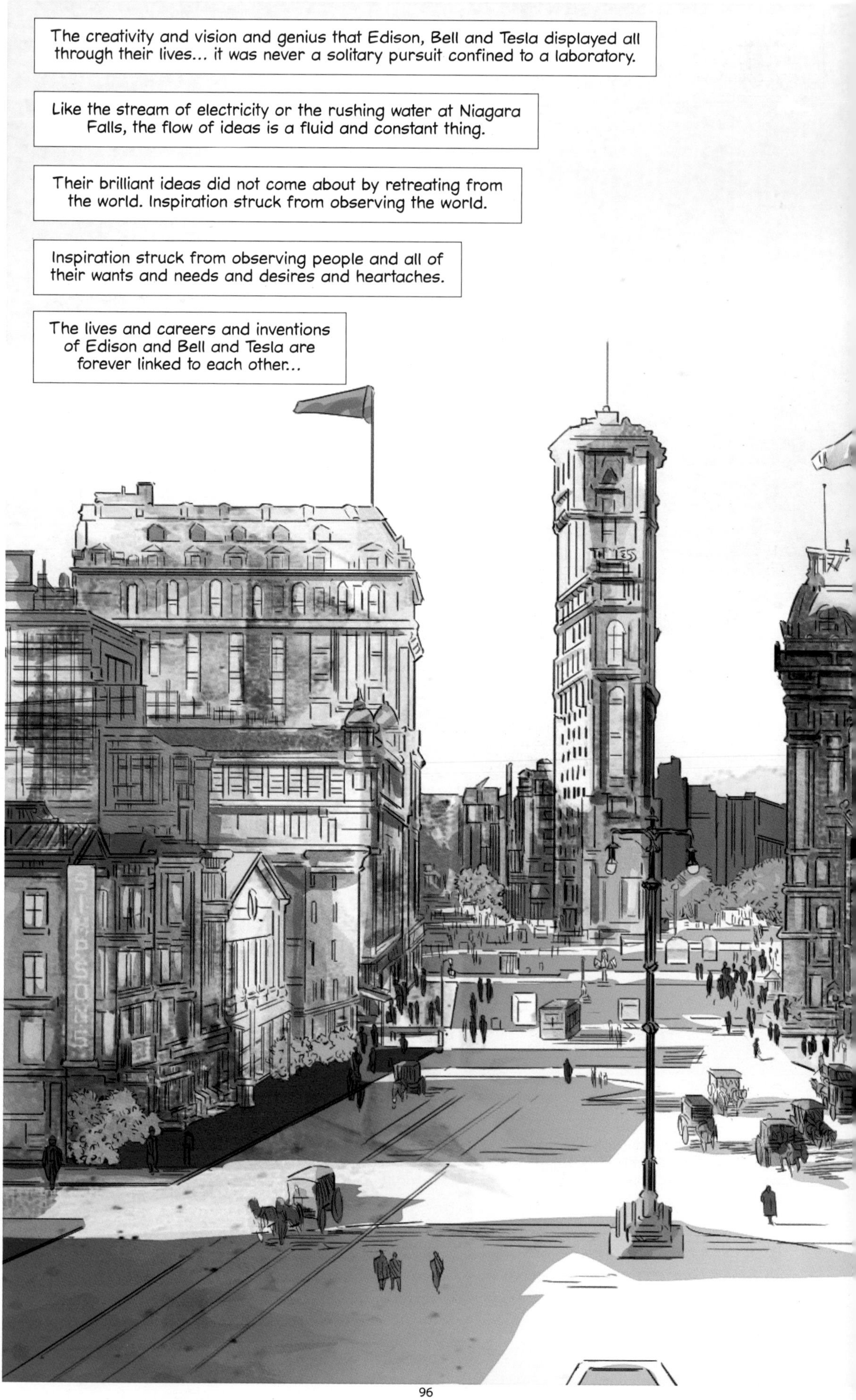
The creativity and vision and genius that Edison, Bell and Tesla displayed all through their lives... it was never a solitary pursuit confined to a laboratory.
Like the stream of electricity or the rushing water at Niagara Falls, the flow of ideas is a fluid and constant thing.
Their brilliant ideas did not come about by retreating from the world. Inspiration struck from observing the world.
Inspiration struck from observing people and all of their wants and needs and desires and heartaches.
The lives and careers and inventions of Edison and Bell and Tesla are forever linked to each other...

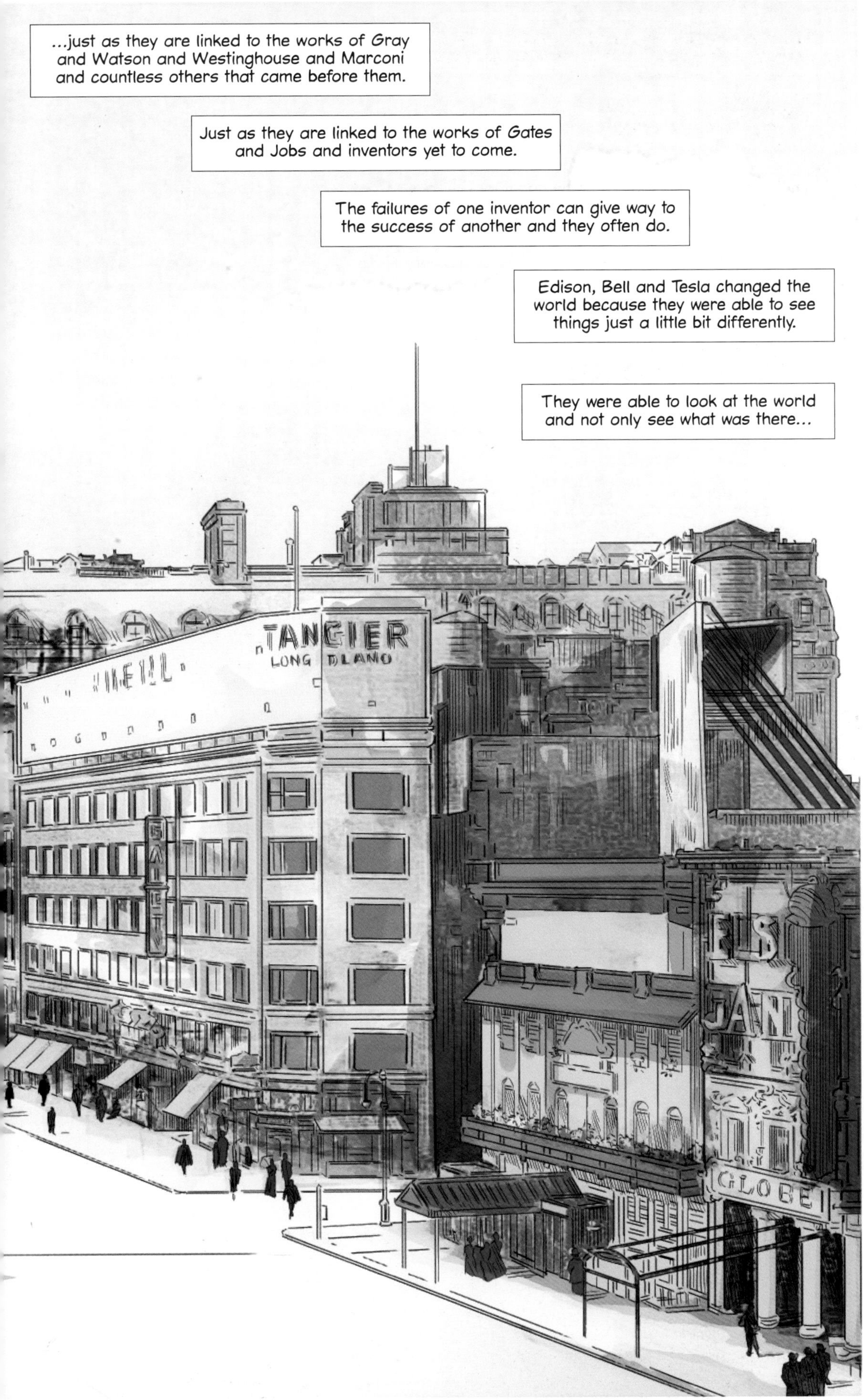
...just as they are linked to the works of Gray and Watson and Westinghouse and Marconi and countless others that came before them.
Just as they are linked to the works of Gates and Jobs and inventors yet to come.
The failures of one inventor can give way to the success of another and they often do.
Edison, Bell and Tesla changed the world because they were able to see things just a little bit differently.
They were able to look at the world and not only see what was there...
TANGIER
GLOBE

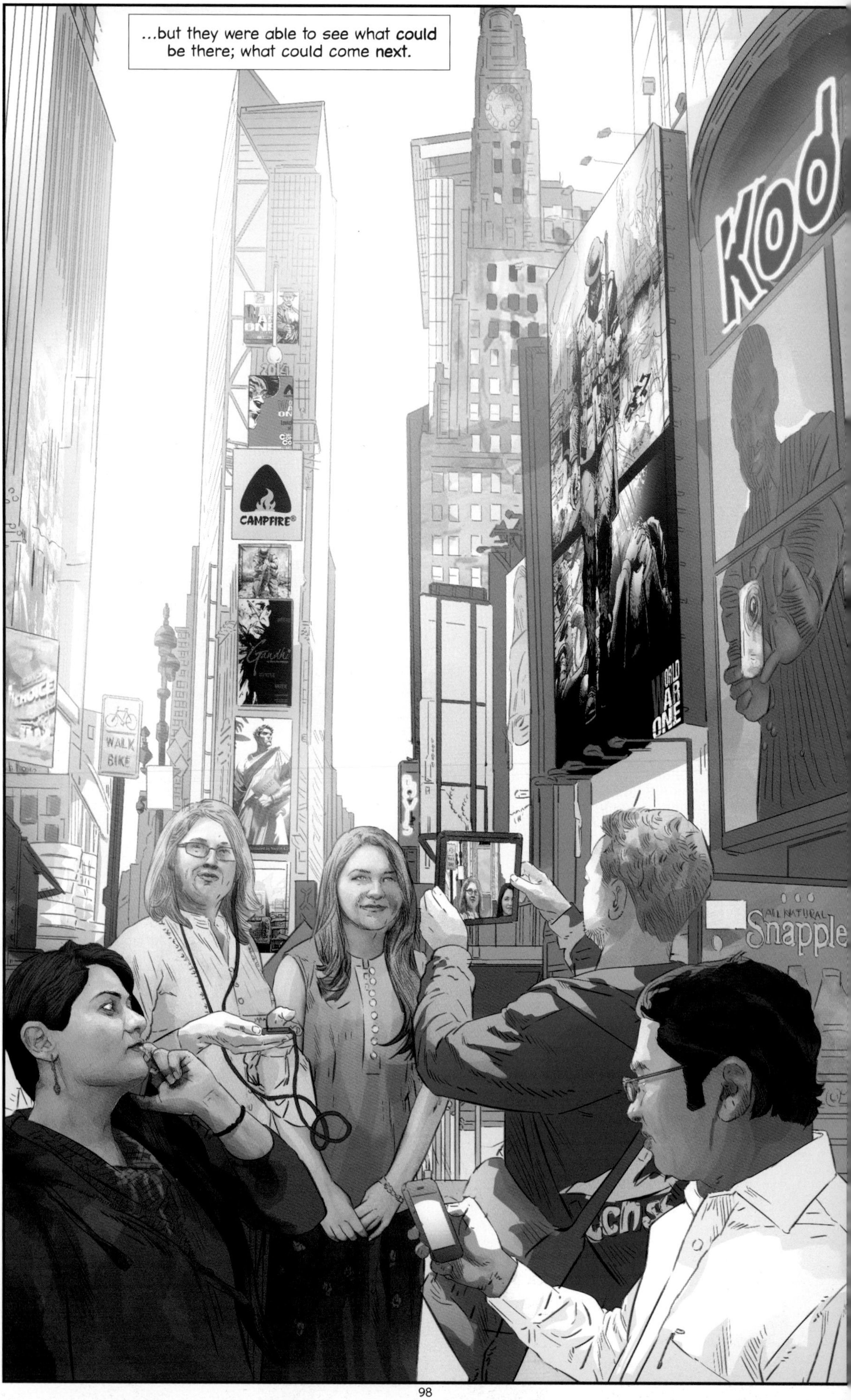

...but they were able to see what **could** be there; what could come **next.**
CAMPFIRE®
WALK
BIKE
WORLD WAR ONE
Snapple

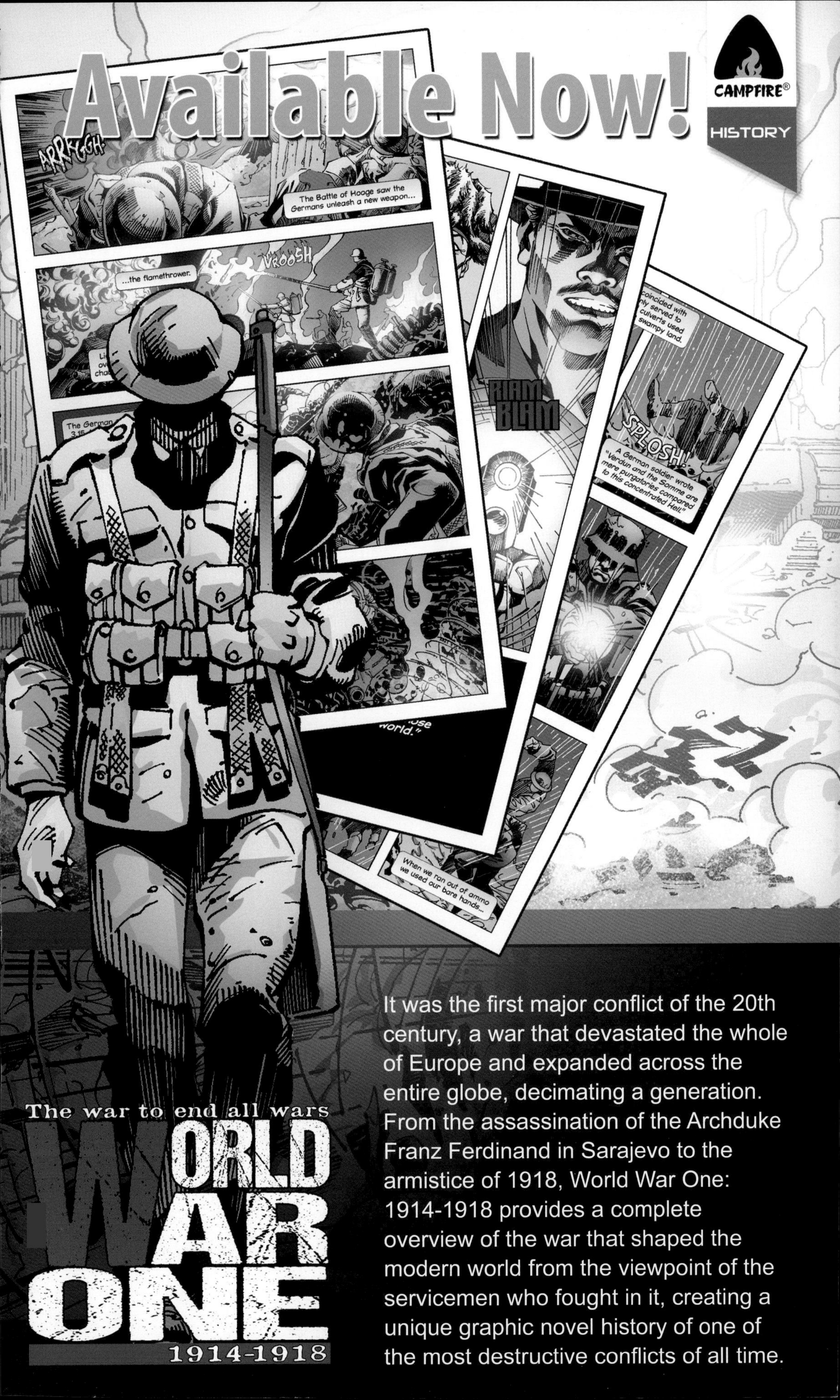
Available Now!
CAMPFIRE®
HISTORY
The Battle of Hooge saw the Germans unleash a new weapon...
...the flamethrower.
VROOSH
BLAM BLAM
SPLOSH!
A German soldier wrote "Verdun and the Somme are mere purgatories compared to this concentrated Hell."
When we ran out of ammo we used our bare hands...

BUILD YOUR OWN TELEPHONE

'Mr Watson, come here, I want to see you,' these were the first words ever spoken over a telephone, as Alexander Graham Bell called out to his assistant. This was on March 10th, 1876, just three days after Bell was granted a patent for 'transmitting vocal or other sounds telegraphically by causing electrical undulations...'. Bell was working on a liquid transmitter at that time. Speaking inside a diaphragm, he was able to make a needle vibrate in water, thereby varying the electrical resistance in the circuit. Sounds complicated? Well, back then it was. With research in electricity still in its infancy, experiments such as these were often a hit-or-miss. Today, though, you can build a small-scale liquid transmitter at home!

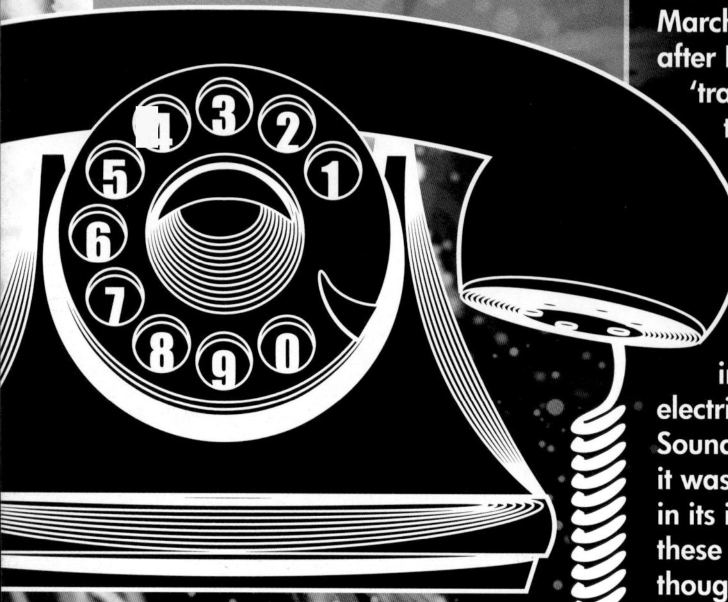
4 3 2 1
5 6 7 8 9 0

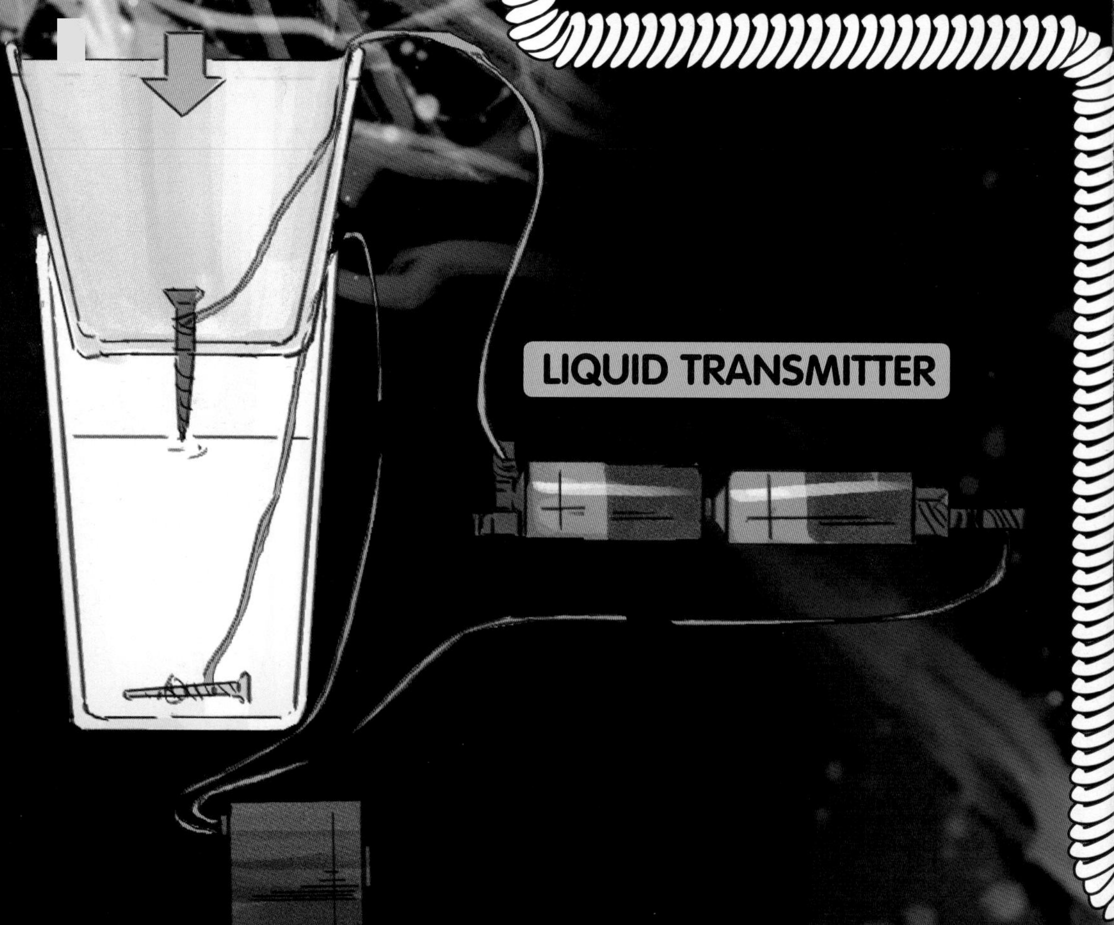
LIQUID TRANSMITTER

Things You Will Need:

1. 1 plastic cup
2. 1 glass about half-filled with water
3. 4 nails or screws
4. 1 magneto receiver (available at any electronics store)
5. 2 AAA batteries
6. 3 meters of wire

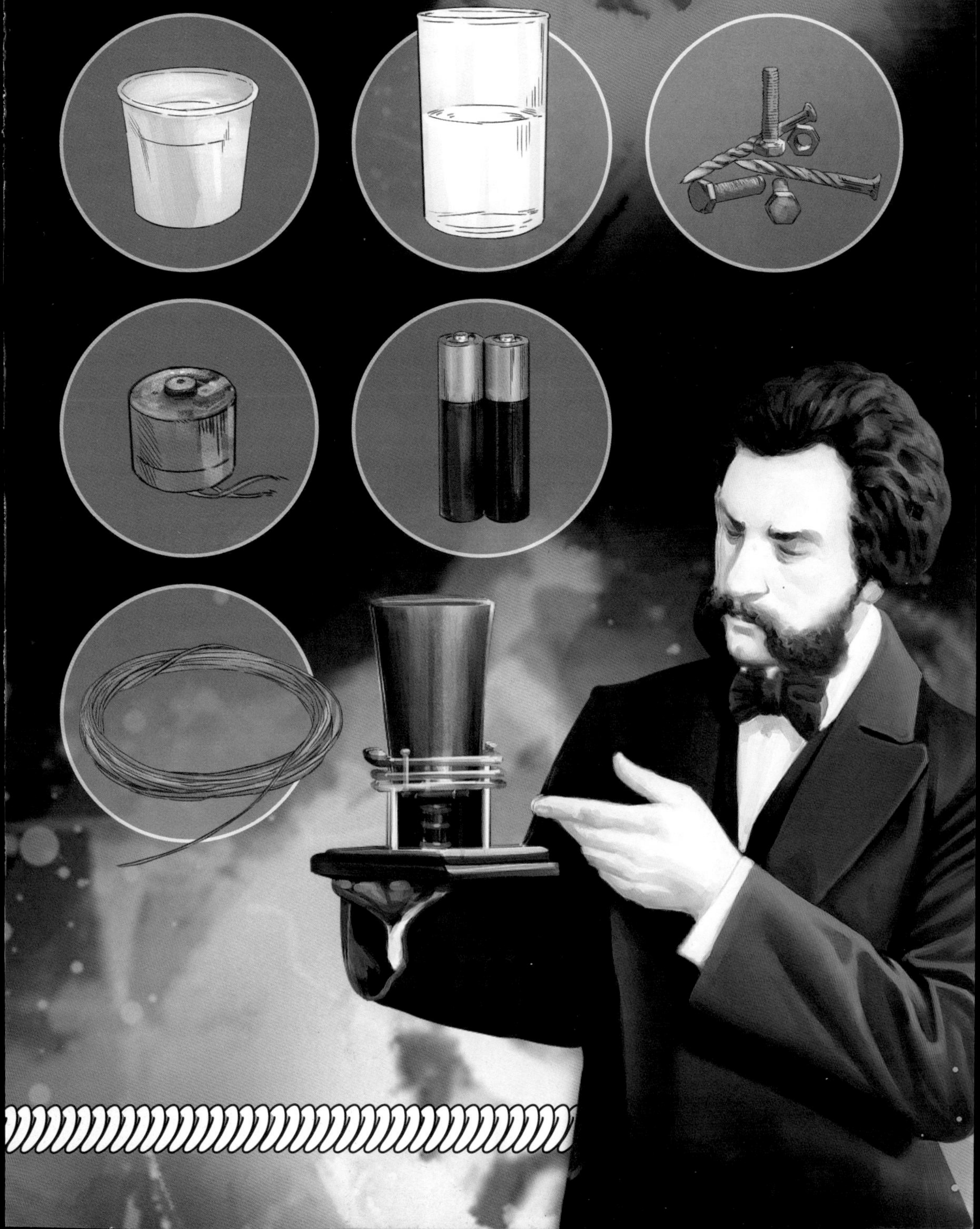

How To Make!

1

1. Connect one nail to a length of wire.

2

2. Poke the tip of the nail through the bottom of the plastic cup as shown.

3

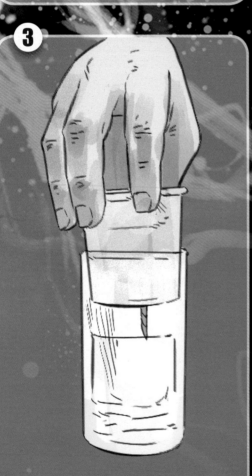

3. Now place the plastic cup inside the glass. Make sure that only the tip of the nail touches the water and the rest of it is dry.

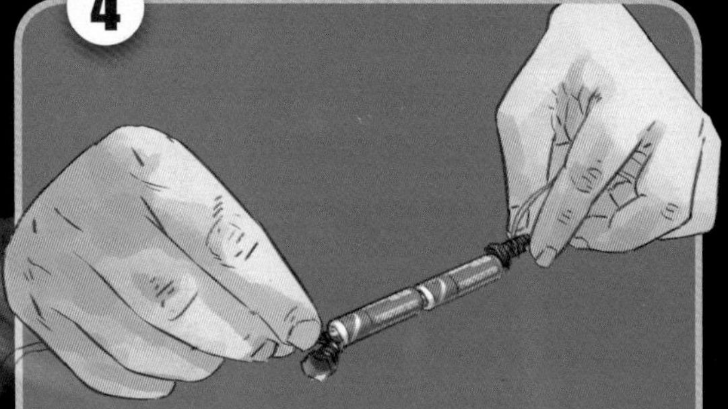

4

4. Connect the other end of that wire to the positive pole of the AAA batteries as shown, with the help of nails.

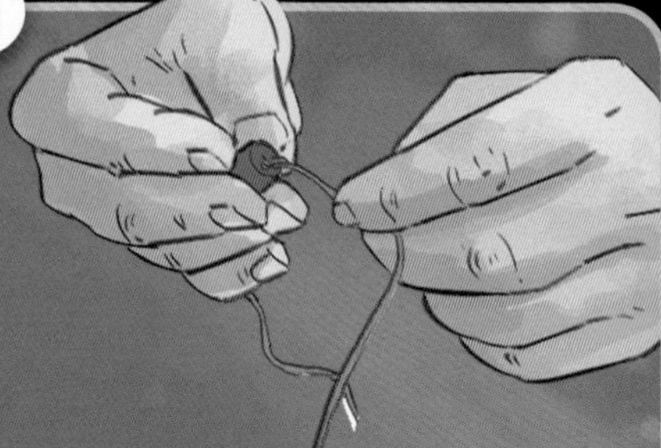

5

5. Take another length of wire and connect one end to the other pole of the batteries, and the other end to the magneto receiver.

6

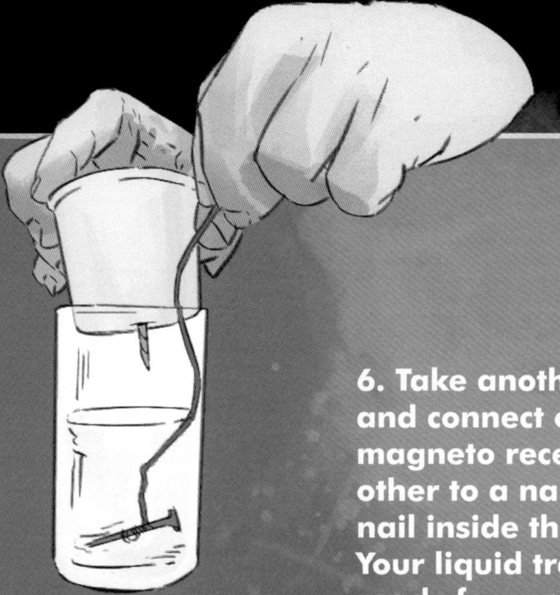

6. Take another length of wire and connect one end to the magneto receiver. Connect the other to a nail and place that nail inside the glass of water. Your liquid transmitter is now ready for use.

7

Liquid Transmitter

7. Ask a friend to speak into the plastic cup. Stand at a distance and hold the magneto receiver in your ear. If all goes well, you should be able to hear your friend speak through the receiver. Sure, this sort of a 'telephone' is not exactly as portable as we are used to, but it will be a fun experiment to try with your friends.

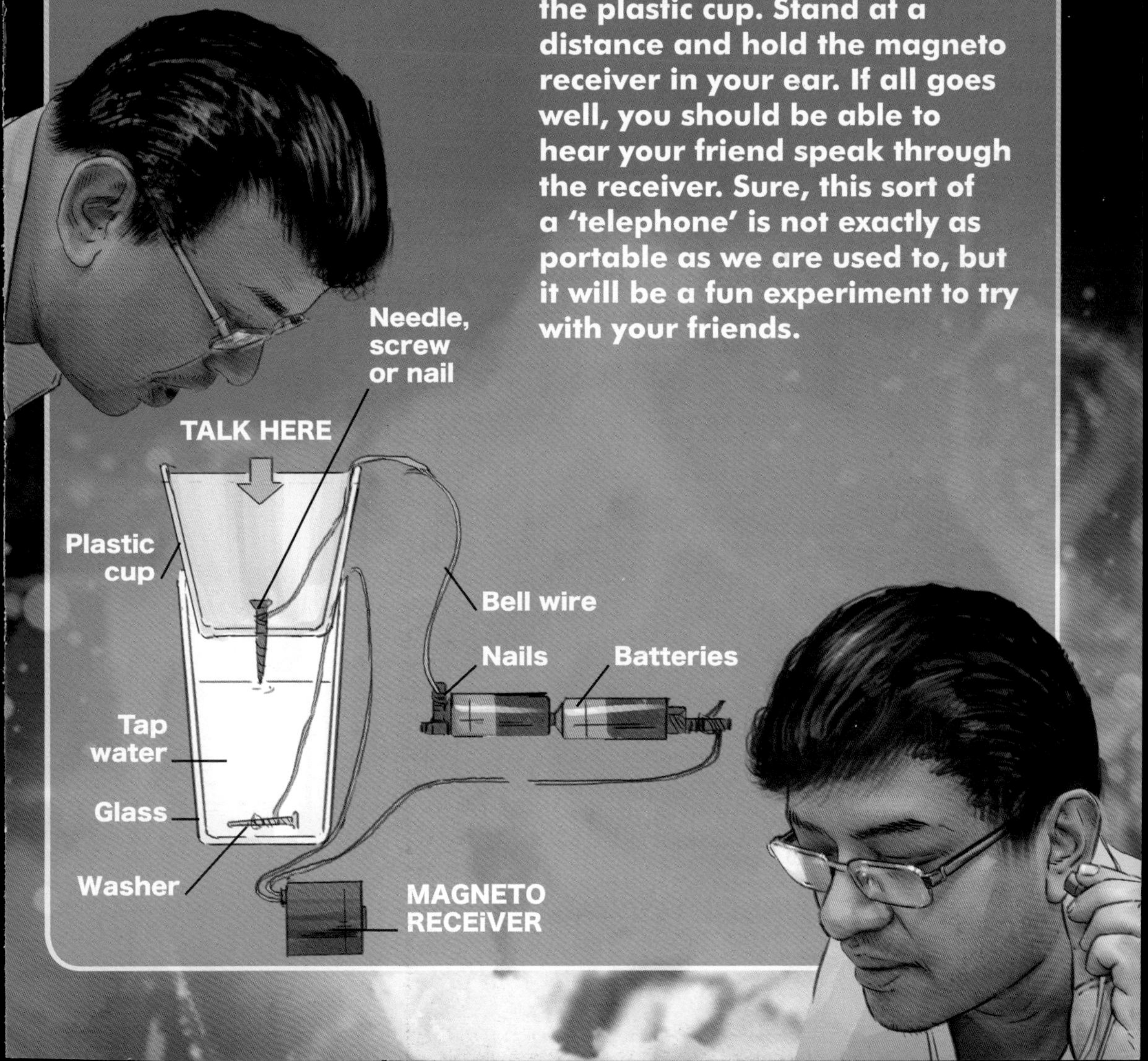

Needle, screw or nail
TALK HERE
Plastic cup
Bell wire
Nails
Batteries
Tap water
Glass
Washer
MAGNETO RECEiVER

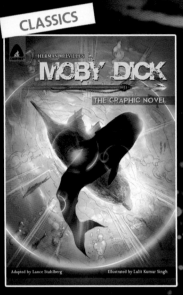